AMERICAN BUSINESS
AND THE PUBLIC SCHOOL

AMERICAN BUSINESS AND THE PUBLIC SCHOOL

Case Studies of Corporate Involvement
in Public Education

MARSHA LEVINE
ROBERTA TRACHTMAN
Editors

A COMMITTEE FOR ECONOMIC DEVELOPMENT PUBLICATION

Teachers College, Columbia University
New York and London

Published by Teachers College Press, 1234 Amsterdam Avenue,
New York, NY 10027

Copyright © 1988 by Teachers College, Columbia University

Chapter 2 © by Metropolitan Life Insurance Company

Library of Congress Cataloging-in-Publication Data

American business and the public school: Case studies of corporate involvement
  in public education/Marsha Levine, Roberta Trachtman, editors.
    p. cm.
  "A Committee for Economic Development Publication."
  Bibliography: p. 252
  Includes index.
  ISBN 0-8077-2880-2
    1. Industry and education—United States—Case studies.
2. Interorganizational relations—United States—Case studies.
3. Public schools—United States—Curricula—Case studies.
I. Levine, Marsha. II. Trachtman, Roberta. III. Committee for
Economic Development.
LC1085.2.A48 1988
370.19′31—dc19   87-18152
                                                 CIP

Manufactured in the United States of America

93 92 91 90 89   2 3 4 5 6

Contents

Foreword

OWEN B. BUTLER

As an independent nonpartisan research organization, the Committee for Economic Development (CED) has been concerned with the quality of education in the United States for the past 30 years. Beginning with the 1959 report *Paying for Better Public Schools*, CED has continued to assert that the private sector has "a responsibility, as citizens, to participate in the local, state, and national effort to improve the schools." The relationship between economic development and the quality of public school education is recognized as an issue of prime importance by CED. In recent years, CED has become increasingly concerned with the ability of American business to compete in world markets. The Committee's study of productivity trends showed that the decline of educational standards in the United States, despite the existence of many fine schools, is linked to the nation's flagging economic competitiveness.

However, problems with public school education must also be measured in humanitarian terms. The basic skills and work habits taught in the schools are essential for the pursuit of higher education and success in the workplace. In addition, the public schools should prepare youngsters to become responsible citizens who can make informed decisions on essential personal and public issues. Ultimately, the quality of public school education can be a positive or a negative influence on the economic development of both the individual and the nation as a whole. With this in mind, in 1982, CED undertook a broad range study to assess the overall quality of our educational system, pinpoint the problems impeding its success, and suggest solutions to improve the public schools. The result, *Investing in Our Children: Business and the Public Schools* (1985), reaffirmed CED's earlier assertion that the private sector must play a crucial role in educational reform.

American Business and the Public School: Case Studies of Corporate Involvement in Public Education is an extremely important outgrowth of *Investing in Our Children*. A compendium of descriptions of successful working relationships between businesses and schools, it is meant as a resource for both education and business leaders in bringing about school reform. Indeed, the case studies recounted in this book illustrate the major thrust of the recommendations from *Investing in Our Children*—that businesses and schools can join together to create effective partnerships to improve education.

Both editor Marsha Levine, co-project director of *Investing in Our Children*, and co-editor Roberta Trachtman have done an outstanding job in developing these studies. Their knowledge and expertise in the field ensure that, like *Investing in Our Children*, this book will have a major impact on education in the United States.

We are deeply grateful to the NYNEX Foundation for its generous support of this project.

Acknowledgments

We wish to thank the many people who gave their time and knowledge generously in the preparation of these case studies. We are particularly grateful to the contributors, persons interviewed, and those who reviewed the drafts. Also, we would like to acknowledge the support and assistance we received from the Committee for Economic Development during this project.

And, finally, we would like to thank our families—Leslie, Sara and Rachel, and Steven and Alison—for their encouragement throughout the preparation of this book.

Marsha Levine
Roberta Trachtman

Introduction

MARSHA LEVINE

BACKGROUND

In September 1985 the Committee for Economic Development issued a policy statement on American business and the public schools. Chaired by Owen B. Butler, then Chairman of the Board of Procter & Gamble, CED placed the American business community at the center of the education reform movement. It drew upon the perspectives, expertise, and experience of business to address some of the main issues in public school improvement: financing, curriculum, and the organization, management, and work force of the schools.

WHY THIS BOOK?

In the course of preparing that policy statement, it became clear that it would be useful, even necessary, to expand on the ways business was and might be involved in public education. While the CED statement provided the opportunity to develop a rationale for corporate involvement and a strategy for making decisions on private sector/public school collaboration, much more could be learned from looking in depth at some of these collaborative efforts. It is to this end, to provide insight from inside the collaborative ventures, that this book was produced. A great deal has been written about business involvement in public schools, but little of it attempts to get underneath the descriptions or beyond the conceptualizations to what actually happens in these collaborative efforts. It is our hope that the seven major case studies will do that. The people involved tell their own stories directly or through an intermediary, and their strengths and weaknesses, trials and errors, motivations and hesitations come alive. In addition, as editors we have chosen to illustrate the breadth of relationships that have grown up between business and policy makers, administrators, teachers, school principals, and education analysts concerned with public education. To do this, we have included numerous samples, which we call mini cases, of very different forms of business/education relationships.

And finally, the book offers the reader new information on business/ education relationships generated by two previously unreported research studies: one, the findings about partnerships from the CED survey conducted in 1984 and updated in January 1986; and the second, findings of research on the impact on teachers of involvement in programs with business.

We hope this volume will be used as a resource on strategies for corporate involvement in education and as a companion to the CED policy statement *Investing in Our Children*.

METHODOLOGY

Selecting the Cases

The longer, in-depth case studies were selected to represent a range of involvement. In addition, we wanted to include the perspectives of both corporate and school people as well as the views of well-respected policy analysts in education. In selecting the corporations for case studies, we identified corporations with different emphases in their education programs, from different sectors of industry operating in different civic environments. Those finally chosen should be viewed as representative of a larger subset of American corporations that have made investments in time, talent, materials, influence, and money toward the goal of improving the quality of public education.

Selecting the Mini Cases

The mini case studies were chosen to reflect the three generic categories of business/school interactions identified in *Investing in Our Children*: (1) involvement focuses on donations of funds or material resources that the business partner shares with the school; (2) involvement of the private sector focuses on in-school programs, where employees work directly with youngsters and/or teachers (at school or on the work site), where information about the employing community is provided through participation on school advisory committees, or where students and teachers are invited to participate in activities held at the business site; (3) involvement has progressed beyond the level of minor funding or programmatic participation to the area of policy participation—the business partners are involved in educational issues relating to finance, management, and human resource development.

We learned about these activities in a variety of ways. There already exists a fairly large body of literature describing these public/private sector interactions, some of which was written by participants, some by analysts. (See the annotated bibliography.) We learned about some of these programs as a result of our own studies and from the CED survey of small and large employers and postsecondary institutions (see Appendix B).

WHAT DID WE WANT TO KNOW?

Each of the authors of the longer case studies was presented with a set of five questions to use as guidelines for developing the material. The questions were:

Civic Context: How does the local climate for public/private sector partnership affect the degree and form that involvement will take?

Motivation for Involvement: What are the internal and external considerations that influenced corporate decision makers to become involved in public education?

Process: What are the institutional requirements, demands on leadership, and communication requirements?

Outcomes: What determines the kinds of outcomes that are sought and identified?

Lessons Learned: What lessons about successes and failures have been learned?

These questions were posed to all authors. In addition, each author received another set of questions that were specific to his or her case study.

WHAT DID WE LEARN?

The case studies and descriptions of corporate involvement reveal a good deal about the requirements, process, outcomes, obstacles, and incentives to business involvement in public schools. Several crosscutting themes are identified and described briefly below.

The Importance of the Civic Context

The history and tradition of public/private partnership varies from city to city. In some places, such as Minneapolis, the corporate community has played a strong, long-term leadership role in civic responsibility. Philanthropy and community responsibility are expected within the corporate sector. Problems seem to be manageable, and there is a history of different sectors working together on finding solutions. The community is relatively small, leaders in each sector can and do get to know each other; thus a personal dimension is present and can be used as a lever for participation.

This is a far more fertile environment for the development of public/private partnerships in education than is found, for example, in New York City. In Minneapolis there is one business community, whereas in New York there are many. In Minneapolis the size and scope of the problems seem manageable; in New York the numbers can be overwhelming. On the other hand, New York's strength comes from its diversity, the presence of many multinational corporate headquarters, the richness of human resources, and the abundance of activity. This scope and size are mirrored in the schools. But it is these very same conditions that make it more difficult for the private sector to engage with the public schools in long-term meaningful ways.

Philadelphia, in contrast, presents a different civic environment from either Minneapolis or New York. There a latent private sector potential was harnessed by The Philadelphia Committee for the Public Schools. This organization was established with a limited time frame— it plans to put itself out of business once its goals are achieved. This made "getting involved" easier, since it did not represent an indefinite diversion of effort and resources.

Boston provides yet another context and another scenario. In that city, working relationships between education and business had been established by court order in the 1974 Boston school desegregation case, and the sectors worked together somewhat uneasily through the Tri-Lateral Council. As a result, the business/school relationship evolved toward some understanding, and by 1982 the Boston Compact represented an active commitment by both business and the schools. The Private Industry Council and the Chamber of Commerce played roles in arriving at the Compact. Perhaps most influential in its support was the Coordinating Committee, known as the Vault, in existence in Boston since the 1950s. The Vault represented 25 of Boston's most influential CEOs and functioned as an information and coordinating link among them on public policy issues. Programs like the Summer Jobs Program and the Jobs Collaborative Program had similarly laid the groundwork. Thus, in Boston, a city in which the business, education, and public sectors are often in disagreement, the way was paved over the last several years for the kind of agreement that the Boston Compact represents.

The Economic Context

In addition to the civic context, the economy is often an important barrier or incentive to involvement. It is impossible to conceive of an effort such as the Boston Compact even being thought of without an economy that was creating jobs at an impressive rate. Hewlett-Packard's involvement, described in Part II of this book, was driven by the need for employable graduates, prepared with the skills and ability to learn new jobs as they are created in a high tech industry. The statewide efforts in Minnesota and California, similarly, must be viewed against the prospects for continued economic growth.

The lesson to be learned here is to be sensitive to these contexts and to be realistic about what they make possible. The fact that they change is also a part of the reality.

What Is the Collaborative's Objective? While most of the collaborative arrangements described in this book share the overall goal of improving the quality of public education, they do not all have the same objective. Some involvements are clearly aimed at supporting and enriching—but not changing—a generally good school system by ensuring that adequate resources are available. Some public education funds serve this function.

Other cases describe activities directed at incremental change or improvement in the public schools. IMPACT II changes the rewards and incentives for good teaching. The Committee to Support the Philadelphia Public Schools leverages the resources of corporations, universities, and foundations in an effort to deal systematically with the financial and management issues of the schools as well as to encourage educational initiatives and provide avenues for recognizing achievement. Burger King's teacher recognition program, In Honor of Excellence, draws attention to the need for different rewards and incentives for good teaching. Those programmatic efforts that deal with enhancing curricula or employability of graduates also fall into this general grouping. The Jobs for America's Graduates, Honeywell's involvement in the development of Summatech, New York City Partnership's mentoring program, and Join-A-School are similarly directed.

Some cases show corporate involvement aimed at system-wide

change. The most obvious are the efforts of the California Business Roundtable and the Minnesota Business Partnership. In each state the business community sought to influence the policy structure of public education. In California, there was a quid pro quo: increased support in exchange for higher standards and greater productivity. In Minnesota, changes in the structure of the schools were recommended to better meet the future needs of society—looking toward the twenty-first century. The Boston Compact seeks systemic change as well: not by influencing state policy but by providing an incentive for the schools to change and improve. The influence being brought to bear is indirect, but may be substantial.

What Is the Focus? Many of the cases deliberately focus on efforts involving either students or teachers. We believe that to have an impact on the quality of education, involvement must focus on the instructional core of schooling, where education actually takes place. We have selected a variety of examples that do just that. It is critical for business and education partners to ask this question if they are serious about having an impact. Metropolitan Life's entire effort is focused on enhancing the professional role of teachers; IMPACT II focuses on rewarding and recognizing teacher initiatives; PATHS in Philadelphia recognizes the importance of responding to the needs of teachers for renewal, recognition, and reward, as does the Burger King program In Honor of Excellence. Alternatively, programs such as Jobs for America's Graduates and the mentor program in New York City attempt to deal directly with the student.

What Is the Role of Leadership? The case studies affirm that top management must be involved if business/education collaboration is to have any impact. Support from the top is necessary if the resources of both the corporation and the school are to be made available in any joint effort. The importance of this cannot be overstated. Changeovers in leadership can mean difficulties in sustaining or regaining momentum for action. In other places, where collaboration was dormant, new leadership has been able to awaken it. There have been outstanding leaders in both sectors. Some of them are described in the cases: Constance Clayton, Superintendent of Schools in Philadelphia; Floretta McKenzie, Superintendent in the D.C. schools; Robert R. Spillane, Superintendent in Boston at the time of the Boston Compact; John Creedon, CEO of Metropolitan Life; Ralph Saul, Chairman of CIGNA; and William Woodside, retired Chairman and CEO of Primerica (formerly American Can Company). Again, these are only representatives of those school and corporate leaders who have stepped forward and taken an outspoken leadership role in business and school issues.

It is important to point out, however, that the CEO does not have to play a visible, "up front" role for the involvement of a corporation to be significant. The example of the support role played by Edson Spencer at Honeywell or John Young at Hewlett-Packard are testimony to that fact. Those companies have deep, institutionalized commitments to quality public education, with their leadership maintaining a much lower profile on this issue.

Is There Change Over Time? Several of the case studies provide some insight into what happens as partnerships mature. Informal evaluations reveal that corporate involvement has changed attitudes and understanding among the private sector volunteers. They suggest a greater corporate understanding of issues facing teachers and students, and fewer stereotypical expectations. Corporate people also report real personal growth and satisfaction. Similarly, the teachers report satisfaction at establishing meaningful relationships with the volunteers, reduced feelings of isolation, and increased feelings of self-respect. Co-editor Roberta Trachtman's research on teachers in 85 school districts across the country reports similar findings among teachers at those locations (see Appendix A).

Honeywell's involvement has broadened and deepened over time as the corporate and school people have learned better ways to communicate, how to respect their differences, and how to leverage their resources together. Initially a programmatic effort, Honeywell's involvement has moved into the policy arena with participation in the Minnesota Business Partnership. The same direction is observed in the involvement of Primerica. Initially that company focused its efforts on Join-A-School. Primerica's leadership believes that such programmatic involvement is essential to building the kind of understanding that is necessary for business to make a commitment to school improvement that needs to be supported through strong financing and public policy. The Primerica Foundation has moved into support of projects such as the Mentor/Internship Program for new teachers. An American Federation of Teachers/university/school system collaborative in several cities, this project has important policy implications for teacher education and professionalism. William Woodside's leadership of the New York Partnership is moving that public/private effort in new policy-influencing directions.

There is a pattern discernible here. Over time, at least some business and school relationships seem to move from programmatic to policy issues as the two parties learn about each other. As partnerships grow, they tend to become institutionalized to ensure staying power. Judging from the many, many people interviewed for these cases, the partnerships tend to have committed, knowledgeable people involved in these efforts.

One of the mini case studies, The Philadelphia Story, suggests an alternative view of change. When the Committee to Support the Philadelphia Public Schools was formed, it was clearly stated and agreed that the business involvement was not intended to be open-ended or institutionalized. The goal was, instead, to have the public sector strengthened sufficiently so that it would be able to assume responsibility for programs undertaken in the partnership. This represents a definite, but contrasting, plan for change from that identified in some of the other cases.

Unilateral vs. United Action. It is clear from the cases studied that companies prefer to do some things unilaterally and others in coalition with other corporations. In the case of Hewlett-Packard, the donation of equipment and involvement in research projects, which are a large part of the effort, are clearly unilateral programs. Other activities are identified as partnerships with schools, other companies, and third-party agencies. Hewlett-Packard selected to work in this way in the development of the Peninsula Academies, a project that required a high level of integration with the educational system. Organizations that link the public and private sector, such as the Allegheny Conference or the New York Partnership, or already existing coalitions of business, such as local chambers of commerce or business roundtables, are frequently used in the establishment of business/school relationships.

Public education funds create a way for corporations to leverage their resources, and provide an organization that can be a surrogate in interacting with the school system. In this way, some corporations can make significant contributions without the demands of interinstitutional collaboration.

Some corporations prefer coalitions for high-risk activities, such as policy and funding initiatives. Such coalitions have the advantage of leveraging the influence the business community can bring to bear. The California and Minnesota stories, and increasingly the activities of the New York Partnership, bear witness to this observation.

How Does the Institution View Collaboration? In the cases presented here, both corporations and schools take collaborative efforts very seriously. The cases written by the corporate people establish the need to link the objectives of their educational involvement not only to the real, identified needs of the schools but to the needs and culture of the corporation itself and the ways in which it is organized. For example, Honeywell, Hewlett-Packard, Burger King, and Metropolitan Life all demonstrate thoughtful, self-conscious attention to these requirements. Interviews with corporate people in many instances revealed a similar combination of sensitivity and self-interest.

From the schools' perspective, there is often the same sort of awareness and sensitivity. Barbara Christen, principal of the Murry Bergtraum High School, writes of the importance of the contribution of the business community in making the curriculum in her magnet school relevant to the employability of her graduates. Providing internship and supervision for students, donating equipment, and serving as advisors are illustrative of the many roles the business community plays in that partnership.

To be sure, involvement of the business community can be controversial. In both California and Minnesota educators did not all agree that the role being played by the business group was appropriate. Although business clearly was viewed as an interested constituency of the public schools, there was not, and is not, unanimity on the kinds of recommendations business has made with respect to how to improve public education.

Additionally, there are those who fear interference of the business community in the substance of the curriculum, on the grounds that it is self-serving. There are those who would clearly seek to keep the business interests out of the schools entirely. Some observers argue, however, that in the 1980s the needs of the business community and the goals of public education are converging. Each is interested in a liberally educated society, equipped with basic skills and higher-level cognitive abilities. They share the objective of educating people who can and will continue to learn for their own growth and development, as well as to be able to advance in their workplaces.

A few lessons stand out when we look back over these cases:

1. Effective business/education partnerships are strategically planned and goals are clearly identified. Simplicity in goal setting is very useful.
2. While goal setting is strategic, opportunities for implementation must take account of the realities of each situation.
3. Clarity is important, and so is consensus. But this need for consensus should not be at the expense of the partners' need to see something in it for themselves.

4. Building commitment within a corporation requires involving people from all levels in the planning and decision-making process. In that way, they feel ownership for the program and commitment toward it.
5. Some things are better done individually, and others benefit from collaboration. Policy involvement and programs requiring substantial resources are often done cooperatively with other corporations.
6. Projects that require substantial, intricate involvement across sectors often benefit from a linking organization.
7. There are limits to what one can reasonably expect from different types of involvement. Career-day programs do not improve test scores, but they often can improve communications across sectors.
8. CEOs need to be used appropriately—to set goals, provide leadership, assert influence, control resources, and provide a wealth of expertise on management and organizations.
9. The companies we describe are not looking for quick fixes. They understand the nature and depth of the problems and issues in education. Metropolitan Life Insurance Company's focus on the teacher is a good example.
10. Effective partnerships take time.
11. The companies described have put effort into understanding their own motivations. They know their basis for involvement. They can state why they are involved.
12. Effective collaboratives are characterized by awareness, sensitivity, and an effort by the partners to know each other.
13. Effective leaders in both sectors are aware of the conflicts that may arise.
14. Sometimes companies need to act together. It is the only way many companies are willing to deal with controversial issues.
15. Companies are aware of their need to work with each other, as well as with the community at large. From this awareness a broader view of partnership emerges and with it far greater opportunities for success.
16. In each case the corporations involved have a clear notion of what is at stake for them and why quality schooling is important to their central purposes.

CONCLUSION

Business/school collaboration has become a trendy piece of the education reform movement. Business/school partnerships are being developed against a background of major legislative reform in the states and concerted efforts by numerous task forces at the national level to deal with the problems of how to move from mass public education to mass quality public education. They are also being played against a history of business involvement that is often questioned and sometimes questionable.

But there has been a real and fundamental change in the level of business involvement with the schools. Where earlier efforts in this century focused on vocational education and narrow skill development, business has now turned its attention to the need for more broadly, liberally educated employees. Where business once advocated techniques that produced schools modeled after factories, many businesses have now learned that participatory management and leadership that empowers people can lead to far greater productivity.

The case studies illustrate that motivation is strong on both sides. Businesses refer to their own self-interest and their role as corporate citizens; educators point to their need for a strong constituency, their need to provide relevant education for young children, and their appreciation for the expertise that is available in the business community.

Important changes are taking place as a result of this new alliance between business and the schools. Private funding, although marginal, has provided important support to teachers in the form of mini grants and recognition programs. Funds have been used to target areas that have been overlooked, such as the middle schools. The welcome reception of local education funds illustrates the importance of school-site budgeting and flexibility in spending. Successful programmatic involvement has targeted effective practices such as tutoring, support for counseling, mentoring, and teacher development. Policy involvement has resulted in new financing for public schools and major policy changes at the state level in curriculum, structure, teacher education, and graduation requirements.

The involvement of large corporations has tended to have a ripple effect—spreading from headquarters throughout the decentralized corporate network and from corporation to corporation.

Undoubtedly, other themes may be extracted from the case material included in this book. As such, we hope it will be a continuing resource for those interested in pursuing these relationships. One final point needs to be made: The teachers, administrators, and businesspeople who were interviewed or wrote the materials for this book were serious about the need to ensure that today's children have a chance at a bright tomorrow. They were trying to find ways to work together toward that future.

Part I

SEVEN CASE STUDIES OF CORPORATE INVOLVEMENT IN PUBLIC EDUCATION

The Case Studies in Brief

MARSHA LEVINE

The corporate cases, Honeywell, Burger King, and Metropolitan Life Insurance Company, were each developed by or with the people most responsible for planning and implementing those efforts. As such they provide the reader with some insight into how corporate people think about, plan for, organize, and implement their companies' external education programs. Corporate readers will learn how others approach involvement with public education. Educators will gain an understanding of their business partners' approach to education issues and will see how some corporations are organized to carry on these efforts.

The companies used as case examples here tie their education effort to the central mission, culture, and strategy of the business. This is, of course, not true for every business that has an involvement in education. Some companies view their involvement in education as an add-on, public relations activity—an adjunct to the corporate philanthropic activities. Such companies were not chosen as case studies here. Instead, the editors chose companies that see sustained successful involvement with education as growing out of the corporation's central goals and purposes.

In each corporate case the voice of the chief executive is clearly heard in setting corporate goals and establishing a commitment to quality education, a commitment that grows out of the recognition of the importance of good education to the survival of the company, the health of the economy, and the sustenance and maintenance of a free and democratic nation. These companies are not doing what they do only to get good publicity or to be nice to the kids. It is a highly developed and enlightened sense of self-interest that drives them.

Although the goals are set forth by top management, it is the program director who defines the objectives and develops the program in ways that are consistent with the way the company does business.

Summary of Major Cases

Honeywell. Rita Kaplan, former Manager of Education Programs at Honeywell, developed Honeywell's education program as an extension of its corporate culture. Honeywell's commitment to education is carried out in the broader context of a commitment to employees, volunteerism, and a developed structure for corporate community involvement.

Honeywell's education efforts emphasize the use of strategic planning and the tools the business has used to manage change. Leveraging resources, sharing risks, and managing change are important parts of the strategy and are developed here for the reader. The emphasis in Honeywell's programs is on the effective use of human resources. While funding and equipment donations play a part, Honeywell's people are central to the partnership. Honeywell's role in the policy arena is deepening. Kaplan's discussion of policy initiatives raises some of the concerns all corporations must have about entering the education policy arena. Political, economic, social, and philosophical questions are raised in the policy agendas.

Metropolitan Life Insurance Company. Metropolitan Life's focus is on the teacher as the pivotal person in school improvement and the achievement of educational excellence.

Prepared by Chava Willig Levy, Met Life's consultant for corporate social responsibility, the case outlines the company's historic interest in the American teacher. The structures that support this commitment are described as they were developed. They include an Advisory Educational Group established as far back as 1924 and the establishment of the Metropolitan Life Foundation in 1976. The decentralization of the company in 1971 had an important structural effect on the development of national and local efforts in education and created a network for influence and communication in this area. The Met Life story is a good illustration of how the involvement of a large corporation can have both national and local impact on quality education.

Burger King. Barbara Gothard, Director of Corporate Affairs for Burger King Corporation, is a former high school principal. She came to Burger King with public school experience and a commitment to quality public education. Her commitment was convincing and contagious. Gothard has developed a corporate education program at Burger King that is formidable and still growing. As the author of this case, she details the decision-making process and describes the motivations that led this company to target education as the primary focus of its corporate social responsibility program.

Burger King employs 250,000 teenagers a year; 70 percent of its work force is under 21 years old; 41 percent is minorities. The skills, knowledge, and attributes that students develop in school are of primary, direct importance to this major corporation, which has restaurants and franchises all over the country.

Burger King's education programs center around its scholarship programs. In addition to the direct impact these programs have had on students, employees, teachers, and principals, Gothard describes the effect involvement with education has had internally on company communications and interdepartmental cooperation, as well as on external agencies of government and education associations.

Murry Bergtraum High School for Business Careers. Barbara Christen, principal of the Murry Bergtraum High School in New York City, has worked with the business community from the time her school, specializing in business careers, was on the drawing board. New York businesses have been involved in every phase of the school's development and are an integral part of its internship program. Christen offers the reader her views on this involvement, as well as on what she, as a school principal, thinks employers need to know about schools, youth, and work readiness.

The school's official charge has been to develop, with the business community, programs that would enhance the employability of the school's graduates. But, really, the school has two mandates: (1) to produce employable students, and (2) to produce students who are ready to go on to college. The story of how the high school principal, faculty, and administrative staff work with the business community offers several principles for successful business/school collaboration. Credibility, communications, and contact are the key factors in their partnership. As much attention is paid to the invisible curriculum (the signals the school sends to students that influence their work habits, values, behavior, and attitudes) as to the formal curriculum.

Public Education Funds. Because many businesses prefer to join with other corporations and leverage their resources—both financial and in-kind—public education funds have grown as a significant vehicle for private/public partnerships. These funds create new organizations that play important linking roles between sectors, facilitating and mediating communications and relationships. They are also new players to be reckoned with in the politics of education and can sometimes complicate the horizon. David Bergholz is the Executive Director of the national Public Education Fund, an organization funded by Ford Foundation to provide technical assistance and seed money to generate public education funds at the local level. In this case, Lies and Bergholz place public education funds in the context of other kinds of private sector involvement and tell us what we may reasonably expect from them and what we may not. They view public education funds as a part of the larger community involvement and thus give us a broader picture in which to evaluate them.

After the Signing: The Boston Compact 1982 to 1985. "On September 22, 1982, an extraordinary press conference took place in the main hall of the Boston School Department. Sharing the stage were the chief executive officers (CEOs) of two prominent Boston corporations, Mayor Kevin White, School Superintendent Robert Spillane, and the President of the School Committee, Jean Sullivan McKeigue. This gathering was unprecedented in the history of the city; it brought together the leaders of Boston's traditionally warring factions: the schools, the city administration, and the business community." Thus begins Eleanor Farrar's and Anthony Cipollone's case study of the Boston Compact. This case examines what the Compact really is, the people involved, how they view it, and what they think about why it is successful.

To help readers understand what made the Compact possible, Farrar and Cipollone describe its history and how business and education related before its founding. The success of the Compact shows the importance of good communications and forceful leadership. Its goals are set in quantifiable terms, yet it seems to mean different things to different people, which is an important part of its strength. The authors tell us that it is indeed an agreement with the ability to be used by many for different purposes, allowing individuals and institutions to "buy in." Because of this, it has been able to achieve a remarkable level of agreement among several groups traditionally more opposed to each other than in harmony—the school system, city hall, the business community, and labor unions.

Farrar and Cipollone take the reader to two high schools to see how the Compact has been used and how effective it has been. One of their conclusions is that is has become an important instrument for the development of school-based education improvement. Initially conceived as a work and employment program, pledging jobs for Boston high school graduates, it has apparently been successful in shifting the focus to improving the quality of the schools. Although there are still formidable obstacles to overcome, the Compact has established an important measure of credibility on both sides of the agreement.

A Tale of Two States: California and Minnesota. Education consultants Paul Berman and Rick Clugston compare and contrast the involvement of the business community in state-level education reform in California and Minnesota. In each state, the business community, acting through an organization of business leaders, became major players in a political process leading to system-wide education reform. In each state, business succeeded in placing its agenda in the center of the political arena and became recognized players, for the first time, in state education policy.

Berman and Clugston describe the four stages of involvement: deciding to get involved, developing an agenda, working it through enactment, and continuing involvement. The processes of political engagement, negotiation, information gathering, decision making, and public outreach are all described. In each case, the political climate, the need for reform and the availability of committed leadership form the context for business involvement. The authors relate that although the processes were similar, in each state the outcome in terms of the business community's agenda was different. This suggests that there is no monolithic business approach to education, but rather a pragmatic approach determined by what is needed and what is possible in the political context.

Since these cases were developed, important economic changes have occurred that have had significant implications for at least one of the programs described. In a brief epilogue, Rita Kaplan notes that a restructuring of operations at Honeywell precipitated by external economic pressures has resulted in major reductions in staff and programs. The fact that Honeywell's programs were linked to the corporate philosophy and received broad internal support contributed enormously to their effectiveness and significance. They were able to, and did, draw on the strength of corporate personnel in diverse positions, and they were able to influence the development of education programs in many Honeywell locations. These characteristics contributed to their success. If education partnerships did not grow out of Honeywell's philosophy, they would not have worked as well or been supported as much. However, their integration did not make them invulnerable in the context of the company's primary need to retain its competitive position. Being "institutionalized" made the education programs stronger, that is, more effective; it did not mean they would not be affected when the company was faced with the need to restructure its resources.

The Honeywell case broaches what has been thought to be the ultimate test of business/education partnerships; for example, what happens when business must respond to economic pressures and change its role in collaboration? In Honeywell's case it is too soon to tell how its commitment will be manifested. The context of public/private partnerships, however, has grown and broadened locally, regionally, and nationally. Changes in tactics employed by one company do not mean that the basic strategy of corporate involvement in public education is necessarily weakened. The motivations for such involvement, if anything, have deepened. It is probably now true that no task force on economic development will ever convene without the public education sector playing a central role. Furthermore, events such as those at Honeywell have implications for the way in which the public sector approaches such partnerships. They suggest that public schools take more of a leadership role in establishing priorities for collaboration and not be merely the passive recipients of the private sector's largesse. The reality of economic pressures suggests also that public schools need to be more dynamic in their ability to deal with change at the same time that they maintain their character as institutions charged with essentially a conservative responsibility, the transmission of knowledge and culture.

*   *   *

The companies described in Part I of this book each reflect the use of corporate strategies and direct action. But some issues are fraught with conflict, and inevitably corporations will have to come to grips with the internal conflicts they will arouse. *New York Times* education columnist Fred Hechinger speaks of this "schizophrenic posture" of American business vis-à-vis the public schools.* At the same time that many support local schools and speak out for quality education, many also support legislative measures that either undercut the ability of the schools to carry out their missions, or draw financial support away from the schools.

---

*Fred M. Hechinger, "Turnaround for the Public Schools?" *Harvard Business Review, 64*(1), Jan.–Feb. 1985, 136–144.

Coming to grips with the policy role that corporations can in fact play will mean supporting a presence and taking a position that may challenge other priorities of the company. In the final analysis the business community can be the most powerful constituency the public schools have; the decision to play that role is a difficult one.

1 Honeywell

RITA KAPLAN
Former Manager, Education Programs, Honeywell Inc.

Banking, food, commerce, high technology, and musical recording and production are part of the Twin Cities' diversified business mix. On a per capita basis, the area is home to more corporate headquarters than is any other American city except Boston.

One of them is Honeywell, a Minneapolis-based international high technology corporation with revenues of more than $6 billion. With 18,000 employees in Minneapolis (94,000 worldwide), Honeywell is one of the three largest employers in the state. Its major markets include computers, integration and automation systems, aerospace and defense, and residential, environmental, and industrial controls.

COMMUNITY TRADITIONS

The values of Minnesota's early business settlers, combined with the state's populist traditions, produced a milieu where sharing in community concerns is expected. The standard for corporate involvement in community affairs was set by George Nelson Dayton, founder of Dayton's department store chain in Minnesota, and his five sons, who inherited the business. Their efforts forged many corporate traditions of working with local political, educational, cultural, and other civic leaders to improve the quality of life. With the Daytons' leadership, the community initiated the 2 Percent/5 Percent Club for corporate philanthropy. As other companies became involved, corporate community programs flourished. These include corporate volunteerism, management and technical assistance for nonprofit organizations, and executive and employee service on boards and commissions in the public and nonprofit sectors.

Beyond Minnesota's deep-rooted tradition of community involvement, its ethnic makeup (predominantly German and Scandinavian), population size, and scale of problems make problem solving more manageable.

The Twin Cities' reputation as a metropolitan area that works is a mixed blessing. Successes from the cooperative efforts of business, public, and nonprofit sectors generate an appetite for collaboration on community issues. But success sometimes breeds complacency. If there's anything, however, that helps keep Minneapolis and St. Paul sensitive to community needs, it is a recognition that there's a thin line separating the two attitudes.

A healthy skepticism keeps Minnesota's tradition of community participation intact. Lines of communication among leaders—corporate and community—are easily accessed in the Twin Cities. The leadership at the grass roots level helps keep corporate programs sensitive to *real* needs and the larger context, which may or may not be addressed. A number of local organizations were established about 15 years ago to make it easier for corporate members of the community to work together to identify and define the issues and develop solutions.

The Honeywell Foundation granted $212,000 for the program in 1986, from which more than 35 programs received grants. Some examples include a Professor Academy, complementing the Teacher Academy, which brings important educational programming to universities with a major priority to serve minority students; Kindertech, a K + 4th grade program with emphasis on math, science, and technology, pulling together resources from Augsburg College, the Minneapolis Public Schools, the Hubert H. Humphrey Institute of Public Affairs, and Honeywell to develop new interdisciplinary curricula and teacher training and parent involvement models; and a Honeywell employee organized program to increase the numbers of teachers and employees trained in collaboration and school improvement issues.

Two new organizations, led by CEOs, were established: the Minnesota Business Partnership and the Minnesota Project on Corporate Responsibility. Honeywell has been very involved in both organizations.

HOW HONEYWELL GOT INVOLVED

The urban riots of the 1960s triggered Honeywell's community involvement. Stephen Keating, then President of the company, brought area businesses and minority groups together to talk about mutual concerns. This action led to the formation of the Minneapolis Urban Coalition and the channeling of dollars into programs and projects for the minority community. It set the tone for Honeywell's community commitment.

In an even more visible commitment, Honeywell decided not to move its corporate offices to the suburbs but to remain in its original inner city location. That decision led to an increased understanding about neighborhoods and what keeps them working. Honeywell revitalized the neighborhood surrounding its offices, viewing this action as an important means for strengthening the community. Along with working on neighborhood housing and providing residents with jobs, Honeywell recognized that getting involved with schools was necessary to keeping neighborhoods vital.

In retrospect, Honeywell's early community involvements seem more miscellaneous than strategic. Yet they demonstrated the company's commitment and provided the foundation for personal and company interest in the community. Keating's leadership and personal involvement set an example for other Honeywell executives and employees and signaled that it was now legitimate for business to be interested in public and social policy issues. When Edson W. Spencer became Chief Executive Officer and President in 1975, he carried Keating's ideas forward and began a more strategic integration of the company's community programs. Under his leadership, a Honeywell philosophy on community responsibility took shape, and the company established operating principles to guide its strategies and practices. Citizenship was one of those principles.

The company's public affairs activities helped it to become a key player in discussions on public and social policies. Credibility was established through these early programs and later by the company's work on key urban issues, such as housing revitalization, jobs, women's concerns, and minority vendor purchasing, and by its continuing commitment to education.

Early Honeywell activities included the United Way, Community Service Awards for employees' volunteer efforts, and a loaned-executive program and dollar support to a Minneapolis inner city high school. In 1979, the company organized its community involvements into the Public Affairs Department, coordinating the functions of community relations, the Honeywell Fund, and government relations.

THE HONEYWELL APPROACH

Over the years, we at Honeywell have learned that corporate responsibility is not discharged simply by random grants to good causes. We have come to understand that it is intrinsic to all functions of the corporation. We see with greater clarity that Honeywell's affairs are interwoven with the social fabric of the communities where we do business. As a consequence, we recognize a practical and ethical obligation to get involved, to contribute to the public well-being where we can, and, above all, to maintain a dialogue with the world outside the corporate walls.

The company has developed a four-level philosophy that reflects its approach to corporate responsibility. The process starts with the contribution of dollars, progresses with the involvement of employees, is further built on partnerships with community groups, and finally is internalized in Honeywell operations. Each level is built on the preceding one, and together they develop responsible community initiatives.

Of course, dollars alone can't meet community needs, but they represent a conscious corporate decision to support community projects. More important than contributions is the company's most valuable resource: people. As active volunteers, employees channel the energies and actions of the company in more effective and creative ways for the benefit of the community. Our employees pave the way for broader, cooperative ventures between Honeywell and community organizations. Using the strengths of Honeywell people and those of other concerned companies, Honeywell can join forces with community and public organizations to form partnerships, an effective method for solving problems. The final level, internalization, involves incorporating commitments made in the community into day-to-day company decisions. Keeping company actions consistent with practices in the community ensures the unity of Honeywell's business and community profiles.

Top management sets the tone for community responsibility and plays an important role in community relations programs. Senior management, including the general managers of the operating divisions, take on significant commitments as volunteers. They serve on boards of organizations such as the Urban League, Opportunity Industrialization Centers, orchestral societies, museums, and family service agencies. Often, they are elected or appointed to serve on public-sector boards and commissions such as school boards, community development agencies, prison industries, universities, and colleges.

The company gives approximately 2 percent of its U.S. pretax profit (about $7 million in 1986) to the Honeywell Foundation (formerly called the Honeywell Fund). The Foundation's Board of Directors earmarks 45 percent of its annual contributions for education programs. Most of these funds are directed to higher education, but the dollar amounts to elementary and secondary schools have increased significantly over the past four years.

SUPPORTING EDUCATION

Employee volunteers work with school administrators, teachers, and parents in several of our major locations. There are over 60 Honeywell school projects in cities such as Boston, New York, Minneapolis, Chicago, Denver, Phoenix, Seattle, and Clearwater, Florida.

In the late 1970s, we regarded K–12 education issues as relatively safe and noncontroversial. It somehow seemed logical that as a high tech company with a highly educated work force, we should recognize and support education programs. It was a comfortable area of involvement for our executives and employees. As we worked at it, the pattern of our involvement shifted from a reactive to an active stance. In 1980, a group of employees responsible for managing our local contributions process in the Twin Cities decided to initiate a project with the Minneapolis schools rather than wait for a request. The group contacted school administrators and offered to augment district resources for an important project that school resources were unable to cover. Because district resources were focused on the average student, we developed a program for high-potential students. In this way, we could help round out the district's focus.

Our experience in education programs and in neighborhood development began to demonstrate some congruency in underlying assumptions. We became increasingly convinced that economic growth and stability are tied to an effective and efficient public education system.

Early on, Honeywell recognized its important stake in elementary and secondary education. The communities in which we operate are more attractive to our employees if quality schools are accessible to their children and to their own continuing development. Strong neighborhoods are enhanced by effective schools with high teacher and student performance and parental involvement. Moreover, we know that our self-interest as employers dictates that any effort is worthwhile if it ensures a stream of qualified people for universities, colleges, and the future work force. Because a poor educational system destroys neighborhoods and derails economic stability, business, as a key stakeholder, should share its expertise and resources where appropriate to enhance the quality of education. We therefore join the education enterprise in the conviction that business cannot afford to give its future work force less than the best.

Many of Honeywell's education programs support company strategies. Programs that help students make successful transitions from school to the workplace support our employment strategies. For example, our summer youth employment programs integrate work, learning, and the building of self-esteem to help young people make the transition. In keeping with our affirmative action and equal opportunity strategies, many of our involvements with education emphasize access and opportunities for specific target populations. The Defense Systems Division provides scholarships to senior students from the communities in which it is located. The Division looks for students who have demonstrated high potential for scientific, engineering, or technical careers in industry or the public sector. The Division scholarship program for minority and handicapped students takes a three-pronged approach: full four-year scholarship, summer employment with specialized tutorials, and employment after graduation. We know that when more people—particularly minorities, women, and the handicapped—are encouraged to pursue the disciplines in demand at Honeywell, our work force can better reflect the ethnic and cultural diversity of the population.

The way we get involved in education issues is consistent with all our community involvements. We try to be sure at the start that we understand the line between our self-interest and the community's interest. The broad picture anchors the mission for any undertaking. In this way, we can be clearer about what expertise we have and what we do not have; where we can collaborate, take the lead, or follow; and how we can leverage our resources for significant impact on the issues.

Always, we begin by listening. We meet with administrators, teachers, parents, and students to find out their impressions about needs and solutions. We build stronger alliances when we bring to the table implicit respect for diversity, individual expertise, and the differing objectives of those with shared goals.

Over the years, we have learned that Honeywell's special resources and technical expertise make positive contributions to the education establishment. To run such a large and complex corporation, Honeywell employees must have a very broad range of diverse skills. Their own interests, talents, and avocations add even greater breadth to our people resources. We also have experience in management issues that are common across organizations, such as managing changes, providing incentives for risk taking, and rewarding individual development. When these resources are combined with administrators' and teachers' understanding of the educational environment, the ability to address important issues is significantly enhanced.

A Change in Emphasis

After several years of miscellaneous involvements in the public schools, we recognized that an uncoordinated approach was no longer adequate. We began to emphasize programs that would allow us to anticipate needs and initiate efforts specifically designed to meet those needs, from the elementary to the college level.

Our education projects help people develop job skills, give dropouts a chance to earn high school diplomas, and provide teachers with needed training in advanced technology. Our strongest contributions, however, occur in development for curriculum, students, and teachers and in strategic planning associated with managing change, because these are major areas that we deal with in our organization.

In designing community involvement projects, we build in some clear and simple concepts that can be shared with the larger community. Computer scientists talk about the *elegance* of a solution. Community involvements need this kind of elegance. They need to be simple, not simplistic; to have vision, not short-range goals; to meet real needs, not assumed needs; and to be understandable.

Some examples of Honeywell projects illustrate how we use our expertise, leverage our resources, and help create new approaches to old problems. Each project serves as a case study for beginning new ventures, and keeps our vision strategic and grounded in what we have learned from our own experience in working in the community. The programs in each of our major areas (development and strategic planning) demonstrate where small amounts of resources make big differences, how our approach works, and what the outcomes are.

CURRICULUM DEVELOPMENT

Although Honeywell's business focuses on high technology, the diversity of our employees' knowledge, skills, and abilities brings breadth to curriculum efforts. Honeywell people work with teachers on mathematics and science courses. We have adapted software programs to meet specialized demands and helped develop computer literacy programs for teachers. We include elements of liberal arts education, such as communication skills, arts, and language, in our programs because, as employers, we know these are very important building blocks for successful employment.

Adopting Schools

In Tampa, Florida, 550 seventh-grade students have firsthand experience with Honeywell volunteers. Employees at our Defense Communications and Production Division adopted the Belle Witter Elementary School in 1984 as a long-term project.

This adoption involves more than needed financial assistance. Employees volunteer as library aides, participate in mentor programs, conduct factory tours and field trips, and provide technical expertise in computer programming. In addition to donating audiovisual equipment, the Division opened its printshop to Belle Witter, thereby reducing the school's instructional materials expenditures.

In 1985, Honeywell employees adopted more than 40 schools across the country. As a result, we are breaking down barriers between business and education and creating an atmosphere in which collaboration flourishes. In many urban centers, the schools are losing their traditional constituency because under 30 percent of the population has school-aged children. Our employees, once involved in a hands-on way with schools, often become advocates for public education. In this way, business participation is making a big difference in the future of our schools.

Linking Business and Schools

Faced with the challenge of preparing students for a high technology future in a low technology environment, educators in Snohomish County, Washington, joined forces with Honeywell's Marine Systems Division in Seattle to develop solutions. Our Seattle operation invited a group of citizens to discuss community concerns about public education. The group was a cross section of people with a stake in the educational enterprise: parents, students, teachers, administrators, business, colleges, vocational and technical schools, public officials, and key decision makers. After hearing the community's concerns, the Division leadership called on representatives from local business and education to further assess the needs. The result is a partnership appropriately called LINK. The program benefits schools and business by linking their resources, and is funded by participating school districts and businesses.

LINK pairs high schools with business so that students, teachers, and people from business can develop education-enhancement programs on a team basis. Other joint ventures include student and teacher internships, classroom business lectures, professional development opportunities for teachers, plant tours, and career education counseling. The schools give business access to athletic facilities and classroom seminars. LINK, both in creation and execution, represents the creativity that results from working partnerships.

STUDENT DEVELOPMENT

Honeywell employees have worked on programs for average students, alienated youths, dropouts, and high-potential students.

A Working Partnership

The relationship between Honeywell and Horace Mann School for the Deaf and Hearing Impaired in Brighton, Massachusetts, illustrates the company's four-step approach to community responsibility. What started as general support grew to include volunteers, developed into a partnership, and was ultimately internalized in Honeywell operations.

In 1976, instructors from Horace Mann asked employees from Honeywell Information Systems in Brighton to participate on its Business and Advisory Commission. Honeywell's involvement soon expanded from advising the school on job training needs to providing both training and jobs. In fact, Honeywell donated a full-time job training center to give Horace Mann students instruction in electromechanical assembly.

In addition to participating in instructor and student training programs, Honeywell established a work-study program and hired the students after graduation. By 1985, the Brighton facility employed more than thirty deaf individuals in five job clusters: electromechanical assembly, clerical, maintenance, distribution, and micrographics. To make the workplace productive and pleasant for its new employees, the company installed special telephones for the deaf, upgraded safety requirements, and held sign language classes for hearing employees.

After successfully helping deaf people find entry-level jobs, Honeywell employees initiated other collaborative programs with the school to establish new job training programs and additional supportive work opportunities for severely disabled adults.

A Special Initiative for Youth at Risk

In 1980, Honeywell's Building Services Division, the Loring-Nicollet-Bethlehem Community Center, the Center for Community Action, and other companies created the Minneapolis Education and Recycling Center (MERC).

This neighborhood center is linked to an alternative education program. It helps at-risk young people to earn a high school degree while gaining work experience and earning wages in the center's business.

The sponsoring partners share a belief that the societal costs of any failure of large numbers of young people in school or work are too high.

The Building Services Division, as sponsoring partner, brought substantial funding, space in a Honeywell-owned building, and the efforts of more than 100 employee volunteers to MERC. When Division managers formed a MERC management committee, they expanded its use to sharing ideas and job expertise with the program's staff. The staff helped us to understand the students' need for real-world experiences. As a result, students from the center shadow our employees at work to learn about their jobs. Our volunteers work with MERC staff to upgrade the program's facilities to meet the growing number of recycling contracts it receives and the additional students who might benefit from the program.

TEACHER DEVELOPMENT

Honeywell people work closely with teachers on education projects. We ask for their advice on key education issues and for feedback on our ideas. We respect their expertise and offer ours as scientists and managers as we work together to shape a broader range of solutions.

Providing Seed Capital for Enterprising Teachers

While the public was debating education reform and issuing reports, Honeywell worked with six other companies (Cray Research, First Bank of Minneapolis, H. B. Fuller, Inter-Regional Finance Group, Medtronic, and Sperry) to launch a program to provide incentives for teachers with innovative ideas.

Aware that advances in technology come from applying new twists to existing ideas, we borrowed the mini grant idea from the Public Education Fund in Pittsburgh, made some adaptations, and initiated our own unique program. The seven participants formed a holding company, Education Ventures Inc. (EVI), in 1984. The idea was to have an umbrella organization to sponsor several education incentive programs and broaden the base of community investment in education. EVI's long-range goal is to initiate programs that will be attractive investments to other companies, organizations, and individuals who want to play a role in strengthening public education. It envisions investments that can be made in multiples of $100, depending on available resources and commitment. In this way, small neighborhood stores, law firms, and medical clinics can join larger corporations in support of education.

The first program implemented was the Teacher Venture Fund. Two Twin Cities school districts were chosen: Minneapolis and Fridley. The selection of a very large and complex district and a small district with only one high school gave the pilot program some interesting contrasts.

Teachers seeking mini grants are asked only four questions:

What do you want to do?
How will you do it?
How will it enrich the day-to-day learning of students and stretch your creativity as a teacher?
What will it cost?

Proposals are reviewed by teams of employees from the founding companies, with the advice of teachers emeriti from the school districts. Drawing on the talents of retired professionals for service to the community is an important lesson we learned from the Honeywell Retiree Volunteer Project, and enlisting the services of retired teachers makes sense in education.

The direct business-to-teacher link is an important aspect of our program. Because the money and the selection come from outside the district, we encourage risk taking. Also, our employee interactions with teachers help break down barriers between business and schools and convert our volunteers into important advocates for public education.

EVI works closely with the schools in administering the program. Our intent is to provide seed capital (up to $500) for innovation, not to alter district curricular objectives but to generate excitement and creativity within the teaching cadre. The program deals with teachers' basic needs: to ease their isolation, to nurture their development, and to provide them recognition.

In 1985, the mini grant program was implemented in seven Honeywell communities: Elgin, Illinois; Charlotte, North Carolina; Rochester, New York; Valley Forge and Denver, Pennsylvania; Davenport, Iowa; West Covina, California; and Phoenix, Arizona. Interesting modifications based on local traditions and needs are taking place. Although these innovations modify the basic program, the creativity and policy direction thrive with this room for change. For example, in West Covina, our division is collaborating with the Rotary in sponsoring the program. In Phoenix, 13 companies (including another EVI founder, Sperry) joined to develop Teacher Venture Arizona. They decided to offer grants to all fifth- and sixth-grade teachers in Maricopa County, rather than to a single school district.

Our experience with the mini grant program has been phenomenal.

We have learned that as an organization with divisions and sales offices across the country, we can quickly transfer a program to many communities. Dispersed operations present built-in marketing and distribution systems for important community programs.

Turning Honeywell Operations into a Campus

In 1985, when school was out for the summer and classrooms were empty, 22 Twin Cities teachers prepared for fall classes in a unique way: attending summer school at Honeywell. Honeywell teamed with 11 area school districts to establish a teacher academy designed to expose high school mathematics and science teachers to some of the technologies, business practices, and careers at the company. The ultimate goal was to enrich the classroom experience for students so that they might see careers in science and technology as exciting opportunities. Honeywell's history of joint ventures with schools created a foundation for building such a mutually beneficial partnership. The schools and Honeywell leadership believed that a collaborative training program for teachers would stimulate better training for students interested in careers in science and industry.

The Defense Systems Division, which took the lead on this project (along with the Underseas and Military Avionics Divisions), connected the program to three central Honeywell objectives:

1. Encouraging placement of highly qualified employees in scientific, engineering, and technical fields.
2. Improving educational opportunities for families of Honeywell's 18,000 employees living in the area.
3. Carrying out Honeywell's commitment to being a concerned, helpful, and responsible corporate citizen.

The academy turned Honeywell's Twin Cities operations into a campus. Teachers attended classes in the company's laboratories, science and training centers, and several other facilities. The academy's curriculum was divided into two sections, one for each of the two weeks. In the first week, teachers were provided background information on how mathematics and science are used in high technology companies and why problem solving and critical thinking are important skills for students considering careers in these areas. During the second week, teachers developed a project for classroom use, with Honeywell technical facilities and personnel for support and consultation.

Some interesting innovations resulted. For example, teachers built a computer model to better understand how integrated circuits work. They set up and ran a scanning electron microscope for high magnification of selected samples, used a mass spectrometer to determine a sample's chemical makeup, and videotaped Honeywell employees in an interview about high technology careers.

Schools joined with Honeywell in providing the $300 weekly stipend to teachers. Honeywell provided the equipment, materials, and campus. More than 40 employees worked on the design and implementation of the academy. Senior engineers and top-level scientists gave lectures and met with teachers for informal discussions.

STRATEGIC PLANNING

We draw on our own experience in managing change and thinking in terms of the long range when we work with schools. We apply what we have learned, where appropriate, in managing change in our own operations and in the community.

Assisting with Large–scale Changes

Because employees are both the largest resource and the biggest cost in most organizations, Honeywell works with school administrators in a variety of ways to explore effective human resource programs. Drawing from our experience, we have worked with administrators on the overall issues of managing change, relating these strategies to the needs of an education system in an urban center experiencing large-scale changes.

With this background, Honeywell and three other Minneapolis corporations (Dayton Hudson, General Mills, and Norwest Bank) led a drive to help the Minneapolis school district implement a strategic planning process. Our involvement deepened Honeywell's commitment to schools. Stephen Keating and other area business leaders attended briefing sessions at which Dr. Richard Green, Superintendent of Minneapolis Public Schools, laid out the district's concerns. The result was that over thirty companies contributed $100,000 and countless hours from employee volunteers to develop a five-year plan for the district.

When the plan was completed, it offered business a means to interact more consistently with the school district. It defined the district's mission and laid out strategies and tactics to achieve equity and quality in public education. More important, it enabled the Superintendent to lead the district through major changes, including closing 18 schools, reorganizing staff, and revitalizing the school system.

This broadened participation in educational issues made the companies involved realize that helping education deal with tomorrow's challenges means getting involved with today's policies, programs, and financial issues. Again, this realization has brought the two sectors closer together, because managements share common responsibilities for looking beyond the short term. "Education and business suffer from mutual isolation," says Green. "We've traditionally had a look-but-don't-touch relationship. We must foster a dynamic crossover with the belief that we can solve problems together."

At this new level of involvement, business and the school district took risks. They opened themselves up to hard-nosed questions about who was running schools, the Superintendent or business. The questions pointed up a generalized distrust of business and an assumption that the school leadership yielded to business power and resources. In this new partnership arrangement, both Honeywell and the school district demonstrated an effective model for sharing power and resources. As a result, they proved to the larger community that productivity increases when business brings complementary expertise to the problems facing education and when educators help shape the way those resources are used.

The five-year plan withstood the test of critics and asserted the leadership of the Superintendent and the school board in ensuring quality education for all Minneapolis students. To further help, Honeywell provided Richard Green with a loaned executive to assist in developing strategies to create business/education partnerships. Then, in 1983, the corporate leadership worked with the Superintendent to assess the plan's progress.

The first two years were so successful that in 1984, Minneapolis businesses and foundations raised an additional $800,000 (under the leadership of a Dayton Hudson executive) to help the district meet the plan's remaining objectives.

The additional funding was provided on the basis of comprehensive status reports prepared by four advisory committees, cochaired by business and school administrators. The committees worked on major priorities within the plan: teacher and principal development, dropout strategies, educational technology, and marketing. They reviewed what had been accomplished to date, what was needed to come in on plan, how much in resources could be provided by the district, and where the gaps were.

In 1985, the same group of business executives and district administrators continued stewardship for the strategic plans in more formalized meetings held bimonthly. At these meetings, priorities were reviewed, progress was charted, and decisions on use of the funds were reexamined.

The same four priorities (principal and teacher development, educational technology, dropout strategies, and marketing) are moving forward. Moreover, strategic planning has become an ongoing element in the management of Minneapolis schools. Honeywell offered top-level support to the major study of K–12 education in Minnesota, sponsored by the Minnesota Business Partnership and conducted by Berman Weiler Associates (BW). The company provided dollars, printing resources, and, most importantly, leadership to expedite this important initiative. A deputy of the CEO served on the task force that provided guidance and oversight to BW's research and recommendations.

Rethinking Our Internal Strategies

Prompted by declining student test scores, the low performance and interest level of women and minorities in mathematics and science, and industry's need to provide remedial education for new employees, Honeywell established an Education Task Force to study the problem and make recommendations. Employee task force members from divisions across the country developed a series of guidelines for company action in education and recommended specific programs targeted at the elementary and secondary schools.

The recommendations became important community projects in 1986. Each recommendation emphasizes methods designed to enhance the learning process for both students and educators. One idea, for example, calls for establishing a Seminar on Building Collaboration in a variety of company locations. Besides serving as a development tool, the seminar, which is to be tested in seven Minneapolis school districts, will help Honeywell volunteers and teachers collaborate in areas such as curriculum and management development, strategic planning, use of technology, student motivation, and parental involvement. Other recommendations address increasing opportunities for minorities, women, and the handicapped in scientific and technical careers; replicating a mathematics, science, and technology magnet program (Summatech) at the high school level; and forming business and education partnerships in the community.

Designing a Joint Venture

Honeywell helped the district design and implement Summatech in 1981. This state-of-the-art program for grades nine to twelve is particularly interesting because it helped North Community High, an inner city school located in the center of a minority neighborhood, to desegregate its student population and change its image. Students from other high schools in the district were attracted to the program as a quality option. The students and the program itself were forces in altering community perceptions about the school's learning environment from unsafe and unproductive to secure and effective. Honeywell's Physical Science Center sponsors this project.

The idea for Summatech arose during work on the district's five-year plan. A magnet program in mathematics and science was one of the plan's priority objectives. Because Honeywell is headquartered in Minneapolis, it seemed to fit the bill as a partner for this bellwether program. After four months of discussion, district administrators, a curriculum consultant, a Honeywell chief scientist, and our public affairs staff agreed on a plan. During this period, meetings took on the aura of a ritual dance, in which each partner moved closer, retreated, and moved closer again. Both Honeywell and the schools tested the boundaries of the new relationship. Individual and joint responsibilities were carefully defined, and the joint and individual risks were articulated. In the end, Honeywell made a commitment of dollars and volunteers to implement the program, and the school district offered to share in paying the salary of a full-time school district employee to serve as program coordinator.

Honeywell and the Minneapolis schools worked together on many projects during the past ten years, but none tapped the company's skills and resources in as broad a manner as did Summatech. Since the program was implemented, over $100,000 in dollar and equipment resources have been invested. However, the dollars inadequately reflect the value of the total resources Honeywell continues to bring to the program through employee volunteers. More than sixty scientists, including two vice-presidents and a chief scientist, brought significant technical expertise to the program. Furthermore, the program was linked to over 20 volunteers from other Honeywell divisions, to the Institute of Technology at the University of Minnesota, and to parents.

Summatech is managed by a steering committee led by a school administrator and our chief scientist. Together, they have fashioned a curriculum to prepare students for entry into technical positions in the workplace or exploratory and theoretical studies in higher education. The diverse student enrollment, which includes females, blacks, and Southeast Asians, reflects important values shared by the schools and Honeywell. When the first class graduated in 1984, two top students— one white, one black—received Honeywell scholarships for their first year in college.

Our employees have come away from their volunteer experience at Summatech with gains. They tell about the naive perceptions that industry and education used to have about each other's environment and resources. They have learned that educators operate in a system with diffuse and competing hierarchies, and school personnel have learned that business operates within a vertical chain of command under explicit performance objectives. Both have concluded that their partnership is important to students, teachers, business, and the community.

A LEARNING EXPERIENCE

Communities, like business, are living entities that require nurturing, new ideas, teamwork, and a strategic sense of where they are going. Through community involvements, Honeywell has learned that business is an important stakeholder in education, but not the only one. A need exists for more broadly based involvement of business in education reform.

We have learned a lot from the experience. We know that a partnership is a developmental process that requires sensitivity and commitment. We in business need to share risks as well as opportunities with the schools, and both sides need to get rid of naive and suspicious assumptions about the other. Our involvements with education are guided by a clearer understanding of the limits of our resources and expertise, and of the boundaries of our self-interest and community interest.

Many elements of partnership have been well documented in the education and public affairs literature during the mid-1980s. We all know that it is important to have a shared goal, mutual respect, a desire to work together, and the commitment to see the project through. Business and schools have come a long way in communicating better with one another. We have all become careful about using jargon, learning to ask for information where we don't understand, and speaking forthrightly where we have knowledge. The major things that we have learned, however, are more about tone, style, and ways we can effectively bring our resources to broader efforts in the community.

One of our strengths in managing our own company is our people. When we need to get things done, we bring our employees in on the decisions. U.S. industry has learned that in our effort to maintain a competitive edge on world markets, we can accomplish more working with people than through people. Concentrating on short-term gains can compromise long-term objectives. All this applies to the education enterprise as well. Educators have helped us understand what management objectives we hold in common and how to appreciate the differences. We have also gotten better at translating some of the strategies that have worked for us into paradigms that fit the education environment. When we bring our people skills with us to the community concerns, we are more effective in working with others.

We need to continue defining our role as a company and as a corporate citizen. We want to gain a better understanding of things such as school politics, seniority and union issues, performance appraisal and certification conflicts, the quality of the work environment, and the culture of the educational system. Clearly, there are risks involved, but we believe that the risks from not being involved are greater. We look toward building on what we have learned and improving how Honeywell meets its commitment to elementary and secondary education.

EPILOGUE

In 1986, Honeywell completed a major restructuring of its business, which affected every part of the company. The Corporate and Community Responsibility department—which manages the contributions of the Honeywell Foundation, the company's response to social policy issues, and employee volunteer involvements in the community—experienced a deep reduction in staff.

As a result, many questions and concerns were raised about the future of Honeywell's traditional commitment to the communities where it has operations. In response, Honeywell issued a statement expressing its intent to "maintain its longstanding commitment to community issues by reinforcing the work done by employee volunteers and from program grants of the Honeywell Foundation." They have involved other business and community leaders in candid discussions about how public and private sectors function as partners in addressing complex societal issues.

Today's rapidly changing business environment, characterized by mergers, acquisitions, and takeovers, requires such dialogue wherever business and the community interact.

2 Metropolitan Life Insurance and the American Educator

Partners in Leadership

CHAVA WILLIG LEVY
Metropolitan Life Insurance Company

In an educational context, the word *summer* usually conjures up one association: vacation, a time for a well-deserved respite for students and teachers. But does this common word association mean the wheels of education screech to a halt each summer?

No. Take the summer of 1984, for example. In Washington, D.C., John J. Creedon, President and Chief Executive Officer of Metropolitan Life Insurance Company, told over 3,000 educators attending the annual convention of the American Federation of Teachers (AFT) about his company's pioneering survey of the American teacher. He was the only business executive chosen as an AFT keynote speaker in a year of great concern about corporate ties to public education. The choice could not have been more appropriate. As a business executive who earned his bachelor's, master's, and law degrees at night and who taught law at New York University, John Creedon has a profound respect for education and educators.

That respect is characteristic of Metropolitan and its people. During that same summer, a claims manager in Aurora, Illinois, monitored activities at a mathematics and science camp for high-potential minority students in his capacity as member of the program's advisory board. In Tampa, Florida, a medical information coder taught potential dropouts how to prepare for exams and dress appropriately for job interviews. In Tulsa, Oklahoma, a public affairs manager prepared to teach Junior Achievement's Project Business course and recruited co-workers to do the same. In New York City, a retired secretary made a weekly trip to the School Volunteer Program's headquarters to prepare academically weak students for the Scholastic Aptitude Tests.

ROOTS OF CORPORATE COMMITMENT: 1909 TO 1929

In 1909, *The Metropolitan*, a company magazine distributed to all policyholders, announced a precedent-setting corporate policy: "Insurance, not merely as a business proposition but as a social programme, will be the future policy of the Company. We shall adapt ourselves to the public . . . necessity. We must get into the current of the world's thought."[1]

Reaching the Adult

Metropolitan introduced business English classes for its own employees in 1909, but the issues that drew the most attention at that time were such public necessities as fighting malnutrition and disease. Accordingly, Metropolitan's initial social program focused on public health education. Twelve years later, in a major campaign to combat illiteracy, the company's Immigrant Service and Citizenship Bureau began distributing English-language primers to recent immigrants. In 1929, a company flyer encouraged the educated public to teach illiterate adults, both immigrants and native-born Americans, how to read.

Even at this early stage of Metropolitan's social program, a business pattern emerged in which altruism blended with enlightened self-interest. A correlation between health education for adults and longevity had been demonstrated. It was in the company's and society's best interest to strengthen that correlation by distributing health literature. Metropolitan's efforts to combat illiteracy and health problems were closely related. Company literature pointed out that a person who could not read could not take advantage of health information distributed to the public.

Through these early efforts, Metropolitan helped thousands of Americans to strengthen their bodies and minds, while fortifying its leadership position in the insurance industry.

Reaching the Child

Metropolitan's initial efforts at health communication had been designed for an adult audience. But in order to bring about a long-term improvement in society's well-being, the company recognized the need to reach the child directly. On December 19, 1924, Metropolitan embarked on a new endeavor in support of health education: Metropolitan's Advisory Educational Group met for the first time, and the company's interest in the educational needs of children took root.

The Advisory Educational Group (which met regularly until 1964) was made up of outstanding educators, including classroom teachers, from all parts of the United States and Canada. It served a consulting role, helping the company to extend its health education activities beyond the home and workplace into elementary and secondary schools. This novel partnership was a harbinger of the joint efforts that Metropolitan has recently initiated with educators.

The minutes of that first meeting reveal an extraordinarily modern approach to education and a wide array of innovative proposals, all of which were implemented by Metropolitan. These included publication of *Health Heroes*, a series of pamphlets featuring biographical sketches of scientists who made major contributions to health; the introduction of audiovisual instruction into the schools through the production of health "lecture films"; and the publication of an illustrated booklet about health to be distributed by art teachers.

Reaching the Teacher

Reaching the teacher first was certainly the key to the goal of reaching the child. Therefore, the Advisory Educational Group's first meeting not only formalized Metropolitan's commitment to school children but also helped to establish something equally important: a partnership with and advocacy for teachers. Of the twelve proposals made at that first meeting, three were for the direct benefit of teachers: to conduct a survey of teachers' health; to finance a teachers' health education travel fellowship in Europe, with the recipient preparing a report on the experience to be disseminated to other teachers; and to secure statistical data and local health laws for use by teachers of history, civics, and geography.

Establishing these lines of communication with the American educator made ethical and economic sense. It would have been presumptuous for the company to offer ideas about school curricula without consulting educators. Furthermore, by identifying the key person through whom Metropolitan's health experts could funnel needed data to children, the company created a multiplier effect, reaching many through few. Finally, Metropolitan saw its relationship with teachers as reciprocal: teaching teachers while learning from them. This attitude ensured that its health education activities would be pedagogically sound and, therefore, cost-effective.

THE GROWING EFFORT: 1929 TO 1975

Metropolitan's pioneering efforts at partnership were to have a long-lasting effect on the American educational system. Over approximately the next half century, these endeavors grew steadily, resulting in curricular and in kind contributions to health and safety education totaling nearly $200 million. However, most of these activities still centered on health and safety education.

The company increased the range for publications and filmstrips designed for children and for teachers and expanded its contacts with professional educators through participation in scores of annual conventions.

AN EXPLOSION OF EDUCATIONAL ACTIVITY: 1976 TO THE PRESENT

Given Metropolitan's history, it is not surprising that by 1976, the commitment to educational excellence was deeply embedded in its corporate culture. A number of internal and external developments during that year propelled the company to new dimensions of educational involvement.

Organizational Changes

In 1976, the Metropolitan Life Foundation was established and announced that projects in education would be one of its key priorities. At that time, the company's decentralization efforts, initiated in 1971, were completed, giving Metropolitan a network of new offices across the nation, and consequently a major presence in many communities. These two developments allowed for a synergy of both national and local initiatives.

The Foundation, located at company headquarters in New York, has contributed over $42 million to support nonprofit health, education, civic, and cultural activities throughout the United States, and has committed more than $9 million in program-related investments. Approximately 30 percent of its funds have gone toward programs on behalf of education, including health education initiatives.

In addition to business advantages, decentralization made it possible to reach more people in more places for the support of education. For example, each key office has established links with local educational institutions and initiatives. Each office works closely with the Foundation on financial contributions and consult frequently with headquarters' Corporate Social Responsibility Division on nonmonetary (in-kind) support.

Societal Changes

While it was undergoing expansion and internal changes, the company witnessed a series of external developments that also shaped its role as a business concerned with education. The company saw societal ills becoming increasingly relevant: a troubled and academically shaky younger generation, weakened by the erosion of the nuclear family; a growing dependency on drugs and alcohol among young people that, as John Creedon has asserted, "leaves even the most talented, most dedicated teachers helpless to educate their students"[2]; and new members of the work force unprepared for the responsibilities of a job. In short, the company saw a need to address itself to an array of new threats to education, health, and family.

Whereas the health education problems first tackled by Metropolitan were diagnosed and treated with relative ease, these complex social problems defied any single diagnosis or solution. They demanded, instead, a complex, multifaceted response.

AN ARRAY OF MOTIVATIONS

That response has grown, particularly since 1984. The result is an evolving array of activities on behalf of education, motivated by both ethics and economics as Metropolitan maintains its responsibilities to itself, its employees, and the communities its serves. Specifically, the company is motivated by three complementary roles: corporate citizen, employer, and insurer.

As a Corporate Citizen

In an interview with *Financier, The Journal of Private Sector Policy*, John Creedon explained that the motivating force behind all these initiatives is the conviction that "the public-school education system is a critical factor in the success of our country."[3] Underlying that statement is the axiom that business is obligated to consciously foster that national success, as well as its own.

An an Employer

The enlightened self-interest behind Metropolitan's educational initiatives is closely linked to the company's status as one of America's major employers. (It has 32,000 employees.) The home office alone employs 8,000 people, and Metropolitan has taken a strong interest in New York City's educational needs. However, because Metropolitan serves the country as a whole, the overwhelming majority of its efforts are national.

Creedon describes the company's "employer" perspective on education this way:

> Part of the effort on the part of business has to be a recognition that our schools are important to business as such, not only as a matter of corporate responsibility, but also as a matter of economics, because the people who will be our employees in the future are the people who will be coming out of the public schools. That's our market, and if they are not given the skills, training and ability to learn in those schools, they won't have it. So it's a matter of self-preservation, in a way.[4]

As an Insurer

Metropolitan is also influenced by its perspective as an insurance and financial services organization. In an era when people need to make increasingly complex financial decisions, a sound education is more critical than ever. Just as health education is an obvious area of concern for an insurance company, education in the broadest sense has become an equally obvious concern. The continued success of the company depends on it.

AN ARRAY OF ACTIVITIES

Although Metropolitan's motivations have evolved, one thing has remained constant in all its educational efforts: the double objective of serving the child and, more important, the teacher.

Reaching the Teacher

At a time when America's schools are facing harsh criticism, Metropolitan has continued to view teachers as a key to better education. In fact, the company's current emphasis on the needs of teachers has amplified its significant efforts on behalf of students. Chief among the many corporate and Foundation initiatives are the Metropolitan Life Survey of the American Teacher and the Foundation's Teacher and Education Division.

Metropolitan Life Survey of the American Teacher. The spate of reports on the educational crisis prompted many to solicit solutions from leaders of government and academia. Metropolitan found it surprising that in all the discussion and debate, the opinions of the teachers themselves were not sought. Therefore, in 1984, the company commissioned the Metropolitan Life Survey of the American Teacher, to be conducted periodically by Louis Harris and Associates. The first survey showed that although teachers feel beleaguered by a lack of both respect and remuneration, they are eager for reform. Moreover, they wish to take an active part in the process. The 1986 survey had as its theme "Restructuring the Teaching Profession." It examined current issues, including teachers' certification, attrition, and participation in school management. Like its predecessors, the survey ensures that the voice of the teacher is heard.

Teacher and Education Division. In 1985, the Metropolitan Life Foundation established the Teacher and Education Division, whose projects are aimed at teachers, particularly at giving them a greater voice in improving the schools. Shortly thereafter, and perhaps mindful of a similar partnership's success over 60 years earlier, the Division formed an Education Advisory Council, comprising distinguished teachers, administrators, union leaders, teacher educators, and scholars from around the country. The Council examines critical challenges faced by the public education system and helps to guide the Division.

Other Initiatives. Metropolitan undertakes many other initiatives on behalf of educators. Here is a sample.

- *Education Forum.* In January 1985, the company sponsored its first Education Forum. Held in New York City, it brought together over 1,000 business, education, labor, and government leaders to explore ways to pursue educational excellence. In 1986, the focus was on strengthening the teaching profession. In future years, the Foundation plans to take similar educational forums to other key metropolitan areas.
- *Future Teacher Scholarship Program.* In 1985, the Metropolitan Life Foundation established a Future Teacher Scholarship Program for outstanding students who are entering their third year of college and who have decided to become teachers. The program which is administered by the Citizens' Scholarship Foundation of America, is open to applicants from 72 colleges and universities located near Metropoli-

tan's head offices. It also offers scholarships for students attending historically black colleges and universities.

- *Regional Forums on Teacher Education Reform.* Starting in the fall of 1986, the Metropolitan Life Foundation began to sponsor, together with the Education Commission of the States, a series of regional forums on teacher education reform. By the end of 1987, forums had taken place in Tampa, Little Rock, San Francisco, Denver, and Boston.
- *Grants for Research and Policy Development.* The Teacher and Education Division has funded three educational research and policy development projects.
  - *Partnership with the Committee for Economic Development.* In 1985, the Foundation collaborated with the Committee for Economic Development (CED) in printing and helping to distribute its study *Investing in Our Children: Business and the Public Schools* and by cosponsoring five Teacher/Business Roundtables. These meetings, held in five major cities, ensured that the dialogue among classroom teachers, school administrators, and business leaders would continue.
  - *Study of the Teaching Profession.* The Foundation's $100,000 lead grant to the Rand Corporation's Center for the Study of the Teaching Profession is producing research on issues that affect teachers, and will result in data useful for policy makers engaged in educational reform.
  - *Study of the Teacher as an Ally in Reform.* The Foundation awarded a $100,000 lead grant to the Work in America Institute for a national policy study entitled "The Teacher: Ally in Educational Reform." The project examined models for encouraging teachers to participate more fully in school management and reform.

Reaching the Child

Metropolitan's efforts to reach school children are concentrated in three major areas: health and safety education, support for academic curricula, and an elusive commodity called the *invisible curriculum.*

Health and Safety Education. The Metropolitan Life Foundation and the Health and Safety Education Division of the company have joined forces to bring new health education programs to the public in general and the student in particular. This blend of philanthropy (funding comes from the Foundation only) and subject matter expertise has resulted in nationally acclaimed initiatives. They reflect both the company's long-standing concern for the health of children and its commitment to ease the formidable task faced by today's teachers.

- *You Can See Tomorrow* (1980) is a film on maintaining children's health and is directed to teachers, teachers in training, and parents. More than 400 prints are in distribution for use by schools, community groups, and television stations. An estimated 6.5 million viewers have seen the film.
- *"The Chemical People"* (1983) is a two-part public television series on drug and alcohol abuse among children and teen-agers. To sustain the program's impact, the Foundation funds the monthly *Chemical People Newsletter*, written and published by WQED Pittsburgh and distributed nationwide to 10,000 task forces founded as a result of the broadcasts. Metropolitan's long-term commitment to the prevention of substance abuse converges with its determination to curtail the negative impact of substance abuse on teacher effectiveness.
- Met Life is the sole corporate sponsor of "A Generation at Risk: Chemical People II" (1987), a sequel to the "Chemical People" program. Produced by WQED Pittsburgh's public television station, the show has two goals: to report on the Chemical People task forces' success stories, and to explore societal issues influenced by drug and alcohol abuse (e.g., the dropout rate, teen-age pregnancy, teen-age suicide, etc.). Metropolitan's funds are targeted for production costs and outreach materials.
- *The Alcohol Education Film Package* (1984) is a series of alcohol-awareness films for children in grades K–6. It is designed to supplement curricula produced by the Automobile Association of America's Foundation for Traffic Safety.
- *Healthy Me* (1985) is a multimillion-dollar initiative rewarding schools for innovative health curricula for grades K–12. Awards are also made to community coalitions that support and work for health instruction in schools. During the first year of this four-year effort, the focus was on programs in the public schools.
- *"Eat Well, Be Well"* (1986) is a series of eight programs, each fifteen minutes long, on nutrition for grades 1–4, prepared especially for the Instructional Television Service of the Public Broadcasting Service (PBS).[5]

Support for Academic Curricula. Metropolitan provides supplementary materials that support existing academic curricula. Here are two examples.

- *"The Shakespeare Plays,"* a BBS–TV and Time Life Television coproduction, presented by PBS, was co-underwritten by Metropolitan from 1979 to 1985 and promoted by the Instructional Television Service to schools across the country. It continues to be used by schools. The company and its co-underwriters also distributed over 300,000 teacher kits to 37,000 public and private secondary schools.
- *Remedial Reading Series for Teachers.* The Foundation has sponsored a two-pronged program with Laubach Literacy International in support of remedial reading instruction. First, the Foundation funded the development, printing, and distribution of a guide containing easy-to-use teaching concepts for remedial reading instructors. The guide, *Growing Literate,* has been distributed to over 43,000 junior and senior high school teachers. Second, the Foundation funded the printing and distribution of the seven-volume "Challenger" reading series to approximately 10,000 teachers. This new collaboration with Laubach was preceded by the "Help Yourself to Health" remedial reading program which fostered two Metropolitan objectives: health and literacy.

The Invisible Curriculum. The CED report—*Investing in Our Children: Business and the Public Schools* (1985)—whose distribution was facilitated by a grant from the Metropolitan Life Foundation, introduced the term *invisible curriculum* to describe social skills such as cooperativeness, perseverance, and honesty, that a school should impart to its students. Over the years, Metropolitan's education initiatives have reflected a strong concern for that invisible curriculum. Reliability, self-discipline, and other traits critical to success in the workplace have been fostered in students through company-sponsored programs.

- *Summer Jobs.* Metropolitan has participated in the New York City Partnership's Summer Jobs program since its inception in 1981. In 1985, Met Life served as the lead company (headquarters) for the program. During that year, the program provided more than 31,000 young people with work experiences, often their first. The program is an important source of career education, encouraging its enrollees (cumulatively over 100,000) to stay in or return to school in order to meet their career objectives.
- *"Working."* As part of its Summer Jobs '85 effort, Metropolitan produced "Working," a videotape that teaches job readiness skills. The company has distributed this award-winning film nationally, together with a 16-lesson teachers' guide and a summary booklet for students, to schools, job training organizations, government agencies, and professional educators' associations. Metropolitan ensured the quality of

these supplementary materials by having them tested and critiqued by New York City public school teachers.

- *Junior Achievement.* Metropolitan employees in nine departments at corporate headquarters and twenty-five offices across the country have served as Junior Achievement consultants, teaching junior and senior high school students about the free enterprise system. The academic data these volunteers impart are supplemented by the hands-on experience of running a business. With the help of their guest instructor, students learn to divide responsibilities, meet deadlines, produce a product or service, and make a profit. They absorb another aspect of the invisible curriculum by observing their instructor's mode of dress and interpersonal skills.
- *School Mentoring Program.* Metropolitan headquarters recently joined with Manhattan's Norman Thomas High School to participate in the Board of Education's School Mentoring Program. Employees ranging from clerk-typists to vice-presidents volunteer to serve as mentors and are paired with students. Each pair meets for two hours a week at the mentor's work site, where the student observes and internalizes both social and work skills. Several Metropolitan offices across the country have developed similar initiatives, establishing links with local schools.
- *Volunteers in the Schools.* Metropolitan's support of education is a company-wide commitment of individuals who wish to make a difference. This commitment takes many forms.
  - The Employee Volunteer Program puts active and retired personnel in touch with opportunities to serve the community. At their request, many retired employees have joined the School Volunteer Program. They tutor public school children who need extra attention in particular areas of study.
  - The company's computer professionals frequently help students and schools with projects requiring their expertise.
  - Several young actuarial employees have founded the Actuarial Science Career Awareness Committee, a group that helps to acquaint local high school and college students with the profession.

THE RIPPLE EFFECT

Etymology (the study of word origins) can often provide insights of great practical value. Take the word *problem*, for example. Funk and Wagnall's defines it as "a perplexing question or situation, especially when difficult or uncertain of solution," adding that its etymological root is *problema*, Greek for "something thrown forward (for discussion)."

When people are grappling with a problem, what they throw forward for discussion are possible solutions. Just as a stone thrown into a pool of water sends ripples outward from its point of impact, a successful solution triggers a ripple effect that ultimately has influence beyond its target. Such is the case with Metropolitan's activities in support of education. The ripple effect has long been in motion within the organization and is now making itself felt outside.

The Internal Ripple Effect

Metropolitan's history of educational involvement has made an internal impact along two dimensions: space (the influence on company facilities across the country) and time (the influence on successive generations of Metropolitan employees).

The Dimension of Space. The internal ripple effect has been felt across organizational lines in a number of ways, including executive initiatives, partnerships between local offices and the New York City headquarters, and self-generated activities in all company locations. Here are several examples.

- *Executive Leadership.* Met Life's President and CEO, John Creedon, has made a personal commitment to give teachers a greater voice in educational reform. One way he is meeting that commitment is by spearheading the CED Teacher/Business Roundtables. By co-hosting the first Roundtable event, he has set an example for other Metropolitan executives who have assumed leadership roles in subsequent meetings.
- *Interoffice Partnerships.* Nonmonetary contributions have resulted when various company offices have exchanged information. In 1984, for example, the National Urban League asked Metropolitan to participate (as it has since 1978) in its Summer Intern Program by hiring black students in key urban areas. The League's liaison at Met Life contacted the company's Great Lakes Head Office in Aurora, Illinois. Within weeks, a student from Chicago was getting a career education there.
- *Local Initiatives.* Some of the most rewarding company activities on behalf of education were developed autonomously in local offices. These efforts were actively encouraged by the company. One such initiative was the Wichita Electronic Installations Center's involvement with a local Board of Education project to design a new data processing center. Another was the Western Head Office employees'

efforts to teach English to newly arrived Asian children, preparing them to enter the San Francisco public school system. Still another has been taking place since 1981 in Aurora, where the Great Lakes Head Office participates in the School/Business Partnership program, which acquaints students and teachers with the business world.

Some local activities have been generated by corporate communications affecting every company facility. For example, headquarters encourages each office to make its building facilities available to nonprofit organizations, such as educational groups, for meetings and other activities. From 1979 to 1981, headquarters hosted monthly meetings for the New York City Board of Education's City-Wide High School Principals' Conference. This enabled the Board to save several thousand dollars when its budget was extremely tight. Perhaps more important, the meetings facilitated much-needed dialogue between the business and education communities. Similarly, in 1985, the company provided meeting space for IMPACT II, a teacher-to-teacher networking program that fosters the exchange of creative curricular innovations. (See pages 165–169 for a discussion of IMPACT II.)

The Dimension of Time. The internal ripple effect can easily be seen by taking a look back at some examples of the company's willingness, through its people, to sustain educational progress over the long term. For instance, Charles A. Siegfried, a former Vice-Chairman of Metropolitan's Board, was appointed to the President's Committee on Health Education in 1971, two years before he retired. At the Committee's recommendation, the National Center for Health Education was founded in 1975, and a Metropolitan officer served as its first president and was reelected to a second term. In 1946, before retiring as head of Metropolitan's School Health Bureau, Pauline Brooks Williamson cofounded the American Association for Gifted Children. Today, Metropolitan officers serve as President and Treasurer of the Association's Board of Directors. Furthermore, the company's chief economist serves as President of the New York City Council on Economic Education. His predecessor at Metropolitan was also a Council officer.

The External Ripple Effect

Metropolitan's intraorganizational patterns of involvement are now being replicated interorganizationally. This relatively new phenomenon is enabling various institutions to share initiatives and work together to achieve common goals.

The *Tulsa World*, one of Oklahoma's largest newspapers, contacted

Metropolitan's Central Head Office requesting permission to administer the Metropolitan Life Survey of the American Teacher to Tulsa's public school teachers. Similarly, Burger King Corporation, whose efforts on behalf of education and educators are described in Chapter 3, administered the survey to teachers whom it had singled out for special recognition. In turn, Burger King has supplemented Metropolitan's current knowledge base by sharing these survey results with the company. Metropolitan's Government and Industry Relations Department then distributed the survey to the nation's key legislators. One recipient, a congressman from California, asked for additional examples of the company's educational initiatives, explaining that such data would acquaint him with activities that others might emulate.

CONCLUSION

At the core of Metropolitan's corporate partnership with education and educators has been a long-standing objective: stronger, healthier, better-educated children.

John Creedon, along with other corporate leaders, recognizes that meeting this one objective will, in turn, create a stronger, healthier, and better-educated society. His vision of what can be achieved when the talents of business and educational leaders converge is reflected throughout Metropolitan. The result: initiatives, both large and small, that give teachers a stronger voice and a stronger profession; programs on the prevention of substance abuse, without which even the most talented teachers may be doomed to failure; and programs that supplement the teacher's invisible curriculum, enabling a new generation to enter the world of work.

An organization is a living organism constantly undergoing change. This biological analogy reflects Metropolitan's evolution over the past 75 years. At its early stages of development, the company had simple needs and, accordingly, a simple set of responses. As society and its needs grew more complex, so did the company's efforts on society's behalf, particularly in the area of education.

As the insurance industry grew more complex, so did the company's structure. Metropolitan's new departments, offices, and Foundation became specialized organs functioning both independently and in conjunction with each other. Decentralization did not dilute the company's commitment to education. Rather, the commitment was enhanced, allowing for even greater diversity of efforts on education's behalf.

However, one thing remained quite simple: the belief that the teacher is the pivotal person in the educational process. Accordingly, Metropolitan is committed to strengthening the teaching profession. The company's leadership has strongly asserted that this commitment will remain long after the current educational crisis is resolved. It is only through a long-term commitment from business and community leaders alike that dignity will be restored to the teaching profession.

That dignity is well deserved. Moreover, it is a critical ingredient of effective leadership, and leadership is the essence of education. Metropolitan is confident that its partnership with American educators will contribute substantially to educational improvements. But ultimately, it is the educators who will lead the nation's schools out of the difficulties they face today.

NOTES

1. "An Important Announcement to Our Policy-holders," *The Metropolitan,* *XXV*(1), February 15, 1909, 2.
2. John J. Creedon, "Business, Teachers and the Schools," presented at the Metropolitan Life Insurance Company Symposium on the Education Profession, New York, March 13, 1986. The Metropolitan Life Survey of Former Teachers in America was released at the symposium.
3. W. C. Rappleye, "John J. Creedon: 'Heed the Teacher,'" *Financier, The Journal of Private Sector Policy, IX*(11), November 1985, 40–43.
4. Ibid., p. 43.
5. There are two previous "Eat Well, Be Well" series, both for adults.

3 Burger King Corporation
Education Enriches Everyone

BARBARA GOTHARD
Burger King Corporation

A MARRIAGE OF ALTRUISM AND SELF–INTEREST

Some one million low-income youths aged 16 to 24 have dropped out of high school, are not in college, and do not have jobs, according to a report in *Business Week*.[1] Most have a sixth- to eighth-grade education. More than 50 percent are minorities. Another 700,000 teen-agers are unable to get initial job experience.

Burger King Corporation, through its company and franchise system, needs to find 200,000 workers each year. With 70 percent of our work force under 21 and 41 percent minorities, the availability and retention of young workers is of prime importance.

Where will these workers come from? Demographic studies suggest that the pool of potential workers in their late teens and early twenties will shrink markedly in the next decade. Retention in the fast-food industry is poor; each crew job is filled two-and-a-half times in the average year. Given these circumstances, Burger King became very concerned about an impending manpower shortage. Moreover, because of the difficulties some young people have with work habits and attitudes, we also became concerned about the corollary need of preparedness for the world of work.

Fundamental Values

Burger King Corporation is a young company, barely 30 years old, and it is part of the fast-food industry, which until recently has not enjoyed a reputation for corporate philanthropy. From the beginning Burger King Corporation's goal in the marketplace has been to satisfy customers' needs for quality food, convenience, and excellent value. Although the company has grown dramatically and has undergone many changes, its fundamental values remain the same. We believe the importance of the customer must always be the cornerstone of our business.

In 1967, Burger King became part of the Pillsbury Company, which gave us the capital and support to expand faster. It has been a good partnership. We manage our own affairs but share with Pillsbury a set of principles regarding the mission of our business and the values that guide our actions and plans.

Partnerships have been critical to our success: with Pillsbury, with the 1,600 franchisees who own 80 percent of our restaurants, and with our employees. Especially important in our scheme of things are the crew members and restaurant managers who form the core of our customer service teams. This commitment to partnership extends to each community in which we do business. We believe in being an excellent corporate citizen. In helping our communities, we ultimately help ourselves.

A New Direction

By 1983, the question of how best to meet community needs was nagging Burger King Corporation's top management. The company was contributing millions of dollars to a broad array of civic programs, ranging from arts to health and human services. Yet to Jeff Campbell, Chairman and Chief Executive Officer (CEO), and Kyle Craig, Executive Vice President for Marketing, there was something unsatisfying about these efforts. True, good works were being done, but perhaps more could be accomplished by channeling support in a single direction.

Jeff Campbell's view of what might be achieved was shaped by family history. His father had dropped out of high school and never forgave his own parents for allowing him to do so. As a result, Campbell learned early to revere the importance of education. As Burger King Corporation's CEO, he had been further sensitized to the need for company support for education through his discussions with the company's 70-member minority franchise association. Recognizing that education is the key to upward mobility for minorities, the association pressed its case for more and better company-supported education programs and minority involvement in them consistent with representation on the company's payroll.

Kyle Craig (now president of Steak & Ale, another Pillsbury unit) was influenced by his wife, a teacher. With his marketing background, he recognized the wisdom of focusing the company's contributions strategy. At a meeting of the National Association of Secondary School Principals in Orlando in late 1983, Craig became convinced that support of education made sense for Burger King.

The idea had the virtue of being utterly consistent with the corporate vision. It was keyed directly to the need to motivate and upgrade the quality of present and future employees. It offered the potential for meaningful involvement at the national, state, and community levels. It also offered an opportunity for Burger King to assume a leadership role in an area that we felt desperately needed corporate involvement. So it was that Jeff Campbell announced, late in 1983: "To demonstrate the company's social responsibility to the communities we serve, Burger King has dedicated its corporate contributions to the support of education."

Both Jeff Campbell and Kyle Craig hoped that ways could be found to benefit the teen-agers who are the backbone of the company's work force. This direction was clearly established in January 1984, with the creation of the Corporate Affairs Department. It was charged with developing and implementing educational programs to target three groups: employees, teachers and principals, and students. I was hired to be its Director. My background as an educator added to the credibility of Burger King Corporation's approach.

While Burger King's education programs were still a loose concept, Campbell and Craig sought the opinions of minority and other key franchisees. Because the majority of Burger King restaurants are franchisee owned, the company cannot simply mandate participation in any program. Franchisees are independent businesspeople who need to be persuaded that a new product or program has value. In January 1984, the concept was formally presented to the National Business Planning Council (which is made up of Burger King franchisee representatives) to get additional thoughts on program design and implementation. The enthusiastic support of the franchisees at that meeting was important in the ultimate success of the program.

Under the umbrella theme "Education Enriches Everyone," Burger King Corporation embarked on a number of education programs for its target groups. I believe these programs can be aptly described as a happy marriage of altruism and self-interest.

EDUCATION PROGRAMS

Employee Programs

An early key decision was that Burger King Corporation's responsibility to education must begin with its employees. Our immediate aims were to strengthen work incentives, build loyalty, and reduce turnover.

Crew Educational Assistance Program. The Crew Educational Assistance Program was begun in June 1984. The goals of this scholarship incentive program were to increase recruitment, reduce turnover, raise productivity, and enhance Burger King's public image. We began with pilot programs in the company's Atlanta and New York regions and with Davgar, a franchisee in Orlando, Florida. The program was subsequently extended to all 500 company-owned stores, and franchisees are beginning to adopt it.

Crew members may earn bonus credits for up to $2,000, to be used for postsecondary education. These credits are based on length of service with the company and maintenance of at least a C average or its equivalent in school. The bonus credits may be used for educational expenses at any licensed or accredited college, university, or vocational or training school. The course of study need not be related to restaurant work, but it must lead to a degree or certificate.

To be eligible, crew members must complete three months of continuous service, averaging at least fifteen hours a week. Participants must be continuously employed and enrolled in the program to accrue bonus credits. The individual restaurants limit the number of participants, so additional applicants are placed on a waiting list.

Crew Member Scholarship. A second scholarship program builds on the first. A $100,000 annual company expenditure supports competitive scholarships of as much as $1,000. The minimum requirement for consideration is a B average. An outside nonprofit organization, Citizens' Scholarship Foundation of America, makes the award decisions on behalf of the company.

Crew member scholarships were tested during the 1985–1986 school year and expanded company-wide in the 1986–1987 year. More than 600 employees applied in the first year.

McLamore Scholarship Program. Scholarships for dependent children of Burger King employees are available through the James W. McLamore Scholarship Program (named for the company's founder). A $50,000 award fund has been established with Citizens' Scholarship Foundation, which selects the winners on the basis of achievement and leadership. The program offers up to twenty-five one-year scholarships of $2,000 to assist with tuition and expenses of attending an accredited postsecondary school. Winners may compete for more than one year of aid.

Teacher and Principal Programs

Jeff Campbell believes that "our company's educators have all too often been neglected and insufficiently appreciated for their efforts to provide quality education."[2] Although teachers and principals are the people with the ability to improve conditions in our schools, they are seldom accorded the recognition to spur them on to new heights. Upgrading the quality of the school experience was identified as a key objective for Burger King.

In Honor of Excellence. In 1984, Burger King created a national recognition program for teachers and principals, In Honor of Excellence. One outstanding teacher and one outstanding principal from each state, the District of Columbia, Puerto Rico, and American Samoa were invited to attend a five-day symposium at Captiva Island, Florida. The program was designed to enhance the educators' professional development and also to afford them the opportunity for relaxation and enjoyment. In Honor of Excellence has since become an annual tribute.

In July 1986, the recommendations of seminar participants were distributed as a monograph to professional organizations, opinion leaders, and other corporations known to be interested in education issues. A one-hour documentary film has also been made, and became available for distribution in September 1987.

Student Programs

We are also funding innovative endeavors in schools, colleges, and universities.

Cities in Schools. Cities in Schools is a program begun in 1974 to prevent students from dropping out and to encourage dropouts to return to school. This end is accomplished by coordinating public and private support services in the schools, to be delivered to at-risk youths. However, much of the counseling takes place outside the school setting. Plans call for expansion to five additional cities.

Burger King supports this nationwide program with a one-time $100,000 grant. The cities in which it participates are Allentown, Bethlehem, Pittsburgh, and Philadelphia, Pennsylvania; Atlanta, Georgia; Bridgeport, Connecticut; Baltimore, Maryland; West Palm Beach and Tallahassee, Florida; Charlotte, North Carolina; Portland, Oregon; Houston, Texas; Seattle, Washington; Lawrence, Massachusetts; Los Angeles, California; and Washington, D.C.

Washington, D.C., Public Schools. Burger King's financial support for an employability skills program in the District's predominantly minority public schools predated its current emphasis on education programs. Our support is enabling the school system to evaluate the success of innovations in the grammar and writing curriculum. The end product of this program, which was begun in 1981, will be a curriculum guide that other school districts can adopt.

Fast-Food Management Courses. In 1984, we helped the University of Wisconsin—Stout construct the first fast-food restaurant management curriculum in the United States. We built a prototype restaurant on campus, and fast-food management students are employed as interns in Burger King's Minneapolis regional office. Since that time, we have helped other collegiate fast-food management programs get started. These include the first minority program, at Bethune-Cookman College's hospitality management school, which began in the fall of 1986. Other schools aided are Northeastern University, Cuyahoga Community College, Miami Dade Community College, and Florida International University.

Consequences of Crime. We supported the publication of *The Consequences of Crime*, a highly acclaimed curriculum program for middle and high school students. It teaches young people that breaking the law has serious and long-lasting implications for their lives.

Miami, Florida Programs. Burger King has a special obligation to support educational programs in its headquarters community. In 1986, the company endowed a $1 million chair in the University of Miami's College of Business Administration to honor James W. McLamore, who serves as Chairman of the University's Board of Trustees.

Art Path, a program initiated by the Junior League, encourages visits by students to Miami's Center for the Fine Arts. Related school-based experiences before and after the trip enhance the value of the visit. Financial support from Burger King helps make it possible for students to receive printed materials about the museum and to visit it free of charge.

Inside Track provides internships for minority students. Its purpose is to prevent a brain drain of young people, mainly blacks, who go away to college and choose not to return to Miami to live and work. Burger King is one of eighteen firms offering these three-summer internships.

Burger King gives financial support to the Foundation for Excellence in the Dade County Public Schools. This organization gives mini grants to teachers to foster creative teaching, encourage interaction between students and teachers, and reward teachers by giving them the opportunity to put exciting, long-cherished ideas into practice. I am a private sector representative on the Foundation's Board of Directors. In 1986, 85 projects were funded, and the program was expanded to include grants to principals.

The company underwrites the cost of printing program materials for the Criminal Justice Program, which is administered through the county court system. This program aims to prevent troubled adolescents from repeating their mistakes.

Hunger projects are the focus of Pillsbury corporate philanthropy: Through the Hunger Project, Burger King funds the purchase of hardcover books that demonstrate techniques of proper nutrition and are given to schools.

We contribute scholarships to University of Miami athletes through the University's Academics for Athletes program. We also contribute financial support to a community conference on ethnic concerns sponsored by the Cuban National Planning Council.

PROGRAM RESULTS

Where possible, Burger King prefers to document results in quantifiable terms. On this basis alone, the company is satisfied with the value returned on its educational programs. The budget for these programs has been expanded from $1.5 million in 1983 to $3.9 million in 1986. Evidence is accumulating of a ripple effect that is indeed forging for Burger King a leadership role in the field of education. However, perhaps the greatest impact from involvement has been on Burger King itself. We have found that one company can, indeed, make a difference.

Impact on Employees

As of May 1986, 1,200 students in 500 company-owned restaurants were participating in our educational assistance programs. For fiscal 1986–1987, we expect 3,000 participants from 900 restaurants. Franchisees wanted to see the company's results before making a commitment and have only recently become involved. Some restaurants in New York, Boston, Orlando, and Jacksonville have already adopted the program. Others intend to manage their own programs using ours as a model. The rate of participation and which franchisees participate will depend to a large extent on the difficulties faced in recruiting crew members. Franchisees in tight labor markets have told us that educational incentives are a powerful recruiting tool.

The McLamore scholarships helped make college possible for 14 children of employees in its first year. Program guidelines are now being expanded to include graduate students.

The cost of training a crew member is $400, so retention is clearly a major concern for Burger King. A study of scholarship recipients after the first six months of the program indicated a 24 percent turnover rate, compared with a 135 percent turnover of those not receiving scholarships. Projections showed that the $1,000 average annual cost per student scholarship would actually save the company money: Savings on training expenses were taken into account, given that a $900,000 savings on reduced turnover was documented.

The company also benefits from being able to offer scholarships as a recruitment tool, ensuring higher quality employees to begin with. Moreover, because these employees stay at their jobs longer, they become more proficient in what they do, and the quality of service improves.

For the crew member, the advantage of being able to accumulate scholarship funds for further education is obvious. We are pleased by the impact these scholarships will have on our crew members' lives; by the program's simplicity and directness, which minimize red tape; and by the condition that satisfactory performance as a crew member and as a student go hand in hand.

We expect some of these young people to rejoin the Burger King professional staff after college. Those who do will have a positive attitude about the company. Their enhanced sense of loyalty and awareness of company values should favorably affect the quality of their work performance.

Our support of education programs has created new avenues for franchisees and restaurant managers to help their communities through personal involvement. Reports come in frequently of employees and franchisees taking leadership roles through service on education advisory groups, creation of partnership programs with schools, and the like. These individuals have expressed gratitude for the conditions that allow them to serve in a meaningful way. Greater visibility and recognition of Burger King people in their communities serve the company's overall business interests.

At the headquarters level, involvement extends well beyond the

Chairman's personal interest and the Corporate Affairs Department's program administration. At least seven different departments contribute to meeting program goals.

Region Human Resources manages the scholarship program, including liaison with franchisees. Feedback on how the program is working is provided by regional human resources managers. The Operations Department, which is the major beneficiary of reduced turnover and higher motivation, assists in the design of the scholarship program. Our educational programs and their positive impact at the community level benefited from the Marketing Department's "Our Town" advertising campaign, which was introduced in the summer of 1986. Management Information Systems designed computer programs for administering the scholarship program and a computer-based recording and tracking system for corporate contributions. Public Relations communicates goals, objectives, and progress to the public, and Corporate Communications communicates that information to employees and franchisees. The Strategic Analysis Group provides demographic studies and labor force analyses and targets need.

For the first time, the company has a cohesive framework to direct employee community involvement and a plan for achieving results. Our corporate affairs plan, which supports and reinforces the company's marketing plan, articulates our goals, strategies, and activities for the next three to five years.

Impact on Teachers and Principals

The ripple effect has been especially pronounced among the 100 teachers and high school principals we honor each year. Outstanding educators spotlighted by Burger King have gained further recognition in their own communities and states. This process is stimulated by Burger King's sending letters to the appropriate governors and legislators, describing the teachers' and principals' accomplishments. Honorees are asked to speak and prepare testimony on the impact of educational reforms, serve on local and state educational policy committees, and appear at community and educational gatherings of all types.

What Burger King has set in motion, others are continuing. We especially treasure our role in stimulating discussion of educational issues. "Our" educators return to their home states and communities refreshed, feeling good about themselves and their profession. They relish walking through the door opened by Burger King to become activists in the cause of educational improvement.

Impact on Students

In Houston, juvenile offenders and truancy cases referred to Cities in Schools improved their attendance rate from 57 to 88 percent. In Atlanta, where over half the Cities in Schools' students had been dropouts prior to program enrollment, attendance rates went up to 82 percent. The success of this program in many cities has earned it the support of Mrs. George Bush, who held a press conference in May 1986 to highlight Burger King's contribution.

The Washington, D.C., school district has revamped its grammar and writing skills curriculum and produced a videotape explaining the curriculum benefits. Plans call for making the tape and curriculum materials available to other school districts and for providing technical assistance.

The handbook *Consequences of Crime* has been used to counsel 7,000 juvenile offenders in Miami and central Florida.

The McLamore endowed chair at the University of Miami will ensure future generations of business students a quality learning experience. Art Path has stimulated visits by 15,000 schoolchildren to Miami's Center for the Fine Arts. The program has led to the creation of a corps of 40 volunteers and an education department at the museum to coordinate activities. Burger King has awarded three, three-summer Inside Track internships to date. In their first year, the mini grants to teachers for special projects awarded through the Foundation for Excellence in the Dade County Public Schools have enhanced the educational experiences of nearly 10,000 schoolchildren. Seventy schools are using books purchased through the Hunger Project to teach proper nutrition.

Impact on Other Groups

Burger King Corporation's request for a ruling by the Internal Revenue Service and the U.S. Department of Labor to ensure that crew member scholarships would not be taxed as income has had interesting consequences. The request led to a position paper that clarified the issues. Both federal agencies ruled in Burger King Corporation's favor, and the position paper, which was circulated among several U.S. senators, gained the company recognition by both the legislative and administrative arms of the government as a leader in the area of educational assistance programs.

Valuable ties have been forged with other organizations interested in education, further strengthening Burger King Corporation's identification with this issue and with opinion leaders in a position to bring about improvement. Company executives have been asked to speak before such groups as the National Association of Secondary School Principals, Council of Chief State School Officers (state school superintendents' organization), and National Association of Independent Schools. Burger King's Chairman and CEO, Jeff Campbell, has been asked to serve on the latter organization's board. Metropolitan Life asked Burger King to administer a survey on teacher issues at one of its In Honor of Excellence conferences.

Also benefiting from Burger King Corporation's educational programs are the institutions that scholarship winners choose to attend. Because the scholarship checks come directly from the company, schools are assured of prompt payment. In an era of declining enrollment because of demographic trends, schools are grateful for any efforts to raise enrollments. Burger King and the receiving institutions are becoming strong allies.

LESSONS LEARNED

Each year, many worthwhile projects across the spectrum of human need come to the attention of a highly visible company such as Burger King. It is tempting to fund as many as possible, especially those that are big and splashy and offer significant one-time publicity benefits. Yet Burger King is resisting that temptation.

Certainly, there is a place for the big promotion. But the company believes this is a weak foundation for an entire social responsibility program intended to produce long-term benefits. When we do promotions, we make a conscious effort to design them to support our educational focus. The long-term benefit we are seeking is a consistent, unified public perception of Burger King as a good corporate citizen. Certainly, the success we have had in publicizing our educational programs among opinion makers and local media indicates that we are on the right track.

Although initially we targeted education and world hunger as our primary concerns, we have found it useful subsequently to identify health and human services, and culture and the arts, as secondary focuses. Often primary- and secondary-emphasis programs are related (e.g., a school program that attempts to deal with a student's home environment, or the Art Path program). We intend to support a recognition program for employees who volunteer their time in worthwhile community activities of any type.

Even in major companies, the corporate affairs director may be asked to produce an educational program like Burger King Corporation's on a shoestring. The resources and budgets in large measure belong to other departments, whose managers must be persuaded of the project's value. In dealings outside the company, we have found that public-sector techniques are often a necessity to stimulate others to support our program goals, without spending vast amounts of company money. Finding reasons for others to take actions you want them to take is at the heart of any good corporate affairs program. In our situation, we developed a rationale that much of the money spent on the program would pay a direct return. Such a rationale is necessary before management can feel comfortable making a commitment to a major program.

There must be a period of internal consensus building before the program gets under way. A corporate affairs director needs the support of key managers, and such support cannot be imposed from the top. Executives need to get used to the idea, and they deserve the opportunity to participate in formulating the program they will later be expected to help carry out. Quiet persuasion and idea sessions in the early stages are part of the strategy for success. If the program is to work, everyone must agree that it is important.

People come to Burger King because of quality, service, and value. But they are also influenced by their perception of how good is the company backing the product. These perceptions formed outside the customers' restaurant experience influence their purchasing behavior. We value nothing as more important than our hard-won reputation, and the education program offers us a way of enhancing it.

THE FUTURE

We are completing a survey of restaurant managers and franchisees to develop a profile or inventory of the company's community involvements. One franchisee said he contributes $600,000 a year to community programs and was pleased that someone cares enough to ask about it. Incomplete results suggest that the Corporate Affairs Department's expenditure is only the tip of the iceberg. The survey results will suggest new directions, in particular how we can organize field staff to get the greatest impact from the money being spent.

We intend to develop a kit of materials and to go on the road with a seminar that will teach restaurant managers and field staff how to conduct an effective community relations program.

Burger King is embarking on a period of consolidating its gains and of developing formal policies to guide future actions. Among the new ideas being considered is the creation of a foundation that would be a focal point for program activity.

A natural extension of the program is to use the credibility and allies we have gained to press for educational reform in the legislative arena on such issues as higher teacher salaries, more effective use of funds already available, and support of worthwhile programs. The people who can make this effort include a number of Burger King executives and franchisees. In the near future, we will be familiarizing them with how the legislative process works and how they can be effective. In this way, we intend to play a more active role in shaping public policies toward education.

NOTES

1. "The Forgotten Americans," *Business Week*, September 2, 1985, 50–55.
2. From program booklet for In Honor of Excellence, the national Burger King recognition program, South Seas Plantation, Captiva Island, Florida, 1984.

4 Murry Bergtraum High School for Business Careers

BARBARA CHRISTEN
Murry Bergtraum High School

When you drive into Manhattan across the Brooklyn Bridge, the panorama of lower Manhattan spreads out before you. Left to the Battery, right up the East River, across the tip of the island to the Hudson and the World Trade Center Towers, the area encompasses the financial capital of the world. In this tight little portion of New York City are clustered the banks and investment houses that are "Wall Street" and the law firms that serve them. As you traverse the last portion of the bridge and turn down the ramp to Pearl and Water Streets, you pass within a hundred yards of the Murry Bergtraum High School for Business Careers.

Since the late 1970s, the name Bergtraum has become well known in the Wall Street community. To those who are interested in public education and especially those who seek to involve business in a partnership with education, this school stands as a model of what can be achieved.

Bergtraum opened in September 1975 with 500 ninth and tenth graders. An *educational option* or *magnet* school, it was given a special mandate by the New York City Board of Education: to prepare students for both college and entry-level positions in the business community. The Board directed that the school create innovative programs in business, establish liaisons with the business community, and develop work-study programs appropriate for secondary school students.

To fulfill its mandate, the school has a number of special resources. Its location is one. In addition, the building was designed with special facilities for instruction in business education; there are a number of typewriting rooms, a computer room, and several rooms for business laboratories (special rooms used for different purposes in business education) in place of the more usual industrial arts shops and home economics rooms. The business faculty is another special resource. Almost one-third of the teachers are business education specialists. They bring a diversity of abilities and talents to the program, exchange ideas and techniques, and build on each other's skills. They create an atmosphere that allows innovation to flourish and that attracts others.

HOW IT BEGAN

In the late 1960s, a number of Wall Street firms felt a need for a high school that would prepare city youths to enter business. Besides its regular district high schools, New York had long had many specialized high schools: Science, Music and Art, Printing, Art and Design, Central Commercial, and others specializing in trades and technology. Discussions began between the Board of Education and a Steering Committee composed of representatives from the Downtown Lower Manhattan Association—the prestigious organization of over 300 firms headquartered south of Canal Street—and several major corporations such as Merrill Lynch and Chase Manhattan Bank. A survey of anticipated employment needs done for the Committee in the early 1970s identified major areas of concentration for the school: banking, accounting, secretarial studies, and marketing. Later, computer science was added.

Because the school would be unique, no special district was designated for it. Rather, students from all over the city would be welcome to apply. In addition, social changes in the 1960s and early 1970s made anathema the idea of an elite school. Therefore, by the time it opened, Bergtraum was mandated to admit a student population that was 50 percent on grade in basic skills, with 25 percent below, and 25 percent above grade. The student body would be a true cross section of the city's students. The formula has worked well.

Most New York City high schools, like schools in cities and towns across the country, exist within a neighborhood. When they arrive as freshmen, the young people already know many others. Local businesses know and often care about the school and its students; local newspapers regard its achievements and shortcomings as worthy of publicity. Many people and organizations have a vested interest in its well-being.

Bergtraum is different. Its entering class each year comes from over 250 public, parochial, and private schools. Students enter knowing perhaps one or two others, perhaps none. They live as far away as the northern Bronx and as close as Chinatown. Some of them travel for over an hour each way to school. They are anonymous in the neighborhood of skyscrapers; only their red and yellow jackets, bags, and T–shirts identify them as Bergtraum students. They come—2,700 of them—because they have asked to come and because they want what Bergtraum offers: a high school diploma *plus* the near certainty of a job. In just 10 years, they have earned for their school a reputation that gives them an entrée to most Wall Street corporations. They have been pioneers in the working out of a dozen different programs that unite the business community and the school. When they leave, most go on to one of more than a hundred different colleges. A great many return after college to the business community that was opened to them while at Bergtraum. They receive much from the business community and they give back much.

By September 1975, the business community had had some unhappy experiences in implementing its recently developed sense of social responsibility. Many programs in the 1960s and early 1970s had placed young people of little skill and no training in business positions in which they could not possibly succeed. Businesspeople, though anxious to meet demands to bring disadvantaged youths into the economic mainstream, had become disillusioned about the abilities and attitudes of young people. Respect for New York City public high schools and their students had plummeted.

At the same time, money was becoming less plentiful in both the public and the private sectors. In New York City, the fiscal crisis began in the summer of 1975: Where public school budgets had been rich, they suddenly became poor. Where the schools had had teachers and money for teachers in abundance, they very suddenly plunged to the opposite extreme; they had to cut programs and pack classes to the contract maximums to provide for the minimum diploma requirements.

We at Bergtraum faced some basic problems: We had to overcome the prevailing negative image. We had to produce students who were capable and caring at a time when our resources for doing so were diminishing daily. We managed to do it. By the beginning of our second year, we had over 4,000 applications and were beginning to make inroads into the business community. Within the next two years, as the student body grew to 1,000, we placed a good number of students in internship and working situations, and our applications for admission rose to 8,000.

HOW DID BERGTRAUM SUCCEED?

How did we buck the tide of negativism and establish the atmosphere in which our students now gain access to many and very prestigious firms? Three things had to be achieved:

1. We had to establish the credibility of the product. We had to produce the can-do kid. We had to make absolutely certain that our students mastered entry-level skills; really could perform the tasks in secretarial studies, accounting, marketing, and computer science; and had the employability skills to be assets in an office.
2. We had to let the business world know that we were doing it; we had to get out the good word about our students.
3. We had to establish contacts in the business community to open doors for internships and jobs for our students and graduates.

The Programs

To address the first challenge, we developed an intensive three-year, hands-on program in each area of concentration. The first three — secretarial studies, accounting, and marketing — were not new as high school subjects; they had long been the stuff of business education. But all too often in recent years, standards had been lowered, and many students had not really mastered significant skills. This was partly attributable to increased emphasis on college entrance. As a result, business subjects were seen as wasteful, negative, and even insulting for a capable student. These students stayed away from business classrooms in droves; what went on in many business classes became less challenging, and the cycle fed upon itself.

We had to recreate the business education curriculum as a true discipline and restore its credibility. We also had to create a program in computer science, which simply had never existed at the secondary level. In addition, we had to make sure that our students learned the value of punctuality, good attendance, good human relations, and responsibility. All this was needed to make our students employable.

We also had to establish credibility, with both parents and students, as a high school. The essential nature of a high school today is that it prepares students for college. Therefore, in developing our program of instruction to attract the cross section of students we intended to serve, we had to be strong in both the academic and the business areas. We wanted to give students more options, not fewer. We wanted students to be prepared to make whatever changes might be necessary in later life. College preparation was a "must," equally as important as job preparation.

Given the dire cutbacks in funds because of the city's fiscal crisis, we made a basic decision: We would offer everything necessary for college entrance, including advanced science and mathematics, but we would concentrate a heavy portion of our resources in business education. We would go well beyond the six-term sequence needed for an area of concentration for the high school diploma and require whatever our faculty and advisors deemed necessary to produce competence. This meant that some students, those in secretarial studies and computer science, would take as many as 16 terms in their specialization. Others took 14. It worked. When our first class graduated, in June 1978, 85 percent went on to college immediately. Moreover, Bergtraum students had begun to establish a positive reputation as really competent employees.

What is the nature of our business programs that gave our students their positive reputation? Most of all, they are *demanding* programs. Students have more than three years of training, including advanced levels. All entering students, grades nine and ten, take typewriting, the basic entry-level business skill. From the beginning, the ninth graders had taken a six-month business introduction course; the tenth graders now do so also. All students must participate in some type of work-study program before graduation.

But the critical factor in our success is that the students start their skills area training in grade 10. With the introductory courses completed in grade 10 and advanced courses completed in grade 11, twelfth graders move into very specialized courses that are usually the counterpart of college courses. Computer science students pursue systems analysis, systems control, and various computer applications. Securities and finance majors take real estate and investment courses and deal daily with the stock market quotations churned out by the tickertape (emanating directly from the floor of the New York Stock Exchange) in their classroom. Marketing students take real estate and insurance courses. Secretarial studies students learn office management and executive secretary skills. They produce itineraries and expense accounts, and work on word processors as well as typewriters. All seniors are thus very much involved in the expansion of skills that can take them directly into the marketplace.

Of course, creating this instructional program involved a certain amount of trial and error. We accepted that from the start. We knew, for example, that we were taking a chance when we taught beginning stenography for a single daily period rather than the customary double period, but our staff developed a well-paced, highly structured approach to teaching the skills of this alternative language. We believe it is an approach that could be effectively adapted to any skills classroom. It paves the way for success by anticipating any difficulties a student may encounter, and provides for frequent, increasingly rapid repetition and for constant review and refinement in succeeding lessons. It has worked very well. In 1975, the first year that our students took the stenography Regents, ten scored 100 and all passed.

In computer science, we began by teaching a computer language

(RPG, the language of our first computer, an IBM System 3) in the first year of the computer science sequence. At the end of that first year, the department head gave me good reasons why the whole order of things should be changed. At the end of the next year, he said that things were better but that the department had learned much more about what our students could do and that therefore the sequence needed changing again. Thus, we worked out a program that resulted in our students developing marketable skills. Now, as the marketplace changes and our business liaisons tell us of new demands, we continue to refine and adapt, recognizing always that change calls for certain risks but more often than not brings rewards.

Our Advisory Council played an important role in the creation of our instructional program. In the early discussions between the Steering Committee and the Board of Education, the Committee recognized that opportunities in the financial sector would burgeon during the 1970s and 1980s. No one foresaw the extent of the impact of the computer, but everyone on the Committee realized that it would assume increasing importance. The Committee laid down the broad outlines of the school's program, including a specialization in money and banking.

When our Advisory Council was established on the foundations of the Steering Committee, members reviewed curricula and pointed out areas for development. They visited classes to note how, as well as what, we teach; they evaluated our interns and cooperative education students on the basis of both visible and "invisible" curricula. When the time was ripe for the development of our major in securities and finance, our Accounting Department worked very closely with Advisory Council members to ascertain what courses would be most useful.

Thus, the development of our instructional program is the foundation of our credibility with the business community. Our graduates must be able to live up to expectations. They must be able to do what we say they can do and in a manner in harmony with the atmosphere and practice of the company for which they are working.

In building credibility with the business community, we were particularly careful, especially at the beginning, to send out students who we were absolutely certain would live up to expectations. We impressed upon our first students that, to the company to which they were assigned, they *were* the school. If they did well, doors would be opened for other Bergtraum students. We still select students carefully to match skills to needs, but those first students really bore a burden of responsibility that they met on every level. They set a standard and created an image that are still major factors in the school's success.

Spreading the Word

In developing business liaisons, we realized that we were breaking ground. We wanted much more than the Alternate Week Cooperative Education Program, which has been successful in New York for more than 60 years. We sought a range of activities and programs that would generate an awareness of business opportunities throughout the school. Clearly this was a full-time job and we designated an Assistant Principal of Activities and Development to work with our Advisory Council and to develop business liaisons of many kinds.

We used all possible means to become known: personal contacts, the media, encouraging visitors, and word-of-mouth publicity. Business, naturally, has a show-me attitude. Accordingly, we set out to show them. Again, we began with our Advisory Council. They toured the school in the fall of 1976, when we had ninth, tenth, and eleventh graders. Their guides were students eager to show off. Council members were far more impressed by the comments of students than they would have been by those of staff, and so we continue to use this technique. The students talk freely about their experiences in school and at work.

From the first tour, much good came. Among other things, the President of the Downtown Lower Manhattan Association wrote a letter to all its members praising the school, describing its programs, and encouraging members to develop internship and work-study programs.

Major New York City newspapers do not give schools the kind of total coverage common in smaller cities and towns. Neighborhood newspapers cover local high schools, but Bergtraum is not a local school. However, as time went on, there were some opportunities. The World Trade Center newsletter, *110*, printed a solid story about the work of our students. Small downtown papers featured various aspects of our program. When students worked at major corporations, stories about them appeared in company publications. *You and Youth*, the national newsletter of the Vocational Foundation, Inc., did a major story about us.

Of course, the best publicity was from the business community itself. An Advisory Council member arranged for the Assistant Principal of Business Education and me to address the monthly meeting of secretarial pool managers of major law firms. The result: a half dozen new contacts and work-study sites. The same thing happened when we met with a group of downtown office managers. Some internships developed after we spoke to the gathered heads of personnel departments of all the city agencies. And more often than we can record, personnel directors contact us because they heard from their counterparts in other companies that our school is a good source of competent part-time and full-time employees.

We continue to bring representatives of business to the school. Several times a year, we have Sponsors' Breakfasts. We find that 8:30 A.M. is a good time to welcome visitors from business. School is in full swing but offices are not. Businesspeople can thus easily visit the school and then go on to their offices. We invite representatives of companies with whom we are anxious to establish contact. Sponsors and students describe the relationships they have developed and the rewards to both. Visitors who want to tour the school are guided by students to their areas of interest.

The exchange is fruitful. Besides goodwill and the sponsor's appreciation of recognition, a broader understanding of the student's background and needs emerges. The representatives of new firms are educated and impressed; many are ready to establish a connection.

One of the most gratifying things that is starting to happen is that graduates from the early classes are now in positions in the business world to begin to bring present students into jobs. Two who are working in personnel offices in banks came to a recent breakfast. A network has begun to build.

A number of additional routes have offered themselves for publicizing the school. As principal, I participate in as many downtown functions and committees as I can. The change in my reception has been a source of delight for me. On hearing the school's name, people used to ask, "Murry Who?" Now they say, "Oh, yes, Bergtraum! Good school!"

Because we are located in an area served by all subway lines and we have a fine auditorium, many agencies, organizations, and private-sector groups ask to rent our facilities. Despite the problems that can result, we always try to accommodate such requests. The building itself and the display of student work in the halls and classrooms have been prime generators of good public relations. Even though a meeting takes place after school, at night, or on a weekend, when students are not present, the evidence of the students' work and spirit speaks volumes.

Our Adult Evening Center, opened in 1977, has also contributed. It offers courses for advancement in city and state government, computer and other skill-building courses, and recreational and cultural courses. (New York City and New York State government workers have a clearly defined career ladder, and recognition is granted for the completion of specific courses intended to upgrade their skills.) Many parents who become familiar with us through the night school not only see to it that their sons or daughters apply for admission but also spread the word about the school through the business community. In this way, Bergtraum has become known to many smaller firms.

Personal contacts have opened up opportunities for work-study programs. Sometimes a relative of a staff member is seeking office help; sometimes one of us will meet an executive of a downtown corporation who is receptive to the idea of hiring students.

Becoming known and accepted takes an investment of time and patience on everyone's part. Visitors take precious hours out of a workday. And although we do it quietly and unobtrusively, bringing them to observe classes for even a few minutes is somewhat disruptive to teachers and students. However, the teachers and students realize the value of the personal image and go right on working, invariably creating a very favorable impression.

The Work–Study Programs

As the connections with the business community began to be established, our work-study programs grew. We realized we had to make certain that businesspeople began to see themselves as partners in education. We wanted to be sure that the experience was truly educational. From the beginning, we sought two kinds of work-study experiences: the unpaid internship, which we had to be certain did not become exploitation, and the paid part-time work experience, which should be a supplement to the educational program.

Each should be structured so that the student grows in skill and knowledge. Accordingly, a major responsibility of the Assistant Principal in charge of business liaisons and the teachers who work under his supervision is to oversee the work-study experiences. In some instances, especially in connection with our intern and Bergtraum Advisory Council Intern Scholarship (BACIS) programs, this requires a number of conferences and a careful spelling out of what is expected on both sides. In our Alternate Week Cooperative Education Program, limited to special areas of study, the Assistant Principal must monitor the work being done to be certain that it ties in closely with the level of the student's area of concentration. In the part-time Cooperative Education Program (now our largest, involving as many as 500 students), the student is paid an appropriate salary for working in the field. The site supervisor's written evaluation and the retention of the student on the job minimize the need for consultation and conference. A visit from the school usually serves the purpose.

In the first two years, when we taught only ninth, tenth, and eleventh graders, we concentrated on the intern experience. We developed the *Student Intern Handbook*, which explores the internship concept and helps the student to analyze and evaluate his or her experience. Interns met periodically in seminars with the Assistant Principal to discuss their work and share their learning with fellow students. The Assistant Principal also met, often at length, with site supervisors and monitored the internships as they developed.

An internship is an unpaid work experience designed to parallel the student's school program. The simplest takes place one period a day in one of the school's offices. Here, the student is trained to answer the telephone, receive visitors, handle inquiries, file, and do other tasks specific to the department. Because all our students take typewriting, they often help with that. The most extended is the full-time internship. Students serve all day for a full semester in an executive's office, shadowing and assisting in many ways.

Most students who choose this type of internship work for city or state officials such as members of the City Council or State Assembly. Students who want to continue science and/or mathematics classes can come to school for the first two periods and still be in the office by 10. The internship work, which involves research, writing, and speaking, earns the student credit in his or her subject areas. Not many students can take on a full internship; but for the right one, it offers a golden opportunity.

Many internships are Day-a-Week spots. For one semester, the student spends one day a week in an office, assisting with clerical tasks, typewriting, working in the company library, and in general learning and doing many things. Day-a-Week interns are responsible for keeping up with all aspects of their studies. They must do all assignments and take all tests. They cannot claim internship as an excuse for nonachievement. Rarely has a student failed in class responsibilities. We have had to terminate only three Day-a-Week internships in eight years. This self-discipline is one of the many rewards of the program.

The experience of being in an office is often an education in itself. Hearing how people speak, seeing how they dress, and observing how they interact are new and fruitful experiences. If a difficulty arises, the Assistant Principal is the troubleshooter, and the student often learns a valuable lesson. The attention and care of the business supervisor help to bring out in the young person a level of initiative and resourcefulness seldom exercised in the classroom. Students learn to keep their eyes open and, with encouragement, to communicate with their supervisors.

For example, one intern working in a bank was helping to prepare a mailing to 900 grant applicants that was supposed to say, "We regret we must reject your application." He noticed that the letter actually said, "We are pleased to accept." He was nervous about drawing his supervisor's attention to the error, but he did, thereby saving the bank much trouble and embarrassment.

Of course, many internships lead to part-time and summer jobs and some to full-time jobs after graduation. But whether or not the experience leads to a job, it does in most instances lead to a fine credential. A student who has interned has a positive answer to the question dreaded by all first-job applicants: "Do you have any experience?" The intern *has*. The evaluation is on file in the school, and the business supervisor stands ready to give a reference.

We have used the intern concept to develop several special programs (the BACIS programs mentioned earlier) planned in close cooperation with a specific corporation and tailor-made to take advantage of the resources and opportunities in that corporation. Our most recent BACIS programs have been developed with Chase Manhattan Bank and the New York Stock Exchange. Approximately 70 students a semester are selected for each program. Each afternoon for a semester, they go directly from school to the company's office. They are assigned to situations that relate to their areas of concentration. Students have worked with management personnel and executives in market surveillance, technology and systems development, member trading analysis, and economic research. Because they are assigned to middle-level executives in their own fields, they learn firsthand about the application of their business skills. But equally important, they become aware of other skills, such as good speech and office decorum. For many, this is the beginning of a process of self-education that supplements their classroom experience.

BACIS interns receive no salary. At the end of their internship, their work is evaluated. If the evaluation is satisfactory, the student is awarded a scholarship of $700. This is approximately the amount he or she would have earned working part-time. But their experience has been much richer. Often, teachers and corporate advisors have modified or created relevant curricula that are taught in classes in the school. Periodic seminars are held during the term, at which school and corporate personnel meet with the students to discuss their experiences. These dialogues often give students the answers to perplexing questions about policy or procedure, and they give feedback to the supervisors about the effectiveness of the program.

The BACIS programs offer very special rewards to the companies and the school. The students selected for the positions must apply and be interviewed. They are ethnically diverse; they bring to the corporations a true cross section of New York City youths. For some in the corporations, these programs are among the few close contacts that they have had with public school students. And our students—motivated, engaging, and willing, indeed anxious, to learn—make a very positive impression.

Over and over, we find that the awakening of a sense of opportunity is one of the greatest rewards of the work-study experience. All our students are deeply aware of the courtesy and respect with which they are treated at their jobs. They begin to see that they are being judged on the basis of what they do, and that if they produce, they will be given opportunity. One young man, reporting to the Advisory Council at its annual fall meeting, spoke with feeling about how proud he was of his new status. He drew attention to his jacket and tie: "No more jeans and T–shirts; I work on Wall Street." He went on to say he had decided to go to college to equip himself to become a permanent part of this world he had recently entered.

DROPOUT PREVENTION

Very early in our existence, we developed a work-study program designed specifically to keep students in school. When our students enter the school, they are admitted to the program for which they applied: marketing, secretarial studies, computer science, accounting, or securities and finance. Twenty-five percent of the students in each area are two or more years below grade level in reading and often also in mathematics. Many of these, by dint of very hard work or by moving into slower-paced classes in their area of concentration, succeed. But by the end of the tenth year, a certain number are in serious trouble. Their problems are sometimes academic, sometimes attitudinal. These students are given the opportunity to transfer to another major, clerical office skills (COS). This is the only program in which a job is a requirement. In their junior year, these students take a full program of classes designed to equip them with both entry-level skills and human relations skills, including keyboarding, employment skills, word processing, and business English. In their senior year, they participate in our Alternate Week Cooperative Education Program. In dealing with these students, the companies are vital educators. The students' business supervisors put a great deal of effort into working with them. The school supervisor, a teacher, watches them closely. If trouble arises, the teacher consults the business supervisor and counsels and supports the student. All the students in this group participate in a special class, Employment Practices, where they talk over their varied job situations. Our graduation rate for this group is about 50 percent—high for a dropout prevention group.

Bella, a student in one of our first COS classes, has become our favorite success story. Bella is a take-charge person. She had little liking for school and was failing many of her subjects. Like so many of her peers, she clearly was intelligent and had "street smarts" and savvy. She did quite well in the more practical COS courses in her eleventh year and really came into her own when she started to work for an investment firm in her senior year. In the office, she showed initiative and resourcefulness; she would carry through on any task. She heeded the advice of her supervisor about speech and worked to upgrade it. She was offered a summer job, then a full-time job. Now, four years later, she is an assistant manager at the company and is going to college at night, with all tuition being paid by her employer. She has been back several times to talk to our students. She personifies for them both opportunity and reward.

WORKING WITH THE BUSINESS COMMUNITY

In dealing with the business community, we have been very much aware that what each company can do for the school is defined by its resources and its sense of social responsibility. In almost every instance, what a company will do is energized by an individual within that company who develops a commitment to fostering education. The farther up in the hierarchy that person is, the greater the chance for significant good. More resources will be made available and greater commitment will be generated right down the line.

Thus, working with business calls for the close attention of at least one school staff member who can dedicate time, energy, and creativity to shaping the liaison with an individual company. Together, the school representative and the company representative can assess school needs and company resources and determine what can be done.

Not all can offer job opportunities, but many can, and these jobs have to be spelled out very clearly. Some companies can offer very special programs: a combination of job opportunity, the development of coordinated curriculum at the school and/or the company, and a range of supplemental experiences. Some can set up seminars to train students for interviews; some can provide a setting for interns; some can offer help in special areas. One company had its graphics department work with us to design and produce our publicity brochure. A company with an enormous printing department duplicated material used in our Introduction to Occupation classes.

We do not ask firms to buy equipment or supplies. But when a CEO's office decor was changed, we inherited several tables and couches that make our Career Education Office look really professional. Similarly, when a major corporation changed its letterhead, our typewriting classes got thousands of sheets of perfectly good paper, and when another changed from green to pink computer cards, we developed a sudden appreciation for the color green. Companies are happy to donate equipment that is outmoded for them but useful to students.

Almost all companies can offer resource people, a standard but excellent way to enable students to understand opportunity and broaden their horizons. Such visitors are a fine supplement to classroom learning. Businesspeople get a great deal of pleasure from sharing with students their insights and accumulated knowledge, and the experience is richer for everyone when students are prepared for the visit with background information on the person and his or her business. If the class prepares questions to address to the speaker, they are likely to profit more from the answers. Over and over, in class after class, these visitors from the world outside bring the message: If you're prepared and willing, opportunity is there.

The students get the same message when we take them to offices for tours. Preparation is important here, too; the student who knows what to look for will see and hear more.

Of all our liaisons with business, that with our Advisory Council has been particularly rewarding. Behind the scene, they advise on curricula and help to open up work-study positions. Up front, their interaction with students is evidence of their interest in the school's well-being.

Graduation is a real celebration of a dual achievement of our students in the academic and the business areas, and our Advisory Council plays a big role on that day. Many members of the Council attend the ceremony. They sit on stage with faculty and special guests. In addition to the regular array of medals and scholarships in academic subjects, prestigious awards are given by Council corporations in the majors most closely allied to their businesses. For example, Dun & Bradstreet gives an award in computer science, and the New York Stock Exchange gives one in securities and finance. Our keynote speaker is usually a CEO of a major corporation.

THE REWARDS OF PARTNERSHIP

What rewards does business get for its contribution to education? The greatest reward a company looks for from involvement in a work-study program is a pool of potential full-time employees. That happens frequently; statistics show that very often the students do stay on as regular employees. If they are going to college, many maintain their connections with the company by working seasonally or part-time during their college years. So the company's investment in these young people pays off.

Now the business community is beginning to look at the larger sphere. Even when young people move to other organizations, other young people similarly trained elsewhere will be available. If the business community ultimately trains a large group of students, a pool will become available to all. That is a dividend on the investment for all employers.

An unexpected reward for businesspeople invariably is the pleasure that on-the-job supervisors get from the experience of working with high school students. The great majority of the young people they encounter in work-study programs are somewhat insecure, quite polite, careful to the point of caution, and very eager to succeed. The supervisors take great pride in the achievements of the students, and bonds are forged that are satisfying to all.

Since the 1960s, many corporations, under pressure to recognize their social responsibility, have established whole departments dedicated to its fulfillment. Lending a hand in public education, especially in work-study programs, is a whole new area in which social responsibility can be exercised. In light of the recent reports on the state of secondary education, assistance in this area is both timely and extremely useful. Money well spent brings satisfaction: It bonds the community and creates needed goodwill.

The corporate community often criticizes today's young people for "poor attitudes" and little knowledge of "traditional values." Business deplores youth's lack of self-discipline, unreliability, and lack of initiative. But how did earlier generations develop these traits? They developed them long before they entered the world of work—at home or in a church group or in the community. Snow had to be shoveled and ashes taken out from the furnace. Food had to be preserved; even daily cooking was far more demanding than food preparation is today. Siblings had to be cared for; laundry had to be washed and ironed. Today's young people have few such tasks. Especially if they live in a city, their only responsibility may be looking after a brother or sister. In doing household tasks, the children and adolescents of earlier generations assumed the mantle of maturity. They received recognition or blame for the quality of the job done.

With lifestyles demanding so little of the child and the adolescent, the growth of these character traits is stunted. Certainly they are fostered in school, but there are few opportunities to practice them. In a business office, however, a young person who is willing and guided can quickly learn their value. Business can help to inculcate in the current generation an awareness of the attitudes and values needed for its own growth. Those who learn on the job bring the message back to the larger school community in what they say, in how they look, and in their demeanor. One of the strongest forces for the education of the younger students in our school is the role models provided by the older students. Business contributes mightily to the maturity of those role models.

Rewards from our association with business accrue to teachers as well as to students. The extensive contacts that juniors and seniors have in the business community create an atmosphere in the classroom that stimulates both teachers and students. The teacher of investments may have a student who is working in the market surveillance area of the stock exchange. In the business law class, there may be a student who works in the regulatory services area. Input from these students adds reality to the class.

As we continue to work with the business community, we expand and refine our course offerings. Teachers have an opportunity to develop their skills in new and unique ways. Keeping up with the advancing technology of computers presents a challenge they can meet right in the school. Frequent contact with resource people in the field alerts the staff to new trends and patterns.

WHAT LIES AHEAD FOR BERGTRAUM?

As we move into our second decade, we know that we will reach out in new directions and that changes will take place. The commitment of business to aid education is growing; more companies are adopting schools, accepting interns and student workers, and initiating programs that reward creativity and excellence in all school areas: the arts, sports, and the traditional subjects. What other kinds of contributions can business make in the next decade to expand its role as a partner in education? One possibility that is just beginning to be explored is support for teachers. The pressure of teaching five classes a day and of preparing two or three different lessons leave a teacher little time to keep up with his or her field. Business could help in four ways:

1. It could hire, for six or eight weeks in the summer, teachers who are training students for specific fields, such as accounting or merchandising. These positions would enable the teacher to learn about new developments. We might even consider arranging a leave, whereby a teacher could go into the field for six months to bring his or her knowledge and skill up-to-date.
2. Corporations could sponsor institutes for teachers at universities. The National Science Foundation has done this for years, and the National Endowment for the Humanities has begun a similar program.
3. Companies that are large enough to have conference centers at corporate headquarters might enlarge the horizons of both teachers and students by inviting them to tour or even by sponsoring student conferences there. Every contact with the world of work adds to a student's understanding of opportunity. Subject-oriented conferences for teachers would be welcomed. Staff development programs examining recent advances in a particular field of study would be valued.
4. Developing an audience for the arts could be a very fine contribution of business to education. Good programs already exist, but more are needed.

Perhaps the most significant thing that business can do for and with schools is to expand the dialogue. As we talk about the process of education, more possibilities for cooperation and support will emerge. Teachers are a creative group, and businesspeople are attuned to turning creativity into productivity. From a shared and explored commitment to youth, a wealth of ideas would emerge to further enhance and expand the growing partnership in education.

LESSONS FOR OTHER SCHOOLS

What we have developed at Bergtraum in business programs and liaisons can be adapted to other schools in other areas. Unquestionably, the process for Bergtraum has been facilitated by our location, resources, and special mission. But every school has its own special resources and people who can look at those resources and determine how best to use them to help it fulfill its mission. There are advantages in a situation in which the school and its students are known to local business and in which local pride and concern are strong.

These general principles of our program are broadly applicable and can provide the basis for a sound and productive partnership between business and education in any area and for any school.

- A high school education should create options for students, not close them. Therefore, a program of instruction that leads to competency in entry-level skills should also provide preparation for further education at whatever point in life the student may wish to pursue it.
- In its zeal to achieve excellence in one area, a high school must not overlook the development of many other aspects of a student's ability, character, and interests. Besides its academic program and special programs, it should provide the strongest extra-curricular program its resources will allow.
- If a school promises opportunity to develop a skill, the program of instruction must be challenging and motivating enough to produce students who have that skill.
- Contact between a business and a school in the creation of a partnership should be on the highest possible level (principal and president), with implementation at the next level.
- A staff member should be put in charge of developing liaisons with business.
- The individual should have the time, imagination, initiative, and freedom to accomplish the task.
- All programs with business should be, to the greatest possible extent, individually shaped by representatives of the company and the school and should grow out of the resources of the company and the needs of the students.
- All business/education partnerships should be educational, and business sponsors should come to see themselves as both educators and businesspeople.
- Supervision and evaluation in work-study programs should be a cooperative process, carried on jointly at the school and the work site.
- The number of school staff involved in such liaisons, especially in work-study programs, should be large enough to allow for education through monitoring, supervising, and evaluating.

The greatest resource our country has is its youth. Young people want very much to become contributing citizens in every way. They want to be self-sufficient adults. They want to participate in the economic life of the country so that they can enjoy the satisfaction of work and the rewards of leisure. The time for them to begin is in adolescence, in the secondary schools. By tapping local business resources and using them to build a program that responds to the needs of its own students, the secondary school can help youth to achieve these goals.

5 The Public Education Fund

VALERIE S. LIES
DAVID BERGHOLZ
Public Education Fund

The Public Education Fund (PEF) was established in 1983 as a national nonprofit, tax-exempt organization headquartered in Pittsburgh, Pennsylvania. Its five-year mission was "to establish or strengthen public/private collaborations devoted to improving the quality of public education and increasing support for the public schools, primarily in urban areas across the country."[1]

The conversations that eventually led to the establishment of PEF were stimulated by a series of private-sector initiatives in public education improvement across the country that had attracted the attention of the Ford Foundation. In each case, the Ford Foundation was attracted to the program by the expression of private-sector interest and involvement in the well-being and future of a publicly supported institution, the local public school district.

Since 1978 the San Francisco Education Fund had been providing grants to teachers and principals and to the public schools to enhance educational opportunities for students and provide private-sector support for educational experiences that could not be financed by public money.

In Washington, D.C., an effort of the Washington Lawyers Committee for Civil Rights Under Law to provide equitable financing among the District's public schools led to the establishment of the Washington Parent Group Fund in 1981. Its purpose was to match dollars raised from Washington-based corporations with those raised by parents for school projects designed to increase parental involvement and for special programs to serve the needs of this primarily minority student population.

In Pittsburgh, the Allegheny Conference on Community Development, a civic association of top corporate leaders, undertook a series of beginning efforts in 1978 to effectively link the business and civic sectors with the public schools. This collaboration led to the establishment within the Conference of an Education Fund that raised public-sector resources to support initiatives on behalf of teachers and students.

A Ford Foundation grant was made to continue and expand the operation of the Washington Parent Group Fund. In San Francisco, Ford funds were provided to host a conference of representatives of the new private-sector initiatives in support of public schools that were developing across the country. The purpose of this conference was to discuss the potentials and problems of these collaborations. The Allegheny Conference received a Ford grant to publish information about its programs of small grants for teachers. A handbook and related program materials were developed and distributed nationally to both private- and public-sector groups.

Both local and national circumstances fueled the development of these private-sector collaborations. Over the preceding decade, urban public school systems had become increasingly isolated from the communities they served. The combination of political and financial pressures and two decades of demographic change had caused dislocations in these systems at an unexpected rate.

During this same period, support from business and industry, institutions of higher education, parents, and the general public had declined. A significant segment of the American public believed that the public schools were no longer performing adequately. This perception was particularly strong in the urban centers, where schools serve substantial numbers of children from low-income and minority families. Although the schools were still a central concern to parents, other taxpayers, and especially the business sector, seemed to have lost interest or felt they were supporting a system from which they derived little or no benefit.

Moreover, in the early 1980s, the federal role in local public education changed. At the same time that funding and psychological support for programs critical to urban school systems were withdrawn, there was an increased scrutiny of the schools. With varying degrees of urgency, the reports of the National Commission on Excellence in Education,[2] the Education Commission of the States,[3] the Carnegie Foundation for the Advancement of Teaching,[4] and others called for needed improvements in public education. Indeed, these reports cited the need for greater local involvement and "investment" in public schools and the realization that the larger community has an important role to play in the improvement of local school systems. (These were also the conclusions of the Committee for Economic Development's 1985 policy statement *Investing in Our Children: Business and the Public Schools.*)

Although this growing national concern was often expressed as criticism, some cities were actually attempting to turn the growing disenchantment into an opportunity for constructive collaborative action. Third-party intermediary organizations, often governed by business and community leaders, were being established that recognized the need to improve community confidence, interest, and involvement in the schools as an important corollary to a district's own educational improvement activities.

The Ford Foundation, as a participant in the dialogue about the well-being of the nation's schools and with its long-standing grant-making interest in public education, explored a variety of strategies for encouraging improvement. Edward J. Meade, Jr., Chief Program Officer, decided to follow up on the earlier grants to community-based school support groups in Pittsburgh, San Francisco, and Washington, D.C.

Conversations in 1982 between Meade and the staff of the Allegheny Conference Education Fund culminated in a plan for a national enterprise that could provide a combination of technical assistance and seed money to developing collaborations between the private sector and the public schools. These new coalitions, labeled *local education funds* (LEF), represented a new form of public/private partnerships in relation to the schools. It was hoped that this program might examine the mechanism for developing third-party relationships between school systems and their respective business, civic, and leadership sectors, and demonstrate that this kind of community-based encouragement of innovation and constituency building could lead to improved public education.

AN EARLY LOCAL EDUCATION FUND

The Allegheny Conference Education Fund is an early example of an LEF. The Allegheny Conference on Community Development had its beginnings at the end of World War II. Richard King Mellon, a Pittsburgh financier and corporate leader, believed that a new kind of civic enterprise was necessary to effect the changes needed to diversify the economic base of the city and the region and to provide for a positive economic future. He envisioned a civic organization with top corporate leadership involvement that would work closely with the public sector to accomplish a broad agenda of community improvement.

The Conference's agenda has continued to focus on economic development and downtown improvement. However, during the late 1960s, the organization adopted a social agenda that included minority entrepreneurship, job training, and, most recently, public school improvement.

In 1978, David Bergholz, the Conference's Assistant Executive Director, was asked to explore a potential relationship with the Pittsburgh public schools. In discussions with school leadership, he was impressed with how isolated from the city's business and civic leadership the schools had become. The problems of desegregation, the financial and political climate that faced the schools, and a general insularity of school leadership had created a less than favorable public perception of the schools' administration and, on the schools' side, a feeling that the community lacked the understanding and willingness to assist it with its problems.

Robert Dickey III, CEO of Dravo Corporation, and Fletcher Byrom, CEO of Koppers Company, both members of the Conference Executive Committee, were especially enthusiastic about entering into a series of conversations with representatives of the local foundation, business, and educational communities regarding possible business-sector initiatives to enlist the support of other corporate and private-sector interests.

Numerous conversations involving the school superintendent, the president of the local teachers' organization, corporate leaders, and foundation executives took place. It was easy to agree that the school system's limited ability to market itself and its services contributed to a less than accurate perception of it by the general public. It was also readily accepted that the private sector had considerable knowledge and expertise in the area of public relations and marketing. The question was how to broker those resources most effectively on behalf of the schools.

The answer was the establishment of the Public Information Advisory Committee, a group of public information specialists from both the profit and nonprofit sectors. The Committee met several times with the school district's part-time public information officer and decided to focus on two tasks: A subcommittee would produce an annual report for the school district that could be broadly distributed to Pittsburgh's leadership community and that would be readable by an audience of other than educators; and a handbook would be developed to instruct administrators, parents, and teachers on how they might best market their school in the immediate community. Initial foundation (H. C. Frick Educational Commission) and corporate (Westinghouse Electric Corporation) grants to the Allegheny Conference supported the successful completion and distribution of these publications.

The early trust between the school system and business leadership established by the Public Information Advisory Committee was put to a considerably more difficult test. The issues involved desegregation and thus were at the heart of many of the district's political and public image difficulties. David Bergholz was asked to chair a citizens' advisory committee that would recommend to the board of education a plan for the establishment of magnet schools. The Conference leadership agreed to loan Bergholz to this effort as a signal of its commitment to the public schools.

At the same time, the Allegheny Conference continued to explore ways in which it could broker greater collaboration between school leadership and the business and philanthropic sectors. A series of programmatic initiatives was designed to be politically neutral enough to attract the broad interest of the funding community, encourage the building of a constituency for the schools, and stimulate innovative programs within the schools.

At the plan's core was the creation of a Conference fund that would raise a relatively limited amount of private-sector support for the agreed-upon initiatives. Thus, the Allegheny Conference Education Fund was established in 1978 with initial support of $230,000 from corporate and family foundations.

One of the first initiatives was a campaign of public information support for the new magnet schools (television and radio spots, billboards, bus placards, and general information material). Its goal was to assist the school system in recruiting up to 4,000 students before the opening of the 1979 school year.

A joint venture between the Greater Pittsburgh Chamber of Commerce, the Allegheny Conference, and the Pittsburgh public schools was proposed in the Partnerships-in-Education program linking business and nonprofit institutions with individual schools.

A third program, Educator-in-Residence, was developed to bring distinguished educational leaders into the city for a period of time to work with educators, the business and foundation community, and others interested in the future of the public schools. Its goal was to better inform the local public debate and raise appropriate issues for the Allegheny Conference Education Fund and school system agendas.

A fourth program was a modest effort to provide mini grants to teachers for innovative classroom projects. This program allowed a community leadership, which included the superintendent and president of the teachers' union, to review proposals from teachers and to provide them with small amounts of money (up to $500) to carry out their projects.

The Allegheny Conference Education Fund moved rapidly toward becoming a broker of financial and human resources for school improvement, and utilized its programmatic base to develop an atmosphere of trust in the Pittsburgh leadership community that has created a context in which substantive school improvement has been achieved. Today, the Pittsburgh public schools are seen as a developing asset rather than a hopeless liability.

PUBLIC EDUCATION FUND

Building on the experience of the Allegheny Conference Education Fund and visits with the handful of other local education funds (LEFs) that existed in the early 1980s and that represented more than a mere fund-raising vehicle or foundation for a local school district, a proposal, developed by David Bergholz and Valerie S. Lies, for a national resource to encourage the creation of other LEFs was crafted and presented to the Ford Foundation. Approval was received to establish the PEF, with David Bergholz of the Allegheny Conference on Community Development as president, and in February 1983, PEF opened its doors.

Its mission, to be accomplished within five years, was to strengthen or assist in the development of public/private collaborations focusing on improving the quality of public education and increasing community interest in the schools. The Public Education Fund was to provide financial and technical assistance to a minimum of 40 urban areas whose school districts have significant minority and low-income populations. In its five-year effort, PEF funded 46 local intermediary organizations in cities across the country. In addition, with a sizable grant to the Southern Education Foundation, it has created a rural initiative, the Fund for Rural Education Enhancement, to foster the development of LEFs in seven rural communities in the Southeast.

PEF's mission has been accomplished through its dual objectives: the provision of technical assistance and the allocation of financial resources through a matching-grant program. While the grant program has criteria governing eligibility for PEF financial support, technical assistance is provided to groups not necessarily meeting those criteria, as time permits. On-site visits are an essential element of the technical assistance program. On those early visits, staff members meet with business and community leaders, school officials, local funding agencies, and others to discuss the experiences of similar LEFs and to offer guidance on organization, programs, and resource development.

ESTABLISHING A LOCAL EDUCATION FUND

The LEFs assisted by PEF are, in most instances, relatively new organizations in their communities. In all cases, they attempt to develop broadly based support for the public schools in environments often made inhospitable by school-system politics, neglect by community leaders, and the general vagaries of school finance and management.

Morale inside many school systems is low, and the range of obstacles to accomplishing significant school improvement is sometimes viewed by those both inside and outside the system as overwhelming. LEFs bring to these isolated institutions a focus for community involvement that has produced positive results. They have marshaled community interest, instituted small-scale but catalytic programs that have improved teacher and administrator morale, attracted favorable media attention to the schools, brokered an array of relationships with the outside world leading toward school improvement, and (to varying degrees) firmly placed concern for the future of the public schools back on the agenda of the cities served by PEF.

Local education funds have successfully involved diverse sectors of the community, largely because of their structure and mission. Although they are firmly based in the community, they are perceived as independent from the school district and therefore essentially immune to the political machinations of boards of education, the comings and goings of superintendents, and the ever-present tensions between district administration and teachers. The business community in particular sees involvement through an LEF as more effective than trying to build an independent relationship with the school bureaucracy.

Another attraction for business is that the decisions regarding the distribution of resources donated to an LEF rest with the LEF's community board. Whether justly or unfairly, boards of education have been accused of managing district resources inefficiently, giving little attention to measuring the results of the educational process. School district requests for grants from a foundation or corporation are often met with skepticism about controls and effectiveness. Thus, the LEF is an attractive broker of financial resources from funders who might not otherwise support school improvement initiatives; moreover, it can act as an objective monitor of those funds.

There is an even simpler reason for the appeal of LEFs: In most cities, there has not been a vehicle through which business and school leadership could discuss the issues each faces in relation to public education and how the two sectors might work together to address those issues.

The establishment of an LEF is different in different cities. However, the PEF Evaluation Team has identified three fairly discrete models: those formed in response to a "critical incident," those that are "opportunistic" in origin, and those that emerge as part of a broader "social/political movement."

However, regardless of the precipitating factors involved in the formation of an LEF, the local corporate and business community is involved. Often, as in Los Angeles and San Antonio, the business leadership has in large part shaped the LEF's program. This is not to say that an LEF had adopted a corporate agenda in relationship to public schools. Rather, the business sector has been a true partner with other community leaders in the formation of these entities, and these partnerships have forged agendas that are essentially acceptable to all interests involved.

The "Critical Incident" Model

Perhaps the most dramatic example of an LEF resulting from a critical incident is the Marcus A. Foster Educational Institute in Oakland, California. An important objective for Marcus Foster during his tenure as superintendent was to find ways in which the community could get more involved in the public schools. To that end, he began developing the concept of a *school foundation* to link community resources and the schools, providing an opportunity for even those who had nothing else to give but money to get involved. Foster's assassination in 1973 was the catalyst for the formation, in that year, of a school support organization, the Marcus A. Foster Educational Institute, conceived as a memorial to Dr. Foster. The corporate community in Oakland—specifically, the Kaiser Aluminum and Chemical Corporation, the Kaiser Foundation Health Plan, Clorox Company, and Blue Cross of California—gave early support to this new endeavor. Over the Institute's 13-year history, those companies have consistently chosen it as the vehicle for their support of an involvement with the public schools. In fact, corporate funding has been the Institute's primary support, both operationally and programmatically.

The origins of the San Francisco Education Fund are less dramatic but can also be traced to a specific event. In response to a growing number of deep-rooted problems in the public schools, the San Francisco Public Schools Commission was formed in January 1975, with civic and corporate leadership, as a cooperative effort of the board of education and the state superintendent of public instruction. Its general objectives were to identify problems in the school district and to assist in implementing agreed-upon solutions. One of its recommendations concerned the growing isolation of the schools from the community: "The public must be a partner in the decision-making process, through a variety of techniques designed to heighten their awareness of educational issues and encourage their enlightened participation in problem-solving."

Acting on this recommendation, community and corporate leaders many of whom had served on the Commission, formed the planning group that conceived and organized what is now the San Francisco Education Fund.

The "Opportunistic" Model

Most LEFs were established because an individual or individuals became concerned about the condition of the local public schools and its impact on them personally or on the general health of the community.

In Paterson, New Jersey, Lawrence Rubin, Executive Director of the Business Employment Foundation, was a key figure. Rubin had long been aware of the miserable condition of the public schools. (The adult training programs that his organization runs exist largely because the public schools have not done their job.) "The business people think the school system stinks. The teachers are critical of the schools; there are no resources to do their job. Parents send their children to private schools. Students vote with their feet and just don't go to school."[5] Rubin approached PEF in 1983, and with the assistance of its staff the Paterson Education Fund was established.

Much of the leadership of the Los Angeles Educational Partnership bubbled up through the CORO Foundation, an organization designed to provide public affairs leaders with the skills to deal with the complex interrelationships of society's major institutions. Peggy Funkhouser, whose consulting agency assisted the private sector in grant making, had served on the board of the CORO Foundation. The corporate community, having organized itself around the highly successful Los Angeles Olympic Games, seemed poised to take on another local issue. Atlantic Richfield, Lockheed Corporation, Pacific Telesis, and other companies provided initial encouragement and funding for the development of a private/public collaboration in support of the public schools. Funkhouser brought to the project skills and knowledge of the educational system, derived from her work in art education, and the ability to work with the private sector. This combination of corporate interest and individual initiative made the partnership a reality.

The Broader "Social/Political Movement" Model

The story of San Antonio's LEF, according to its director, David Sugg, has its origins in the city's history and traditions. Historically, the Hispanic and Mexican influence dominated the area; Hispanics were the majority population. But the power structure was closed and Anglo-dominated. In the late 1970s, a referendum that abolished at-large city council elections in favor of single-member districts brought about a dramatic and significant shift in participatory government. After a period of confrontation came the more constructive coalition building and the election of Lila Cockrell, and later Henry Cisneros, as Mayor.

One of the products of this opening-up process was United San Antonio, a corporate and civic organization established under Lila Cockrell's tenure, whose primary mission was economic development. But it was also clear that if high technology was to be persuaded to come to San Antonio, the city would need to have a trained labor force. The Business/Community Network for Education, the city's original LEF, was created to address this need. At the initiation of Mayor Cisneros, a broad-based improvement program, Target '90/Goals for San Antonio, was undertaken. The work started by the Business/Community Network evolved into the Target '90/Goals for San Antonio Network for Education, which actively engages corporate interest in public schools through a variety of school/business partnerships. Southwest Research Institute, Digital Equipment Corporation, and Southwestern Bell provided early leadership in this effort.

The Washington Parents' Group Fund also seems to have some of its roots in a larger social movement. The Fund's strong equity agenda is supported by the assignment of volunteer attorneys to schools in the District to assist parents in resolving problems at the school level that lend themselves to such solutions. Westinghouse Electric Corporation and C & P Telephone have been major partners in this collaboration since the planning stages.

LEF PROGRAMS

As a private/public collaboration, an LEF seeks to reach consensus on strategies to address commonly recognized problems. Although LEFs have fashioned their programs according to their definitions of these problems, all seek to broker the human and financial resources of the private sector in appropriate ways to support and encourage the local public schools. The problems most commonly identified have been:

The growing isolation of schools from the community they serve.
The waning of public confidence and involvement in the schools.
The lack of discretionary resources to target in ways that boost teacher morale and launch innovative improvement initiatives.

Without exception, PEF-supported funds implement programs by targeting small amounts of money for specific purposes. These mini programs have been directed primarily at supporting teacher innovation and creativity in the classroom, improving teacher morale, and signaling community support for teachers. Other teacher-focused initiatives have involved mathematics and science teachers in collaborative programs with higher educational institutions and corporations.

Grants have also been made at the principal or school level to encourage a team planning approach to a priority issue or problem for a particular school. Issues have included parental involvement, dropouts, peer counseling, and school/community interaction.

The common characteristic of these initiatives is that the money is raised from the private sector and allocated by a community-based committee of the LEF. The members of these committees are drawn from educational, business, parent, and civic leadership.

Many funds have also launched public-information efforts to present a more accurate and positive picture of the schools and to work with the media to attract productive attention to school activities.

A number of LEFs sponsor an array of school/business partnerships. Some are based on the Adopt-A-School model. Others focus on a particular issue: teacher internship at companies for professional development, curriculum collaboration, and brokering specific corporate resources to a problem identified by the district, such as transportation fleet management, computer training, or food-service management.

In many cases, assistance to the schools comes in a form other than money. The vast and often untapped expertise and resources of the business sector, higher educational institutions, or other youth-service agencies are brokered, organized, and applied.

Key Issues for LEFs
as Third–Party Intermediaries

LEFs, like other successful collaborative efforts engaging the private sector in the public interest, must clearly define the relationship between the institutions they are linking. Their value lies in their ability to attract, from those who historically have not been involved, participation, interest, and money to address the issue of improved urban public schools.

PEF, brokering and assisting on the national level, has supported these local initiatives. But the long-term survival of LEFs as independent third parties will be determined by the value and usefulness with which their immediate communities and the sectors they link perceive them. Moreover, value and usefulness may be defined differently by different participants. The experience of PEF to date suggests that several factors are necessary to the successful development of LEFs.

The LEF must establish an independent but friendly relationship with the involved school district(s). In every instance (especially where a local fund originated inside the school system), the creation and maintenance of an LEF's independent status is a source of tension. Yet the basic need for the LEF to be seen by the outside world as a friendly intermediary is absolutely vital to its ability to attract committed leadership and private-sector dollars. Many school administrators and school board members are apprehensive about the creation of a new force in their arena. The local fund must develop a mission and a governing structure that will allay these fears and, at the same time, must seek input and cooperation from the office of the local school administrator(s).

The LEF must be broadly representative. The LEF membership should reflect a wide range of local interest in the schools and should include a significant presence by the city's major corporations and the business sector. As CED states in *Investing in Our Children*, the business sector, as an organized constituency, has both enormous resources to share with public schools and compelling needs to be fulfilled by those institutions. LEFs are concerned with building constituencies and greater community involvement, and the business community has much to gain from, and a responsibility for assisting and encouraging, improvements in the quality of schools.

The diversity of interests at the policy-making level ensures that LEFs do not duplicate existing business initiatives and that a much broader agenda is adopted for district-wide improvements and enhanced public understanding of the local school district.

LEFs must determine the appropriate level of development and use of private-sector resources. The responsibility for funding public schools clearly lies with the various levels of government—state, local, and federal. Realistically, against the enormous budgets of urban school systems, the money raised by an LEF from private-sector activities will seem marginal at best. By and large, the LEFs supported by PEF are not endowed organizations. If they build an endowment base, it is often to sustain operating costs rather than to perpetuate specific program initiatives.

LEFs must recognize the primacy of the public financing of the schools and construct their budgets in a manner sustainable by the local private sector. Private-sector support must be allocated in an appropriate manner for innovation and relationship building, not to make up for lost or reduced public revenues. The strategic use of funds and the brokering of nonmonetary resources, rather than the total amount of dollars generated, should be the yardstick for success.

The impression made by the thoughtful application of a resource developed by an LEF can have a profound influence on a school system if it is leveraged as part of a mutually agreed-upon long-term strategy to bring about change in the schools and in the way in which a community's citizens perceive their effectiveness.

The LEF must find an appropriate balance between its abilities to be opportunistic and to move strategically. This juggling act is very much at the heart of being a successful intermediary. The LEF must be entrepreneurial, seizing opportunities for brokering as they arise. Yet, it must operate within a well-defined mission or strategy. It must recognize that not all opportunities are fruitful for the local intermediary to pursue. Staff and community board leadership are critical to an LEF's ability to respond appropriately. Broad community credibility, an entrepreneurial style, the ability to work well with educators as well as with business-people, and a finely honed political sense are necessary to an effective broker. However, fund-raising skill is not a qualification that PEF feels is essential, given an LEF board of directors made up of highly placed business and community leaders.

NEED FOR EVALUATION

Most of the local education funds that fit the characteristics we have described are very young organizations. Only as they survive and develop over time can their effectiveness be measured. The Public Education Fund Evaluation Team has been collecting data on these funds since their inception and will continue to monitor their evolution over the next several years.

Some key questions will have to be asked:

- As new private/public collaborations, are these LEFs organizationally efficient?
- As new, small, community philanthropies, where did they invest their resources, and with what results?
- As catalysts for school improvement, where did they intervene, and with what results?

- As political instrumentalities, did they broaden the constituency for the public schools, and to what purpose?
- Have they been self-renewing organizations, able to institutionalize their presence and the enhanced interest in public education, while continuing to be opportunistic and entrepreneurial?

PEF's initial five-year mission was completed in early 1988. An information-sharing and networking function will be maintained under new governance and staffing. Evaluation of PEF's grantees and its general operating process will continue for at least three years beyond the 1988 closing so that questions about the effectiveness of the Local Education Fund model already raised and others yet to be identified can be better answered.

NOTES

1. The Public Education Fund brochure, 1983.
2. National Commission on Excellence in Education, *A Nation at Risk*, Washington, DC: U.S. Government Printing Office, 1983.
3. A. Odden, *Financing Educational Excellence*, Denver, CO: Education Commission of the States, 1983.
4. E. L. Boyer, *High School*, New York: Harper & Row, 1983.
5. C. K. McGuire, M. McLaughlin, and P. Nachtigal, The Public Education Fund Interim Evaluation Report, Pittsburgh, PA, 1986, p. 19.

6 After the Signing

The Boston Compact 1982 to 1985

ELEANOR FARRAR
State University of New York at Buffalo

ANTHONY CIPOLLONE
Education Matters, Inc.

On September 22, 1982, an extraordinary press conference took place in the main hall of the Boston School Department. Sharing the stage were the chief executive officers (CEOs) of two prominent Boston corporations, Mayor Kevin White, School Superintendent Robert Spillane, and the President of the School Committee, Jean Sullivan McKeigue. This gathering was unprecedented in the history of the city; it brought together the leaders of Boston's traditionally warring factions: the schools, the city administration, and the business community. Said Robert Schwartz, a former Kevin White aide who was present, "To see [former mayor] Kevin White, who had never been in the School Department building before, created such a wave around the place that it was clear that this wasn't just another announcement."

If the gathering created a stir among observers of the political scene, the announcement came as an even greater surprise. These leaders were making public pledges to involve their institutions in an ambitious new plan for improving the education and work prospects of the city's young people: the Boston Compact.

The Compact is a formal agreement among the School Department, members of the business community, area colleges and universities, and the trade unions. In signing it, the business community agreed to hire 400 June 1983 graduates for permanent jobs and to increase that number to 1,000 students within two years if they could meet entry-level requirements. The cosigners from the business community also agreed

This chapter is based on a paper prepared for the Edna McConnell Clark Foundation, which is in no way responsible for the views expressed herein. This chapter is not for quotation without permission from the authors.

to work closely with the Boston Private Industry Council (PIC), a private, federally supported, nonprofit organization established in 1979 to explore private-sector initiatives in employment training. The business cosigners were to help PIC expand from three to six the number of schools participating in the Jobs Collaborative, a school-to-work transition program. Finally, they pledged to recruit 300 companies by 1984 to participate in a priority hiring program for graduates and to increase the number of summer jobs available for high school students from 750 in 1982 to 1,000 in 1983.

On the education side, the School Department made a commitment to reduce both high school absentee and dropout rates by 5 percent annually. It also agreed to implement increased academic standards, requiring that all graduates meet minimum standards in reading and mathematics by 1986. And the department promised a 5 percent annual increase in the number of students who either took a job or went to college after graduation.

Within two years after these agreements were signed, the Compact was expanded to include higher education cosigners and unions. The Boston trade unions agreed to set aside 5 percent of their apprenticeship positions annually for qualified high school graduates. Twenty-five area colleges and schools of higher education agreed to enroll 25 percent more Boston public school graduates through 1988 and to assist the schools in strengthening their college preparatory curriculum. The colleges also agreed to increase financial aid for local youngsters and to develop support services to help them remain in college.

But to listen to those who work with the Compact, it is clear that this is more than just a set of agreements. In many respects, it is also a concept, an idea whose execution depends on how it is interpreted and understood by those assigned to carry it out. The people who work with the Compact have different views. "I characterize this as something of a high school assistance office," said Robert Schwartz, the Compact's Executive Director. "There's a group of people looking out for the high schools, hustling the resources they want, being their advocates. . . . We're also a bunch of people making demands on them." James Caradonio, who heads education and employment for the Boston schools, thinks the Compact has become a "collective bargaining agent for kids" working on behalf of those "who traditionally never got anything." Others see it as a vehicle for convening diverse groups. "You don't just put institutions next to each other and expect that they'll work. There have to be these bridges. There have to be forums to talk," says Al McMahill, Staff Director of the Compact. Edward Doherty, Boston Teachers' Union President, calls it "a recognized forum whereby educators can sit down with business and college representatives to talk about elementary and secondary school problems. It simply is a positive force in this community."

Inside the schools, people see it slightly differently. The new Headmaster of Dorchester High School, Stanley Swartz, says that at the district and city levels, the Compact is "a public relations tool." But as a school principal, he uses it as "an administrative tool" for working with department heads on curriculum and school goals. Craig Williams, PIC Career Experience Teacher in Swartz's school, says that it is leverage to put pressure on kids to shape up and on local businesses for resources. Karen Williams, Compact Development Officer at Jamaica Plain High School, also sees it as leverage, but as more too: "A good way to think of the Compact is planning. It redirected us in the right areas, forced us to sit down and plan and strategize and really get down to work."

For the man who endorsed, promoted, and went on the stump for the Compact, School Superintendent Robert Spillane,[1] it is a "political coalition builder. I use the Compact to legitimize coalition and constituency building." He does not think the Compact is about jobs; he does not care about the big financial contributions local businesses have made to the schools. "You can throw that away. The most important thing is that it has opened lines of communication with the business community. It has made them advocates for the schools." John O'Bryant, a Boston School Committee member who first fought over the Compact but went on to become one of Mr. Spillane's big fans, said, "It's like apple pie and motherhood. Any committee would have voted for it."

These very different angles of vision reflect the Compact's enormous malleability, its projective-test quality. People see in it and make of it the things they want to. According to Ted Dooley of PIC, "The extent to which [people] see the Compact as a program is the extent to which they have already limited its potential influence. I think for a lot of educators it's not clear what the Compact is offering and not clear what the Compact really is."

At one level, it is a politically astute and cleverly crafted agreement that people have used to accomplish a broad range of objectives. But at another level, the Compact is a program that has expanded beyond its initial push to find jobs for Boston youth to a strategy for introducing broad-based improvements in the city's high schools. Part of its success results from the many different and sometimes competing purposes that it serves. This makes it useful to everyone, from the Superintendent pursuing his agenda, to principals and school staff focused on another set of issues, to the students themselves, whose objectives may be entirely different.

To the surprise of some and the delight of many, the original Compact agreement still stands. Over 500 businesses are now participating. In Summer 1985, 876 graduates received full-time jobs and 2,200 students participated in the Summer Jobs Program. And all of Boston's 14 comprehensive high schools now participate in the Jobs Collaborative Program.

Although the Compact has been heralded nationwide as a unique undertaking, it is also grounded in good common sense. It is a mobilization of resources to combat the disturbing litany of negative statistics characterizing our cities. High school dropout rates, after years of steady decline, rose 5-1/2 percent between 1972 and 1982. Whereas one out of four students drops out nationwide, rates in the fifteen largest cities range from 29 to 52 percent and even higher for minority students. Youth employment figures are equally grim; wide gaps exist between the ability of minority and nonminority youths to find work. For example, in the period from 1955 to 1981, employment for minority males aged 16 to 19 was cut almost in half, plummeting from 53 percent to slightly over 26 percent; but during the same period, opportunities for nonminority males hovered near 50 percent. The plight of minority females has been equally dismal. In 1981, their employment rates stood at 21 percent, versus 46 percent for white females in the 16-to-19 year-old range.

What drove Boston's leaders to stand on a stage and publicly proclaim their commitment to combat problems that no city had successfully overcome? And why, three years later, had the Compact become a national success story that annually attracts scores of visitors seeking to find out how to begin similar ventures in their own cities?

BACKGROUND: BEFORE THE SIGNING
OF THE BUSINESS / EDUCATION AGREEMENT

Looking back at the 1982 press conference, one Bostonian noted that it was "the kind of scene that had never happened in this city." To understand what made this congregation possible, it is important to know what had occurred in Boston over the previous few years that made the time right for selling the Compact concept in 1982. Several people, circumstances, and events had converged to create what Jim Darr, Executive Director of the Boston PIC, called "the ripeness of the moment."

First, important working relationships already existed. Business and education had been thrown together by order of the court in the 1974 Boston school desegregation case, and they had been working together, albeit uneasily, since then through the Tri-Lateral Council. The Tri-Lateral was a "mixed success," according to Daniel Morley, Vice President of the State Street Bank and a former PIC President. He characterized it as "mostly a paper arrangement, with small amounts of paper going to the schools and the schools suspicious because they saw business mucking around in curriculum and they just wanted business to get jobs for the kids." But through seven years' experience working with each other on the Tri-Lateral, PIC, the Jobs Collaborative Program, and the Chamber of Commerce, businesspeople and school people had reached several understandings about what the schools needed. "You had an evolution from concern about the school system to concrete action toward improving the schools," according to William Edgerly, Chairman of the State Street Bank and former PIC Chairman. "There was an act of commitment by large employers to get involved with the schools when the Compact started."

A second set of relationships existed within the business community through the Coordinating Committee, better known in local circles as the Vault. The Vault, which has been operating since the late 1950s, was an exclusive group of 25 CEOs of the city's largest firms, who shared information and coordinated company activities in areas of social responsibility and public policy. The Vault's member firms, which included Mr. Edgerly's State Street Bank, were the first companies to sign the Compact—a show of support whose impact is hard to overestimate.

Relationships also existed as a result of the old Youth Entitlement Program, which Boston had participated in from 1978 to 1980. As one part of the Youth Employment Demonstration Project Act under the 1977 amendments to the Comprehensive Employment Training Act, the Entitlement poured over $40 million into the city over a two-year period. It was unique not only for its funding level but also because it guaranteed a job to nearly half the city's teen-agers, provided they were income-eligible and stayed in or returned to school. The in-school employment requirements forced the city's employment and manpower agency and its public schools to collaborate, something they had previously carefully avoided. What was at first a rocky relationship had become downright friendly by the time the Compact entered the scene.

The Summer Jobs Program and the Jobs Collaborative Program were other significant pieces of ground that had been cultivated. "We had had a very successful experience with the Summer Jobs Program starting in 1980," William Edgerly reported. "It was very productive because it put nonschool people in the schools and established stronger links with the private sector." As Paul Grogan, Director of the city's Neighborhood Development and Employment Agency, described it:

We had a hard-boiled, practical program that was linked to attendance and effort in school. This was a real program. It was carefully set up and the jobs were of high quality. We got powerful people, important people to provide leadership. Because of this, the Summer Jobs Program was a success.

"This effort paved the way," Jim Darr believes. "It got high visibility in the companies and gave them the sense that this thing really worked because the kids can work." The success of the Summer Jobs Program was a major turning point in the citywide efforts to find jobs for teenagers. The 125 selected were personable young people who would make the impression on business that the program's staff wanted. "We discovered that inner-city kids, while they might have a somewhat smaller store of general information and experience compared to suburban kids, are otherwise just fine. And their supervisors found them fine and have enjoyed working with them," reported William Spring, Vice President of the Federal Reserve Bank of Boston and President of PIC. "So this really has been a key event in establishing credibility with the private sector."

This success led PIC to develop the in-school Jobs Collaborative Program. A year earlier, PIC had approached the Edna McConnell Clark Foundation with the idea of starting a machinists' training program for high school students. The Foundation said no but was impressed with other things PIC was doing and so sent the PIC staff back to the drawing board. A few months later, they presented the Jobs Collaborative idea, and the Clark Foundation bought it. With foundation support behind it, the Jobs Collaborative Program was the first piece of what was to become the Boston Compact.

Another piece of Compact folklore concerns the people who developed the concept and were instrumental in bringing together partners from the different sectors: Bob Schwartz, Jim Darr, Bill Spring, Al McMahill, Ted Dooley, Paul Grogan, Jim Caradonio, and Jane Morrison-Margulis. They knew and trusted each other and had many years of experience working together on youth employment issues. "The original people—the plotters and conspirators—we all knew each other. We had similar views, similar ends, a very long track record in public life, and accessibility to all the powers in town," Paul Grogan said. McMahill and others agreed. "This was an example of what can happen when you get a group of people together who have known each other for awhile. You've known one another in various disguises so you don't necessarily haul around your turf baggage with you." Bill Spring agreed but thought that their years of working on youth education and employment issues, some of them in Washington during the Carter Administration, were more important. They had just about crafted a new federal youth education and training bill when Carter lost the Presidency; in some sense, they were doing the same kind of thing all over again in Boston. "Because we had worked together, we had a sense of what was possible, something that people in other cities may not have." Spring also believes that the personal styles and credibility of the Compact staff made it easier for business leaders to deal with them, something that Dan Morley agrees with. He believes they were "successful intermediaries with business" because they were very businesslike themselves in background and styles. They did not seem like school people, whom many businessmen would prefer not to deal with.

Perhaps the most unusual part of the Compact story concerns the dramatic show of leadership by the new Superintendent, Robert Spillane, immediately upon his arrival. According to Catherine Stratton, PIC's Executive Director at the time, the key event in Spillane's triumph was a presentation about the Compact to the Vault. His ability to convey his message in terms of management and bargains "provided an instant aura of credibility that no Superintendent had had in years, perhaps decades. Part of it was his presence, part of it was his credibility. And part of it was probably the sense of desperation that existed: 'If this person doesn't make it, what is going to happen to our schools?'"

Before Superintendent Spillane's arrival in the summer of 1981, the business community had fairly given up on decent management of the city's schools. According to Frank Morris, President of the Federal Reserve Bank of Boston, "It was difficult for the business community to accomplish much with no leadership in the schools. We would ask the Superintendents, 'How much money does the school system spend?' And they would say, 'I don't know.'"

Spillane quickly gained their confidence. He learned how much money he was spending; he introduced a number of accountability and management devices that appeared to give order to the system. He behaved more like a businessman. The business community was impressed by the essence of his message: that the schools were going to deliver on their basic responsibilities, that they would teach kids to read and write. As Paul Grogan observed, "It's not that Spillane is such a brilliant educator. It's that he's perceived as a strong leader, someone you can deal with. He's someone who handles himself extremely well with a sophisticated crowd."

Frank Morris also believes that labor market conditions gave "a rational reason" to the business community's interest in Robert Spillane's ideas.

It was very easy to see that we were going to have a labor shortage, and in fact it now exists. And people coming into the labor force from the schools were often functionally illiterate. The school system was not doing its job. But if the city had been economically depressed, there may not have been the incentive for business to do what it did.

For those in the Compact office, the booming economy, with its multitude of entry-level jobs, only magnified the seriousness of the school system's deficiencies. Jim Darr told of examining the records of seniors in three high schools and finding "incredibly obvious" academic deficiencies, even though the students had very positive personal skills.

The schools felt themselves to be victims of circumstances in terms of the budget, their faculty, court orders, et cetera. In many ways, the Headmaster really felt that he took all his orders from somewhere else. So in that context, you couldn't expect an individual school to raise itself by its own bootstraps.

The Headmasters' lack of authority to influence even their own staffs' performance encouraged Compact staff to feel that "it would have to be a basic part of the mission to engage the system in a broader way."

Social and political changes in Boston also helped the Compact. The city had lost its traditional constituency for the public schools. Enrollment had declined from 92,000 in 1972 to under 60,000 in 1982, and projections suggested an enrollment of 40,000 by 1995. These statistics reflected not only the demographic facts of life but also the middle class's option to move to the suburbs or shift their youngsters to the city's larger parochial school system. According to Teachers' Union President Ed Doherty, only one family in eleven has a child in the Boston public schools; 27 percent of the city's school-aged children attend nonpublic schools, mostly parochial. "The electorate used to be people who used the schools. Now people want their tax dollars going to the fire and police departments." Superintendent Spillane said that "as of 1981, there was absolutely no constituency for the schools. Bilingual parents were complaining; everyone was complaining." He needed a new group of school advocates, and the business community was the obvious target. "I wanted them to form a part of the effort to improve the Boston schools so that if, for example, the School Committee were to say, 'Cut the budget by $20 million,' it would be a real slap in the face to the business community." By filling the vacuum created by demographic shifts and population changes with business executives, the school system was embracing a constituency far more powerful than any other.

The city was also becoming less contentious about its schools. After years of nasty fighting over school busing, things had quieted down. "Desegregation had worn itself out as a passion," Bill Spring thinks. "For some reason, the candidates who appealed to racial divisiveness weren't elected in 1980." The five-member School Committee that did win office seemed less interested than its predecessors had been in furthering their own careers. This was signaled in part by their selection of Robert Spillane for the Superintendent's job. He was the first unknown outsider appointed in eleven years—years during which eight other people had held the job. Perhaps his appointment said something about the city's resident population—that people might be tired of fighting and ready to settle down for an honest look at the quality of their schools.

Bill Spring and Frank Morris also believed that the city's residents were beginning to realize that there were limits to what Federal Judge Arthur Garrity's court could do. People were used to the idea that the Superintendent and the School Committee could not be counted on and so had placed their trust in the courts. But they were learning that although busing students and redistributing resources could be mandated, school quality could not. The black community, in particular, began to realize that the court had done about as much as it could do.

The Boston school desegregation case, despite the animosity and turmoil that it had produced, had an undeniably big hand in arranging the conditions that eventually led to the Compact's creation. According to Bob Schwartz, "We couldn't have gotten the citywide agreements with the business community and the colleges without the six or seven years of working together under the court order." The Tri-Lateral Council was formed in the spring of 1974, shortly before Judge Garrity issued his liability findings on the schools. In a sense, the business community had set up the Tri-Lateral to get in under the umbrella of quality education that it seemed likely the courts would push for. The willingness of the business community to work with the schools set a precedent that made it easy to approach the colleges. The four "masters" appointed by the court to oversee desegregation and the two court experts hit on the notion that since businesses had voluntarily paired with the high schools, why not go to the college presidents to see if they, too, would buy the idea of partnerships. According to Bob Schwartz, "It was a lot easier to approach the colleges once businesses were in place." Once the universities had agreed, Judge Garrity ordered the school system to cooperate. The partnerships did not happen by chance; many think that given a choice, the school system would have politely said "thank you" and walked away. The court order forced the schools into collaboration, an opening of their doors to outsiders that previously was unthinkable.

Finally, the Compact idea sold in Boston because of several shrewd assessments of who could be pushed and how far. The Compact document was written by a small core group of people who decided to forego broad-based participation, with its inevitable political maneuvering and haggling, in favor of speed and decisiveness. "It's always a tough choice whether to begin with something at the grass roots level and get a lot of participation or, particularly with something of this complexity, to negotiate behind closed doors with a limited number of people and then deal with the flack you get from those who weren't included," Bob Schwartz admitted. The Compact staff felt they had to operate the latter way because the business community had little understanding of, or tolerance for, the processes required in working with the public sector. "If we had said to the business leadership that in addition to having to negotiate with the Superintendent, we would have to go out and consult with 25 different community-based organizations and interest groups, they would have said, 'Hey, sorry.'" The staff also felt that securing the business community's commitment first would help to deliver the cooperation of other groups.

This strategy apparently worked, but not until some School Committee objections were overcome. "We were presented with it and told, 'Here, take it,'" Committeeman John O'Bryant recalled. It was put together by "the typical Boston group: white males. They didn't consult with the black community or anyone on the School Committee," something that he found astonishing in light of the system's 75 percent minority enrollment. He and Jean McGuire, the other black member of the Committee, told them that "we wouldn't personally sign off until the Compact included assurances that the percentage of minority youngsters employed would reflect their percentages in the school system. And so they were willing to write that in." Now John O'Bryant thinks the Compact is "very worthwhile. I hear the companies are pleased. I think that this is the first experience many of them had had dealing with minority students. If it did one thing, it exposed business and industry to Boston's black kids."

Another group that might have spoiled the party was the Boston Teachers' Union, which at the time was "too busy." Ed Doherty explained that "as a union, we were deeply involved in contract negotiations and layoffs when the Compact was announced. In 1981, 710 tenured teachers were laid off, 500 in 1982, and we were having contract negotiations." But later, when the Jobs Collaborative Program expanded to other schools, the union did not fail to notice that the high schools' PIC Career Experience Teachers were hired at a time when many classroom teachers were being "riffed," as the profession calls a reduction in force. "They were paid less than teachers and had fewer fringe benefits. But an agreement was reached with PIC that preferences for those jobs would go to laid-off teachers." Ed Doherty believes that PIC Career Experience Teachers are "doing guidance work. We could have said that they ought to get full guidance counselor salary and benefits. But we were told unequivocally that if we put up a fuss, they simply wouldn't go into the budget."

Still, at the time, the union had "no major objections to the Compact. The schools need money to operate, and that's tax money. If business is lobbying against the schools or being silent, it doesn't get legislators to vote favorably. If business cooperates, it's easier to get money from elected officials." Ed Doherty also liked the Compact's goals. "They're ones that no one can object to: improved attendance, jobs for the kids, reducing dropouts, increasing college attendance. They are simply and clearly spelled out." Cay Stratton believes that attaching numbers to these goals and putting them in the form of a bargain were essential to winning wide endorsement. "This concept was easy for the business community and the public to understand. When you talk about school improvement as a bargain, it's less abstract. They can grab it. Businesspeople do not relate to terms like *institutional change*."

With this set of actors and institutions, the Compact was accepted, and the ceremonial signing took place. It seemed destined for a bright future and Boston's youngsters for a brighter future. Its supporters included the best and the brightest leaders of the city's business and education communities, who knew what they had to deliver, and a strong new Superintendent determined to shake lethargy from the system and replace Headmasters with people able to get things done. Even the Boston press was on the right side, calling it "the most exciting plan ever put together to benefit the city's public school children."[2] Neil R. Pierce, a syndicated columnist writing for the *Globe*, said, "What makes it noteworthy (and worthy of emulation in other cities) is the serious long-term commitment of all the players, the measurable goals all can grasp, and the extending of the new era of public-private partnerships."[3]

THE COMPACT IN THE BOSTON HIGH SCHOOLS

While people in the universities, in the Compact and PIC offices, and on the Superintendent's staff were busy at work on their blueprints for change in the high schools, how did the school staff view these many efforts?

Certainly, a number of high school Headmasters were on Robert

Spillane's reform bandwagon. This wasn't surprising. Not long after his arrival, he replaced nearly half of the 17 in an effort to bring fresh leadership to the high schools. One of these was Stan Swartz, Headmaster of Dorchester High School, where he had taught and administered since 1969. Swartz allowed that there were many skeptics among his colleagues "waiting to see the [Compact's] track record" before they joined in. But even though the Compact's planning process was required of all schools, he seized on it because "it seemed to coincide with what we wanted to do here, and it seemed to be the one [program] that was delivering resources." Headmaster Swartz also thought that it fit well in Dorchester because the school already had a good relationship with its business partner, New England Telephone. People at Dorchester were familiar with business partners, liked what they offered, and were used to outsiders in their school.

Stacy Johnson, Headmaster at Jamaica Plain High School, believed the Compact "was the right idea that came at the right time. I saw the Compact as leverage, and I saw it as a plus. I bought into the philosophy of the Compact, and it gave me some leverage to do the things I wanted to do. It provided me with some backing."

Ted Dooley thinks the Compact has worked well in some schools but not in others. He cites Dorchester as one of the success stories.

> The Headmaster used it as a rallying force for staff development, reorganization, bringing importance to the curriculum. Working with people at the Compact and their working with [the PIC staff] to have a very effective Jobs Collaborative Program makes them a winner. There's no question about it.

But he also agrees that "the schools are very different. Some schools will say that there has been no change at all, that the Compact is all smoke and mirrors. Other schools will point to really significant change."

What is that change, and how has it come about? Many believe that the success of the Summer Jobs Program and the rapid expansion of the Jobs Collaborative Program right after the Compact was signed were instrumental in producing change. They got the attention of district administrators and school staff. They indicated to the schools that the business community would produce jobs and that that would motivate students. According to Dan Morley, "The Compact didn't invent [the Summer Jobs Program], but it did give it life and visibility. Some think that a summer job and a guarantee of a job after school will justify kids staying in school. I hope that's right!" The two jobs programs that the Compact subsumed were intended to get young people jobs and show the schools that the Compact could deliver. The business commitment to provide jobs was a way to keep them invested in the public school system.

But jobs were only the leitmotiv of the Compact's agenda. Jim Darr said that he "always felt that in terms of the impact of the Compact in the first two years, the business community's side would be much more important than the school's side, but that it would decline and should decline relative to the school's side of it." The role of the jobs program could more easily follow. "What the [Compact] really does inside the school is that it has an impact on the school's climate. More than the impact on individual students, it's the changing sense of expectations that kids find and discover when they enter the building. Preaching job results actually has an impact on more kids going to college because it changes the overall climate of what to expect and raises the level of what to expect." What the Compact is supposed to strengthen are the relationships among teachers, students, and administrators; the perceptions students have of themselves and what they can achieve academically and vocationally; and the quality of the education in each school.

How has such an ambitious task been approached? What steps have been taken to move from a conceptual framework, a philosophy about educational change and improvement, to a working program that has attempted to infuse new life into Boston's weary high schools?

PLANNING FOR THE PLANNING PROCESS

Once the flames of doubt and opposition in the School Committee and minority communities had been put out, the Compact began a planning process to sell the idea to the schools. This was done in a number of different ways.

Early in 1983, a Compact office was formally established; Bob Schwartz and Al McMahill, who were loaned by the Center for Public Service at Brandeis University to consult with the Superintendent, were hired as Executive Director and Staff Director, respectively. Although the office was housed in the School Department headquarters, the Compact was not an official Department program. Rather, it was a "quasiautonomous body." Schwartz claims that this was done for two reasons.

One was symbolism in terms of the outside. We had to say that this was a priority and that "Schwartz reports to the Superintendent." The second, was that given the way bureaucracies work, if you've got three Deputies [Superintendents], if you work for one of them, you have a hard time getting the other two to cooperate. At critical points [such as] getting a memo from the Superintendent to the Headmasters, getting his weight behind us, made a difference.

With the Compact's implementation mandated for each school and an office established to oversee it, the difficult work in the schools began in earnest. What was important was to generate enough enthusiasm among administrators, teachers, and students so that Compact goals could be addressed at the classroom level. Speaking of the importance of having educators accept the Compact as a school improvement effort, Al McMahill said, "We viewed this as the ultimate test. If you're trying to change things and classrooms don't change, then nothing ever changes."

One of the first things done was to identify staff who could represent the various aspects of the Compact in each school. Explains McMahill, "We first identified people called Compact liaisons over the spring of 1983. We basically told each Headmaster to identify someone within their building to work with the [Compact] office on the implementation of activities." These liaisons, later called Development Officers, were to assist the Headmasters in trying strategies that would begin to meet the Compact's goals. As school staff rather than Compact employees, each defined the position differently, a function of the skills they brought to the job, the needs of each school, and what the Headmaster wanted them to do. Karen Williams, the Development Officer at Jamaica Plain High School, says, "My job is to get the Compact in, get people to own it, believe in it, and get involved in it." According to William Fitzgerald, the Development Officer at Dorchester, he works with all members of the faculty. "I report to the Headmaster, but I deal with everyone in the school. The nature of this job is to get along with people at all levels. You can't be viewed as administration by faculty. They want to deal with you on a peer level. It's the same with administrators. It's almost a unique position, where I'm not evaluating people, I'm working with them. I basically supervise no one but work with everyone."

In some cases, Development Officers provide a link with the school's business partner, coordinate the activities of outside agency representatives who might be providing services to the school, or recruit new students. At other schools, they might work closely with teachers to integrate the Compact's goals into the classroom teaching process. For the most part, their specific duties depend on the specific objectives of the school and the wishes of the Headmaster. Al McMahill says that "many of these people felt that their job was to do and be the Compact in their building."

At the same time that the Development Officers were being identified, PIC continued to expand its Jobs Collaborative Program, moving from the original three high schools to fourteen. This program's expansion allowed PIC to add Career Experience Teachers in each school. These individuals taught career development classes and prepared students for summer jobs, part-time jobs during the school year, and permanent positions upon graduation. In addition, they spent part of their time contacting businesses that had signed the Compact pledge, establishing relationships with them, and cultivating jobs and other resources.

People at the Compact office and PIC thought that if the Compact was to have any hope of being accepted by administrators and teachers, it needed to pay particular attention to the culture and climate of each school building so that the new Development Officers and career specialists would be accepted. Ted Dooley says that "what we did was approach the schools the way an anthropologist approaches a culture. You have to go in and learn the lay of the land, the language, the concepts. We've really earned our credibility by knowing the day-to-day business of the Headmaster and the faculty. We've gone in and worked with them at their own level."

One way this was accomplished was in the decision to hire laid-off teachers as Career Experience Teachers. According to Jim Darr, these individuals "had worked in those schools before, [and] could be recommended by the Headmasters. For political reasons, we wanted to relay a message that we were sensitive to the tensions in the system. We were not aware at the time how valuable that would be to us."

One political benefit of this decision was that it served to establish friendly relations with the Boston Teachers' Union. At a time when there was considerable passion regarding layoffs, the hiring of riffed teachers helped the union buy into the Compact.

According to Jim Darr, other benefits were more practical. "They brought us an ability to get schedules changed and help maneuver kids through the system so that they'd be available for our activities. This was more than we ever could have done [without them]." Ted Dooley added, "At one school, our staff person can get things done that the Superintendent couldn't get done."

Finally, the hiring of many former teachers helped make the Compact credible to both the Headmasters and the teachers. It helped instill a degree of ownership in the program. "We've never made any bones about the fact that the Development Officers don't work for us. They work for the Headmasters," Al McMahill explained. "There's no question about that." Regarding the PIC positions, Dooley remarked: "We approached [the schools] and said, 'This is your program, your staff, your position. These people report to us, but they also report to you.'" To illustrate this, he related how "in a few schools where we put people, they were not necessarily the very best we could have hired. But they were the best people for those situations because they were strongly connected with the Headmasters. They had been in the schools before."

As people representing the Compact began moving into each school, it became clear that there was a need for some mechanism to help the schools begin to address the Compact's goals. Initially, this was the role of workgroups. These workgroups, which were the Compact Steering Committee's idea and represented a cross section of school constituencies, were led by a School Department official and a senior staff member of an appropriate agency. Each workgroup was set up to address a specific issue: guidance counseling, higher education awareness, and career counseling; alternative education; job development; remedial education and basic skills; arts, interscholastic and intramural athletics; curriculum development; career and vocational education; computer literacy; research and evaluation; and school management assistance. Some, particularly the job development and counseling/higher education awareness and career counseling workgroups, are still part of the implementation strategy; others expired or never got off the ground.

The use of cross-school workgroups was not the original choice of the Compact planners. They had wanted planning teams to work within schools, with the Compact staff providing technical assistance. But initially the Superintendent did not agree. Bob Schwartz, then a consultant, remembers:

> In June of 1982, when it came time to make a proposal to the Superintendent for budgetary support during the 1982–83 school year, I submitted a proposal which had three parts to it. One part of it was to begin to work intensively with three schools on a pilot basis in the area of school-level planning and development. The memo got returned to me with that whole part of it crossed out, as if to say, "We don't need that."

Although both Schwartz and McMahill went along with the idea of workgroups, they were sure that problems would arise, along with a need to redesign the planning approach. Al McMahill explains:

> What I did was put together as many workgroups as I could, support them as best I could, and sure enough, it wasn't too far down that road that people began scratching their heads and saying, "But we don't have the constituencies in the schools. We don't have a clear sense of what the schools need." At that point, I went out to the schools and formed our local school planning effort in the summer of 1983. That's when we finally started to do our constituency building in the schools.

This effort at constituency building became known as the Summer Planning Institute, an important developmental milestone for the Compact.

THE 1983 SUMMER PLANNING INSTITUTE

In the original Compact agreement, it was specified that the schools would not be judged on their performance during the 1982–1983 school year. Rather, this would be a period of planning, a time to develop conditions for successful entry into the schools. The Summer Planning Institute of 1983, in the opinion of most Compact observers, was critical to entry and in many ways served as a kickoff to school-based Compact activities.

By the summer of 1983, a number of critical developments had occurred in the planning process. First, people who could represent the Compact within the schools were now in place. Second, the Jobs Collaborative Program, which had involved three schools during the preceding school year, had been very successful. These two factors combined to enhance the Compact's credibility in at least those schools. Stan Swartz, Headmaster of Dorchester, observed:

> There were a lot of skeptics as to whether they [the Compact] were going to deliver the jobs, but PIC was very effective and hired school people, people who know the schools and know the politics and chemistry of the school system. I'd say the marriage between PIC and the public schools has been a very effective one. There is good communication between them and the School Department, and I think this has helped facilitate the success of the program.

Another factor enhancing the Compact's credibility was the success of the 1983 Summer Jobs Program. Although the previous summer's program had done extremely well, the signing of the Compact had created more jobs and was viewed very positively by the schools. It was an indication that the business community was indeed taking its Compact pledge seriously.

Finally, by midsummer, the high schools had undergone substantial reorganization. Some Headmasters and a number of department heads had been replaced. There was a feeling in the school system that Superintendent Spillane was making the high schools a high priority in his administration and that Headmasters would be held accountable for school performance. According to one Assistant Headmaster, "There was a feeling that Spillane meant business."

Headmasters and other representatives of each high school met for the 1983 Summer Planning Institute at the Boston campus of the University of Massachusetts for eight days. The Institute was to allow school representatives to get together, away from their school buildings, to devise a written plan spelling out how each school would address the Compact's goals during the upcoming school year. The mornings were devoted to workshops on effective practices that might meet those goals; these were given by practitioners currently working in the Boston schools, who were deliberately utilized to signal that there was indeed a sense of faith and confidence in the school's staff and that there were resources in the system that could be tapped. As Al McMahill points out, "In many cases, workshop speakers got up out of the audience and came forward to present. Only a few 'wing tips' were brought in from the outside." Some of these 'wing tips' were consultant specialists in areas such as school and curriculum planning. In the afternoons, representatives of individual schools met to produce their school plans. Says Jane Morrison-Margulis, "It was the first time anybody paid attention to individuals within the high schools and said, 'Why don't you put down on paper your plans for the school.' During the Institute, people had time to plan, and they were away from the distraction of their schools."

According to Stacy Johnson, Headmaster of Jamaica Plain, "the Summer Planning group put pressure on people to put things on paper and devise a game plan." Yet, because this was a new process, pressure and full participation came slowly to some. To some extent, Robert Spillane's presence and not-so-gentle encouragement helped foster this acceptance. Jim Caradonio explained:

> The Headmasters at our first Summer Institute had to show up with a plan and run planning meetings. I remember in the beginning some didn't take it seriously, so the Superintendent came to the meetings and put their feet to the fire. And, boy, the next day they were busy!

Besides getting school personnel to sit down and actively plan programs for the upcoming year, the Summer Institute had another purpose: It allowed the organizers of the Compact to set what they believed should be the tone for the future. Says Al McMahill: "We made the schools three promises in the summer of 1983. The first promise was that the Compact was not going to go away and neither were we. The second promise was that we had an ideological approach that we were not going to deviate from." This ideological approach involved a strong belief that institutional change must involve bottom-up planning and must instill a sense of ownership to participants. "The third promise," he added, "was that we made no promises. We promised them no quick fix. We promised them long, hard fights."

At the conclusion of the Summer Institute, schools had developed written procedures for addressing the Compact's objectives. These were not how-to guides, but more general in nature, listing objectives, delegating responsibilities, and establishing time lines for their achievement. The quality of the plans, according to Ted Dooley, may have reflected the commitment of each Headmaster. Whereas some welcomed the plans as a powerful tool for plotting the future of their schools, others "paid lip service and went about business as they always did." However, even in those schools where administrators took the planning process seriously, there remained the question of how to sell the plans and ideas to those who were the most important players on the field: the teachers.

THE COMPACT IN JAMAICA PLAIN
AND DORCHESTER HIGH SCHOOLS

Both Jamaica Plain and Dorchester are characterized by Ted Dooley as "stars" of the Compact. They may not reflect the experiences of all or even most of the Boston high schools, yet their experiences demonstrate how the Compact went about integrating itself into the schools.

Reflecting on the initial planning process begun at the 1983 Summer Institute, Karen Williams, the Development Officer at Jamaica Plain, sees a significant flaw. For all the talk of bottom-up planning and participation, the written plans were for the most part authored by administrative personnel. "Quite frankly," said Williams, "the way the Compact was put upon the schools by [the central administration] it was difficult to generate any ownership." Facing the plan in September 1983, the teachers' response was, "Oh, you've got a plan? You do it!" Bill Fitzgerald, Dorchester's Development Officer, paints the same picture of that first year: "We had to sell it [that] year. Some people somehow associated in their mind that the central administration wanted to impose upon them and infringe on their contract. [Teachers' initial] response was, 'Oh, sure, I'll do this for you.' I don't think they took this seriously at all." According to one Dorchester teacher, this response at least partly could be attributed to the fact that only administrative personnel had been involved at the Summer Planning Institute. Classroom teachers had not been consulted, nor did they influence its outcome.

During the first year, there was a conscious effort to make department heads and teachers aware of the contents of the new plans and to promote the Compact concept. At Jamaica Plain, Karen Williams says that she began "quietly monitoring each step of the plan. You know, things like [saying to teachers], 'What's happening? How's it going? Remember the Compact!' I really did a lot of individual public relations. I don't think there was anyone who would say that they were unaware that there was a plan. They may not have memorized it or known exactly what was in it, but they knew it was there."

Department heads at Dorchester were given copies of the plan and asked to review it and make suggestions about possible revisions. According to William Fitzgerald, many of the suggestions were incorporated into the final document. "I think we convinced people. We sold them that this was a plan with realistic goals and that we also wanted their input. [We] showed everyone that this was a living document and that nothing was etched in stone."

At both schools, the final thaw came as a result of student progress that many attributed to the Compact. What is interesting is that in one school this progress revolved around academic achievements; in the other, changed attitudes were the result of the jobs programs. In the case of Jamaica Plain, Karen Williams believes that the first indications that the teachers were being won over was the end-of-the-year testing results. "We jumped up to the number-two school in the district, a jump in average score of over 20 points. And people like success. They like to be part of success. This was the first time that the school as a whole said, 'Wow, maybe this is not so bad! Maybe this Compact idea and the fact that we are all working towards the same goal is not so bad.'"

Dorchester teachers were impressed by both the quantity and the quality of the jobs offered through the Jobs Collaborative Program and, particularly, the Summer Jobs Program. They saw that students were responding in great numbers and that PIC was ready and willing to deliver jobs. This was especially true in the case of the New England Telephone Company, Dorchester's business partner for the past 15 years. Although the company had traditionally provided a variety of resources to the school, there was never any sign of interest in hiring Dorchester students. This changed under the Compact. According to Bill Fitzgerald, the Development Officer who had been the school's company contact from the start, the Compact was the "wedge that allowed the kids to get in." Prior to the Compact's school/business agreement, only three Dorchester students had been placed at New England Telephone. In the summer of 1983, that number rose to 23; the next summer, it nearly doubled. According to Craig Williams, teachers could see many students motivated by their experiences in these jobs.

The Summer Jobs Program [has] served as a signal to both teachers and kids that good things are happening. The word is out now. [As] time progresses, teachers have really been integrating the program into what they do. They see that we've placed over 100 kids in summer jobs. The program [went] through a legitimation process, and the teachers gave it a lot of support; they play a large part and reinforce what I do.

Dorchester's Stan Swartz confirmed this: "We put together a plan, and people might have been reluctant to buy into it, but when PIC began to deliver the jobs and the students began to realize that this thing was working, the teachers jumped on the bandwagon."

As a new round of planning began in the spring of 1984, the various departments in each school went about the business of reviewing previous plans and preparing updates. At Jamaica Plain, Karen Williams was impressed with the tenor of the meetings and believes that they reflected the change in teacher attitudes toward planning. She illustrates this with an account of a business department meeting.

The questions that teachers asked were good questions, and I think it really got the department head to take the Compact much more seriously than she had. They wanted to know why: "Why can't we produce kids who can type 45 words per minute? Why can't kids type after having typing three years?" They put [the department head] on the spot. I was not there to make her uncomfortable, but if I had asked those questions, it would have come across differently than had the teachers asked them. And that was great. They were saying, "We need a plan. What do we do?"

This serious approach to planning was rewarded during the next school year as both schools continued to add to their accomplishments. Year-end standardized test results indicated that student scores had again risen in most curricular areas. Jamaica Plain and Dorchester were included among 26 schools recognized by the Massachusetts Board of Education for excellence in school desegregation. Jamaica Plain received a two-year Carnegie Corporation School Improvement Grant to implement an innovative alternative English and history program and a staff development program. Dorchester got a public commendation from the Governor for its Compact Ventures Program, which provides additional, intensive support services for ninth-grade students. Visitors from around the country have flocked to both schools to learn how the Compact works at the building level.

Public recognition reinforced the importance and value of long-range planning. In both schools, planning is now an ongoing process, not a quick year-end task. For example, Karen Williams indicated that in

February 1985, when it became apparent that Jamaica Plain would have difficulty achieving a goal of 85 percent daily attendance, the attendance committee reorganized its strategies to better attack the problem. The staff conducted a phoning blitz, calling students' homes on days they were absent. There was also stricter enforcement of a School Department policy that makes subject failure mandatory after 15 days of unexcused absences. There is agreement that attendance will be an important item in the 1986–1987 plan.

At Dorchester, ongoing reviews of the 1984–1985 plan also resulted in a clearer sense of direction. Three subcommittees were formed to address a possible restructuring of the school's schedule and ways of improving school communication and school discipline. In April, these subcommittees reported back to the planning team with ideas for the 1985–1986 plan. A decision was made to concentrate resources on four approaches to the dropout issue:

1. The school year would be divided into semesters so that students who had made insufficient progress in attendance or academics could start the second half of the year with a clean slate.
2. A new school social worker would develop outside support services for high-risk students.
3. A peer advisory and peer tutoring program paired new and veteran student help with academic and social transition problems.
4. The successful Compact Ventures Program, which provides academic, social, and emotional support to high-risk students, would be expanded to the ninth and tenth grades.

Principal Stan Swartz and planning team members believed that these measures would help sustain the progress they had made in keeping Dorchester students in school.

Significant to the planning progress at both schools have been the contributions made by their university liaisons, Ann De Placido from the Boston campus of the University of Massachusetts and Bard Hamlen from Simmons College. Each has helped administrators and teachers develop programs that are either operating or in the planning stages: helping one of the Headmasters to assemble a strong administrative team, working with department heads to infuse basic skills instruction into curriculum areas, assisting with program evaluations, and helping staff identify outside support services for students. According to Marilyn Corsini, Assistant Headmaster at Jamaica Plain, Bard Hamlen has served as "a sounding board for [the Headmaster] and me, often helping us expand on some of our ideas." She was instrumental in conceptualizing the project and writing for the Carnegie grant; she helped the English and History Departments implement the alternative teaching strategies proposed in the grant.

Change has been reported in both schools, at least in the way the Compact planning process has been absorbed into their operation. Al McMahill distinguishes between schools that "have it" and those that don't.

> Schools that "have it" have integrated the notion that "it's not the Compact's plan; it's the school's plan." Those schools that treat doing the Compact plan as a compliance exercise rather than as a means within their own building of clarifying, cohesion, direction, and moving forward, those schools don't have it.

By these standards, Jamaica Plain and Dorchester have it.

There may be some speculation, however, about why they have it. No one questions that schools are planning more and working toward specific goals, but some question whether they identify this process with the Compact. Phil Moskoff, Career Experience Teacher at Jamaica Plain, says:

> I'm not sure that if you took ten Jamaica Plain High School teachers, put them in a room and asked them what the Boston Compact was, all ten would know about it. But they would know me and what I do. If teachers view something as working, they get interested in it, and they don't really care what it's called. People around here know I work for PIC. They know that PIC implements a job program. If you ask them what my relationship is to the Compact, they might not know.

According to Joseph Casey, Chairman of the English and Language Arts Department at Dorchester, teachers spend a good deal of time on projects that address issues identified with the Compact, such as increasing daily attendance and bolstering basic skills. He adds, however, that "my perception is, no, the average classroom teacher does not have a lot of knowledge about the Compact."

The Headmaster at a school not closely aligned with the Compact believes that, for the most part, teachers see the Compact as a jobs program rather than one of school improvement, adding that "for all intents and purposes, the Jobs Collaborative is the Boston Compact!"

Perhaps Marilyn Corsini puts the issue of recognition into perspective. She believes that there has been substantial movement in shifting the responsibility for planning from the school administration to the teachers. "I look at the integration of the Compact in phases. In the beginning, planning was primarily done by the administration; but right now we're in Phase II, with the department heads taking a lot of responsibility for developing the plan." Her feeling is that in Phase III teachers will take an even greater role in the planning process and increase their recognition of what the Compact is doing in the schools.

Still, no matter what the degree of actual recognition by the average classroom teacher, the fact remains that at least in those schools that have it, there is a much greater degree of school-wide planning and faculty participation than ever before; there *has* been change. And this, after all, is the primary goal of the Compact. As Al McMahill points out, these schools "will never approach a problem quite the same way again. Planning won't be something that happens because someone else tells them it has to happen. It will happen because they won't think about doing it any other way." In the end, he adds, "what we really want is change, not fame."

SUMMARY OF THE FIRST TWO YEARS

The cases of Jamaica Plain and Dorchester are two examples of how the Boston Compact is playing itself out in the schools. As district high schools, they have received fewer resources in recent years and traditionally serve students of lower academic caliber than the more specialized magnet schools do. It is not an understatement to say that three years ago, they were in very sad shape. Similarly, it would not be an overstatement to say that since the advent of the Compact, there have been significant advances in each school. Nonetheless, their experiences reflect the fact that integrating the Compact into academic practices and procedures is, and probably will continue to be, a slow process. Schools are still assessing and planning and allowing the process to take hold.

The Jobs Collaborative Program and the Summer Jobs Program continue to exceed their goals, and the Compact met its 1985 goal of placing 600 graduating seniors in permanent jobs. Even more impressive than the figures, however, are the differences in the way members of the business community view students. Reflecting on the experiences of Dorchester students, Craig Williams says that businesses have "changed the way they look at Boston school students. They don't see them any more as having basic discipline problems. They know now that we have good kids."

Modest gains have been recorded in both the attendance rates and the achievement scores of students since the introduction of the Compact. And although it can't be said for certain that this is a direct result of the Compact's efforts, many of those interviewed felt certain that a relationship exists. There are other, less quantifiable indications that the Compact is getting its message across, at least in these two schools. According to Phil Moskoff, at Jamaica Plain:

> [The Compact] works far better than I imagined. The combination of putting kids in a work situation with counseling and schoolwork had a great effect. It has increased attendance and done a myriad of other things. For students, the Compact shows the longitudinal picture, that there is a connection between school and work. Seeing this in real life does more to put pressure on kids than anything teachers can say. For teachers, it has made life considerably easier. It has made discipline problems less. And it has helped me in that a lot of kids who didn't see a concrete value in education now do.

Ed Doherty, President of the Boston Teachers' Union, offered a powerful perspective on how teachers feel about the Compact:

> I've been working here in the union office for ten years, and if something is not working well in the schools, we always hear about it. If a program is in trouble or people are unhappy, they call the union and blast us for not protecting them. They let off steam. But I can't think of one call that we've had complaining about the Compact.

The Compact has been expanded and strengthened with the addition of the two agreements with the higher education community and the Boston Trade Unions Council. Some of the Compact's framers envision an even greater number of participants and agreements as time passes. Boston area museums and cultural organizations are mentioned as possible future collaborations, as are a number of social service and health care providers. Plans are under way to make the Boston Compact a comprehensive set of agreements among and between the full range of organizations that can help the city's youngsters.

A LOOK INTO THE FUTURE

The Compact's newly forged relationships among the education, business, and labor communities are a step forward not only for the city but for the entire education-to-work community. The Compact has moved partnerships beyond the old arm's-length agreement between business symbolically fulfilling its civic responsibilities and school systems wary of sharing or losing control. The Compact is particularly noteworthy because it has shifted the central idea away from work and employment experience to improving the quality of education. It aims beyond work training and job placement to ensure that students who seek those opportunities have the academic skills that business and others think necessary for successful, long-term employment.

But moving ahead on this ambitious agenda will not be easy, as the Compact's framers are quick to acknowledge. "There is a mountain of failed efforts that have to be overcome," Paul Grogan pointed out. Efforts to change the high schools in many cities have foundered on weak leadership, foggy goals, stalemated politics, and lack of commitment to carry through. The Boston schools are no exception. They've tried new things, but the failures of the past decade have left their mark. Headmasters and teachers alike need evidence that this program will not go the way of all the others.

The Compact's ability thus far to deliver on its promises is clearly a move in the right direction. Although the numbers of students employed through the Jobs Collaborative Program is still relatively small at under 100 per school, the numbers are growing. In a few years, 40 percent of each graduating class will have had some exposure to the Jobs Collaborative. And the schools are beginning to feel the effects of other resources from the business community. Still, the incentives for schools to buy into the Compact's planning process are less clear. Headmasters like Stan Swartz and Stacy Johnson found incentives in the Compact's ability to help them further their own school plans. But when school heads fail to make that connection, have plans they prefer to carry out their own way, or lack plans altogether, it is not clear what course the Compact will follow. Al McMahill thinks that tough-minded incentives may be called for.

> We've got some more schools to bring along. But that's where the line structure has got to come in and say, "Hey, it's a new day, and you're either going to do some things some new ways, or you're going to have to find some other work to do." Now, if the system won't do that, then I think it's undercutting itself. It will be interesting to see what happens.

Incentives for classroom teachers may be even more important. Some say that teachers have been impressed by better attendance rates and higher test scores and that their morale has improved. But it is doubtful that improved morale alone can reform the school system. There is no question that it is one important ingredient. But school improvement ultimately rests on better teaching, and teachers need their own opportunities to improve through in-service training and new curricula that they want to use. Thus far, these ingredients are missing.

The development of incentives for Headmasters and teachers to take the Compact's school improvement goals seriously is ultimately intended to improve student performance. In the past few years, many more students have gone to school more regularly. And over time, regular attendance combined with a regular job may convince many more that staying in school is better than the alternative. But simply clocking hours in school will not overcome many youngsters' very real academic deficiencies. Jim Caradonio believes that "the biggest problem is still the area of basic skills. If there's any weakness in the Compact, it's not in its approach but in its ability to tackle this problem." Jim Darr concurs: "On the substantive side, the greatest storm cloud is around the basic skills that kids enter ninth grade with and the relative inability of the high schools so far to change that." The Compact, through the Private Industry Council (PIC), has moved to extend remedial work back to the ninth grade. Before he left, Robert Spillane told the business community of the system's need for reading teachers in all its middle schools. That will help younger students, but the Compact needs a short-term strategy for assisting students who have made it to high school without having mastered rudimentary mathematics and reading skills. Such strategies exist, but they are labor intensive and expensive. Thus, dealing with the problem of deficient basic skills is perhaps the biggest challenge the Compact faces. The school system must deliver on its side of the business/education bargain. The question is: How much time does it have to do it?

The Compact faces other challenges as well, many the result of its success and survival. One of the great ironies of American education is that successful programs that catch the public's eye have a hard time keeping it. Interest moves on to other things; yet, that interest and what it brought to the program are vital to the program's success and survival. The Compact must find a way to maintain the business community's involvement in the face of other public demands on its resources. As William Edgerly observed in 1985, "Business is now reviewing its relationship with the Compact, trying to evaluate our alternatives for going forward, to focus our efforts in fewer ways so that resources can be applied effectively and collaboratively. There is a sense among all of us CEOs that we have a project that is successful, and we want to maintain it."

In 1985, many people seemed to think that the way to maintain the Compact was by institutionalizing it in the School Department. But they had different points of view about which aspects should be institutionalized. Most agreed that the business/school relationship, the jobs, and the school improvement process should become permanent fixtures. They disagreed about who ought to support and manage the Compact. "In the jobs context, we've provided the organization and the seed money to see this consortium effort pay off for kids," Dan Morley pointed out. "Then [the school district] can rejuggle its budgets and pay for the staff." Morley thought that the program should become the long-term responsibility of the school system, not of business, which will want to move on to other things. "I think it will never be successful if business has to fund it. It's the kind of test program that can be supported at the start from the outside, but it must be incorporated into the school system."

Among the school people, John O'Bryant agreed, but wanted to wait awhile before the Compact became the responsibility of the School Department alone. "From a logistical standpoint, I don't think anybody should do anything for a year or two. We need to develop confidence in the system so that chief executive officers will feel comfortable working with school people. [Then] it must be institutionalized; otherwise it is too vulnerable to being cut." Superintendent Spillane disagreed and said flatly that the Compact could "never" be organizationally incorporated into the School Department. He believes that if this happened, the support of PIC, the main conduit to the business community, would be lost. Jane Morrison-Margulis explained that for this reason institutionalization "can't and shouldn't [happen]. This will take the clout out. The Compact is a combination of internal and external services. It is not a School Department program and never will be."

Nevertheless, many people pointed to evidence that the Compact was becoming an accepted way of life for some of the partners. William Spring observed that "there is now a cadre of people at the Federal Reserve Bank who take it for granted that one of the things they're going to be doing is having kids from South Boston High School in significant numbers working in part-time jobs." Ted Dooley noted that "the School Department has internalized the activities of the Compact. It's less dependent on the skeletal structure of the Compact." He pointed out that the Compact office and its staff are housed in the School Department and that the PIC Career Experience Teachers' salaries had been picked up by a $300,000 appropriation from the School Committee. Its boosters thought that as both an organizational unit and a new way of doing things, the Compact was becoming increasingly accepted. Morrison-Margulis believed that the Compact was even sinking roots in the schools. "Every day in every high school, a nonunion person is teaching. The fact that this was occurring while teachers were being laid off is astounding." She thought that there were so many different people and institutions publicly linked to the Compact through a deliberate public relations and media campaign that it would be hard for them to renege on their agreements. The Compact "won't go away because there are too many people with their feet in it. There's a great deal of theater attached; the amount is astonishing. But it is also substantive."

But shadows fell over this bright confidence when certain subjects were raised in the winter of 1985. The Compact's independence from the rest of the system bothered the School Committee and the Teachers' Union. John O'Bryant described the Compact as a "semiautonomous unit" and said that "the School Committee is going to have trouble with that. We want all of the people who are working in the schools to be certified. And why shouldn't they be?" He and Ed Doherty noted that the staff the Compact assigned to the schools are not paid salaries comparable to those of other school staff. Yet, according to Doherty, they're doing guidance work. (The Compact staff strongly disagrees.) Doherty suggested that this could become a bargaining issue in the 1986 contract negotiations; however, when the time came, the issue did not come up.

Leadership was another worry, and some people were not optimistic about what might happen if certain key people left, particularly Robert Spillane. If he left, John O'Bryant mused at the time, "the Compact would be in serious trouble," particularly if the job went to an insider who would be under great pressure from some members of the School Committee. Bill Spring and several others agreed that the program was vulnerable there. "The one place where we would really fall apart is if Spillane left and was replaced by somebody who feels that his mandate is not to be Spillane. We're vulnerable on the school leadership side, but not for very much longer, perhaps just for a couple of more years." Others observed that the Compact had already demonstrated resiliency by surviving the difficult transition from a five-member to a thirteen-member School Committee as well as a change in city administration. If anything, these changes were thought to have strengthened the Compact's support. Moreover, it seemed unlikely that any new Superintendent would turn his back on a program that served as a main line to corporate support for the schools. Al McMahill wondered what would happen when others left. "Programs are people, and people are programs to a certain degree. [People leaving] is going to be a tough one." He also believed that, given enough time, the Compact could withstand this. "Time is the critical element. If we can get in another year or two, we will have brought [about] some specific changes in the way the school system functions. People just aren't doing things the same way they used to do it."

*   *   *

A year after this chapter was written, several of these worrisome possibilities materialized. In the summer of 1985, Robert Spillane left to become Superintendent of Schools in Fairfax, Virginia. His successor, Lavelle Wilson, took a low public profile on one of his predecessor's favorite programs, even though Compact staff members said that he was squarely behind it.

The debate about institutionalizing the Compact was no longer noisy; the Compact's school improvement component was absorbed by the School Department. In 1986, it was merged with both the school-based management and school improvement programs and then merged once more with the Department's staff development function. Officially part of the Office for School Assistance, the Compact was settled in the middle of the bureaucracy. Its staff was three layers removed from the Superintendent and reported to some of the curriculum and instruction staff they used to fight with. Paul Grogan, one of the original co-conspirators, also left Boston. And others in the group turned attention elsewhere, devising ways to help other cities get their own local Compacts going. In 1986, people left, attention shifted, and the Teachers' Union was warming up for spring contract negotiations. The Compact's future seemed far from certain.

Still, there are good reasons to predict a sunny ending to this story. For one thing, the Compact's framers did a thorough job of binding in the business community so that it now has a stake in the program's survival. Some of the city's oldest, most respected private-sector organizations have backed the Compact from the start. Their CEOs have chaired its committees and spoken out on its behalf. Regardless of whether the Compact is part of, or apart from, the School Department, in many ways it belongs to these city leaders.

Moreover, the Compact provides business with a service it needs. In 1985, Massachusetts had the lowest unemployment rate of the nation's 12 most industrialized states, and Boston's economic boom was largely responsible for this record. The private sector's enormous labor power requirements in this thriving economy behoove it to care about the quality of the public schools over the long term. But in the meantime, the Compact's short-term payoff to business is a cadre of young people whom the Compact has screened and endorsed as responsible entry-level job candidates. The business community's continuing support thus rests on more than just good public relations and a better-prepared labor force down the road.

The Compact's future may also be ensured by its success in polishing the city's tarnished image after nearly a decade of unflattering front-page stories about desegregation and school busing. The Compact rose to national prominence as a model education/business partnership at a time when partnership ideas were just taking hold. It drew considerable attention to the city for that reason, but also because of its successful jobs component, an idea that had been tried many times in many places with little success. The success of the Jobs Collaborative Program cast a can-do glow on the school improvement part of the Compact as well. People believed that it was working.

And Boston's high schools have improved in some ways. Although the dropout rate rose slightly in 1985 and continues to be a perplexing problem, student attendance and achievement also went up—good news the Compact has not been shy to take credit for. Critics in the school system dispute the Compact's role in bringing about these improvements; they believe that tougher district attendance policies and the upbeat national mood about education are more responsible. They may be right, but these are mere details to a public that for the first time in decades has heard that its city's public education system is something to be proud of. And they have heard this linked to the Boston Compact.

The Compact's success in changing attitudes and perceptions of the Boston public schools may help it to sink roots deeper in the school system. As a symbol of educational quality and community participation, it is virtually without parallel. But whether the city's educators will give full life to this symbol is still an open question.

NOTES

1. When the first version of this chapter was written, in January 1985, Robert Spillane was not known to be a candidate for another job. By the following summer, he had resigned, and the School Committee had undertaken a search for his successor.
2. *Boston Globe*, November 18, 1982.
3. Neil Pierce, syndicated column in the *Boston Globe*, November 28, 1982.

ACKNOWLEDGMENTS

The following people were interviewed in the preparation of this chapter:
James Caradonio, Director, Education and Employment for the Boston Public Schools; *Joseph Casey*, Chairman, English and Language Arts Department, Dorchester High School; *Marilyn Corsini*, Assistant Headmaster, Jamaica Plain High School; *James Darr*, Executive Director, Boston Private Industry Council; *Ann De Placido*, University-School Liaison, University of Massachusetts, Boston; *Edward Doherty*, President, Boston Teachers' Union; *Ted Dooley*, Associate Director, Boston Private Industry Council; *William Edgerly*, Chairman, State Street Bank; *William Fitzgerald*, Development Officer, Dorchester High School; *Paul Grogan*, Executive Director, Neighborhood Development and Employment Agency; *Bard Hamlen*, University-School Liaison, Simmons College; *Stacy Johnson*, Headmaster, Jamaica Plain High School; *Jane Morrison-Margulis*, Youth Program Manager, Neighborhood Development and Employment Agency; *Al McMahill*, Staff Director, Boston Compact; *Frank Morris*, President, Federal Reserve Bank of Boston; *Phillip Moskow*, Career Experience Teacher, Jamaica Plain High School; *John O'Bryant*, Vice President, Northeastern University and member, Boston School Committee; *Robert Schwartz*, Executive Director, Boston Compact; *Robert I. Sperber*, Staff Director, the President's Steering Committee; *Robert Spillane*, Superintendent, Boston Public Schools; *William Spring*, Vice President, Federal Reserve Bank of Boston; *Catherine Stratton*, Associate Secretary of Economic Affairs for the Commonwealth of Massachusetts; *Stanley Swartz*, Headmaster, Dorchester High School; *Craig Williams*, Career Experience Teacher, Dorchester High School; *Karen Williams*, Development Officer, Jamaica Plain High School.

7 A Tale of Two States

The Business Community and Education Reform in California and Minnesota

PAUL BERMAN
Berman, Weiler Associates

RICK CLUGSTON
Springhill Center

By the early 1980s, California's once outstanding elementary and secondary education system was in serious trouble. Financial support had drastically decreased, course work and standards had slipped, and student test scores had dropped. The Governor, State Department of Education, and legislature could not break an impasse of conflicting political interests, and lacked clear ideas of what to do. Many concerned citizens feared that the legislature would continue to debate much but act little. Out of frustration, one public interest group launched a well-publicized petition drive to replace public education with a voucher system.

At the same time, Minnesota education was experiencing deterioration rather than crisis. The state's quality of life and business competitiveness had been built on a solid foundation of a sound educational system, but deeply disturbing cracks had begun to appear in this structure. Declining test scores, traumatic teacher strikes, unfamiliar tensions over minority problems, and reports of student alienation were unsettling to a public that had always maintained pride in its schools. Some citizens' groups and state leaders expressed concern that educators seemed unwilling to embrace change that would enable Minnesota education to keep pace with demands of the future.

Within two years, both California and Minnesota saw intense political dramas culminating in education reform legislation. Their stories have a common element: The states' business communities prodded the political process into action. Without their initiative, reforms might not have happened, or might have been different. Business had become a major player in the political process, countering the educational system's natural tendency to maintain the status quo.

Business activities in both states unfolded in four stages: (1) *getting involved*, (2) *developing a reform agenda*, (3) *working to enact the agenda*, and (4) *continuing the involvement*. Corporate leaders made decisions during each stage that determined the nature and depth of their subsequent involvement. In neither state did they adhere to a predetermined plan with specific objectives and steps to be accomplished. Instead, business leaders learned in each stage about education and the public policy process, while unpredictable events sorely tried their commitment of time, resources, and political capital. We will describe the events in California and Minnesota in terms of these stages, beginning with the California story.

As participant-observers in the events described, we have supplemented our firsthand knowledge with selected interviews of key actors. As participants, we necessarily describe events from only one of the many perspectives from which these tales might be told. Since our focus is the business community, the stories do not examine the contributions of other actors who shaped the complex political events.

REFORM IN CALIFORNIA

During the 1970s, about 25 percent of the nation's new immigrants settled in California; by 1980, almost one-third of the state's 24 million people were ethnic minorities. This immigration has brought great language and cultural diversity and a pressing need for more and improved social services, including education. In 1979, about 15.2 percent of California's children lived in poverty, placing the state thirty-first in the proportion of its children above the poverty level, while at the same time it ranked fifth in per capita income.[1] The state lives with great wealth and great poverty.

California is a land of contrasts in other ways. The urban megalopolises (the areas of Los Angeles-Long Beach, San Francisco-Oakland-San Jose, and San Diego) house the corporate headquarters of some of the nation's largest businesses, whereas California's central valley constitutes the nation's single largest producer of various agricultural products. This urban/rural division, along with the state's heterogeneous population and large economic disparities, is further complicated by a split between the north and south, with each region having distinct histories, life-styles, political values, and economies.

California politics is consequently unpredictable and contentious. Swings between liberal and conservative moods have often foreshadowed national trends. One well-known example is the Proposition 13

taxpayers' revolt. The combination of a robust economy and high inflation during the mid-1970s quadrupled state revenues from state sales,
income, and property taxes. By 1978, the state government had com-
piled a $4 billion surplus. The value of real estate had greatly escalated,
and property taxes, which were assessed according to market values,
correspondingly rose to a point where they became a heavy burden on
the state's homeowners. Despite considerable wrangling, the legislature
could not act either to redistribute the surplus or to reduce property
taxes. A citizens' group gathered signatures to place Proposition 13, a
tax rollback initiative, on the 1978 ballot. California's voters supported
this measure, thus severely slashing property taxes and limiting the level
of taxation that could be raised by a property tax.

Proposition 13 hit the school districts hard. They could no longer
collect substantial local property taxes to finance their schools. The
state now controlled the purse strings for K–12 education. State financial control of education meant a greater centralized policy role for the
state government and for the politically divided legislature.

By the beginning of the 1980s, the legislature had much to worry
about in education. Total funding (in constant dollars) of the K–12 system had dwindled, test scores had declined, many schools had cut back
from six or seven to five periods of instruction per day, newspapers
reported that both course work and textbooks were not demanding,
citizen support for education appeared shaky, and teachers felt demora-
lized. Public education was adrift.

It was in this climate of paralysis that the California business community decided to act.

Stage 1: Getting Involved

Founded in 1976, the California Roundtable (CRT) is an organization of the chief executive officers (CEOs) of the 86 largest corporations
headquartered in the state.[2] Like its model, the national Business
Roundtable, CRT normally concerns itself with broad business-related
issues, rather than special-interest lobbying for a particular industrial
sector. It raises operating funds by membership dues, and looks to other
organizations to prepare analyses or mount lobbying efforts.

By the end of the 1970s, education problems had become salient to
many California corporate leaders. For some executives in the state's
high technology industries of Silicon Valley, education issues arose because of concern about mathematics and science training. The shortage
of mathematics and science teachers had begun to reach crisis proportions in California, and many high school graduates had to take remedi-

al mathematics as well as English course work to qualify for their university majors. Business leaders knew that the state needed a steady supply of competent university graduates if California was to retain national leadership in the competitive technical and scientific fields.

Other business leaders were concerned about the quality and motivation of the pool of applicants for entry-level positions in more traditional industries. Cornell Maier, CEO of Kaiser Aluminum and Chemical Corporation and a respected civic leader in Oakland, had firsthand knowledge of these problems. He remembered, for example, how the Port Authority in Oakland had tested 1,100 high school graduates for jobs and discovered that only 40 percent could pass an elementary mathematics test. At Maier's urging, the Roundtable established the Jobs and Education Task Force in 1980 to determine why so many California students seemed to be inadequately prepared for college and employment.

Task Force members thought of themselves as "rookies" in the education policy arena and therefore proceeded cautiously. On February 10 and 11, 1980, the Roundtable sponsored the Conference on Public Education for corporate executives and school leaders (primarily district superintendents). Bringing business and education executives together helped pave the way for future corporate involvement and began the slow process of mobilizing the business community.

Contracting for an Independent Study. Task Force members knew they lacked education expertise and would be seen by the policy community as unknowledgeable. The CEOs knew they wanted education to improve, but they did not know how. Although the Roundtable had previously funded specialized studies, it had typically dealt with issues where there was already a clear business agenda. Understanding these concerns, the Task Force decided that a comprehensive and well-documented study by independent experts could provide specific proposals that would be perceived as legitimate in the eyes of the policy community.

The Task Force convinced the Roundtable membership to approve a competition for a contract for the first phase of a possible two-phase or three-phase study. Competitive bids were solicited (a CRT member company managed the bidding process and the resulting contract), and a six-month contract was awarded to Berman, Weiler Associates (BW).

The Roundtable's decision to commission an independent study was a bold departure. Prior activity by the business community had largely consisted of donations by individual corporations (often through corporate foundations) to individual school districts. The Roundtable

Task Force questioned the efficacy of simple corporate giving *and* considered it unlikely that individual school districts could improve without state-level reform. CRT's position that the business community should propose concrete recommendations to influence state-level educational policy was without precedent in 1981.

Stage 2: Developing a Reform Agenda

During the first phase of the study, the Roundtable did not systematically contact education groups. Nor did it attempt to influence the research or the consultants' recommendations. However, some CEOs, acting as individuals rather than Roundtable representatives, pursued a parallel strategy to influence education reform. The first phase occurred during an election year for both Governor and State Superintendent of Public Instruction.[3] Although education was not an issue in the gubernatorial race, the nonpartisan contest for Superintendent was bitterly fought. Nightly television became a battleground of spot commercials about education. Although the CRT does not endorse political candidates, several CEOs of the Jobs and Education Task Force, along with other CEOs, gave financial and other support to the challenger for the superintendency, Bill Honig.

Honig's "back to basics" message undoubtedly appealed to some business leaders. Key Task Force members also favored him for a more subtle reason. In their view, Honig stood for change; his opponent did not. Such business leaders as Cornell Maier believed that an action-oriented Superintendent would help establish the proper climate for reform. Observers of California politics credit Bill Honig's victory in part to the backing of large segments of the business community.

BW's Analysis and Recommendations. The BW staff presented their initial analysis in July 1982 to a private meeting of the Task Force. The analysis confirmed what many had suspected: California education was approaching a crisis. Though these findings provided details and highlighted several new issues, the CEOs were more interested in recommendations for concrete action. BW's recommendations from the first phase were unveiled in August 1982 to a full meeting of the Task Force.

Michael Kirst, a keen observer of the scene, wrote, "While the study's results are not very novel now because of numerous (subsequent) national commissions, they were new in the fall of 1982." The Task Force realized that many of the recommendations were bound to be controversial. The recommendation to establish statewide minimum graduation requirements, for example, seemed certain to excite strong opposition. It was widely believed in the summer of 1982 that education interest groups, which had considerable sway in the legislature, would staunchly oppose any "centralized" requirements. The Task Force understood that these and other reforms could not pass unless the Roundtable built coalitions with powerful political interests in the state.

Organizational consensus was needed if the Roundtable was to act. BW had proposed increased funding for education *only if* significant reforms were undertaken. The possibility that CRT might support increased state funding for education surfaced as a disagreement among CRT members. Some business leaders were concerned that if the legislature enacted education reforms, it also would legislate new or higher taxes on business and industry in order to raise the level of spending on education and balance the budget.

Cornell Maier mobilized members of the Task Force to persuade CEOs that the CRT should publicly oppose increased funding for education unless worthwhile reforms were passed. Linking more money to strong reforms became a principle around which a working consensus of Roundtable members was forged; it later became the key to building informal coalitions with the education community. The Task Force so successfully garnered CEO support that the CRT general membership meeting, held two weeks after the election, endorsed the BW recommendations, approved the immediate distribution of the reports, and authorized the second-phase study.

The second contract, from December 1982 to July 1983, called for the development of reforms of the teaching profession and strategic advice and other implementation assistance for the 1983 legislative session that was to begin in January. With these actions, the Roundtable committed itself to an agenda for the reform of California's education system.

Stage 3: Working to Enact the Agenda

Maier and the Task Force wasted no time in entering the thick of education policy, meeting with representatives of the major teachers' unions to demonstrate the business community's commitment to reform. He said CRT firmly believed in the basic principles articulated in the BW recommendations, but was flexible on details of specific legislative proposals and was interested in discussing these or other reforms with all groups.

Over the next few months, CEOs and deputies met with numerous interest groups and educators and gave many speeches throughout the state. In addition, the Roundtable launched a public relations campaign that included press releases, wide distribution of the BW reports, and a brochure about the reforms.

The Roundtable's legislative campaign began in January 1983, while the new legislature was constituting its committees. The election of Superintendent Honig was widely interpreted in the legislature as a mandate for reform. The State Senate responded by appointing a newly elected Senator, former Assemblyman Gary Hart (the Assembly's chief architect of a variety of innovative school improvement measures) as the Chair of the Senate Education Committee.[4]

One week before Hart's appointment, several Roundtable CEOs and deputies met with the Democratic and Republican leadership of the legislature to personally advance their agenda (see Figure 1). One day after Hart's appointment, a similar contingent met with Hart to offer support for reform and to present the Roundtable's agenda. This personal involvement of business leaders was unprecedented in California's education policy arena.

By the middle of February, the balance of forces for reform appeared strong, and the chances for significant education legislation seemed high. For example, education leaders were privately negotiating about statewide standards that might be acceptable to the various interests. Superintendent Honig circulated the first draft of his program (which was similar in most respects to the CRT's agenda but added provisions about teacher discipline and tenure restrictions).

The CRT's proposals for concrete and comprehensive reforms in the area of standards helped crystallize ideas within the policy community that had previously been too vague to withstand the criticism of various interest groups.

The personal involvement of CEOs unambiguously signaled business's commitment to press for reform. An article written by Cornell Maier, which appeared in the *Los Angeles Times*, the state's most widely read newspaper, stated the Roundtable's message: Business support for increased funding for education would be forthcoming *only if* there were reforms. Democrats, who had a majority in the legislature, favored increased funding, although some did not support significant reform; Republicans wanted reform, but were not willing to raise the state budget or oppose new Republican Governor George Deukmejian's wishes; the Governor opposed increasing taxes to provide more money for education but favored cuts in other services, which Democrats adamantly rejected. Education interest groups and other political actors believed that the Roundtable might influence the Governor and the Republican swing vote in the legislature to support more funding.

FIGURE 1. CRT's Legislative Agenda, January 1983

The California Roundtable has adopted the following principles for legislative action:

Raise educational standards
Upgrade math and science education
Strengthen the teaching profession
Increase funding for education (particularly secondary education)

CRT recognizes that new legislation in these areas will require additional state revenues. CRT will support measures to raise revenues provided that appropriate legislation and other actions are taken to achieve these four principles.

In support of these principles, CRT has formulated an initial legislative agenda relevant to raising educational standards. This agenda includes:

Minimum graduation requirements
Required local use of state curriculum guidelines
Strengthened state testing of student performance
Textbook upgrading
Strengthened attendance and discipline laws
Longer school day and year

CRT considers each of these items to be open to discussion and will be talking to interested parties to reach a consensus on the legislative agenda that would best help improve student performance. Other items, particularly in the areas of finance and personnel, will be added in the next few months as a result of these discussions.

At the beginning of March, the Roundtable raised the reform stakes. During the second phase, new proposals introduced included the master teacher plan, a requirement that entering teachers take professional exams and serve an apprenticeship, a stipulation that teachers who had not recently taught a subject they were assigned to teach should take a subject-matter examination, a tightening of dismissal and lay-off procedures, an increase in the beginning salaries of teachers, and a raise in the general teaching salary level *if* economic conditions in the state permitted.[5] The CRT's Executive Committee approved the principles underlying the new proposals, despite reservations about the funding provisions, and Maier returned to Sacramento with the enlarged agenda.

Over the next month and a half, Senator Hart and Superintendent Honig reached a compromise on the reforms dealing with dismissals and layoffs. The Assembly leadership added more elements and more money to their version of the pending legislation, and Hart negotiated with the interest groups over what would be included and in what ways. Lobbying became frenzied as the legislation approached a finished bill. The Roundtable had difficulties in these final moments "working in the trenches," as lobbyists call the day-to-day work of influencing the drafting of legislative language, because it had not hired a lobbyist. Toward the end of May, Hart hammered out a compromise legislation, Senate Bill 813 (SB 813), that the teachers' unions were willing not to oppose and that Assembly Democrats could support.

The last act of the drama did not involve the substance of education reform: It involved money. The Governor opposed full funding of SB 813 at the level proposed by the Democrats because it would require tax increases. The CRT attempted to play a broker's role in this dispute by using its influence with the Governor and the Republican legislators. In serving in this role, the Roundtable leadership had to avoid accepting the Democratic tax increase position while not abandoning the call for increased funding for education.

There was a perception, especially among Democrats in the legislature (who were asking for a $900 million increase for education funded through a tax increase), that CRT was "with them all the way to the boat." That is, some Democrats felt that business was pressuring for reforms and increased funding for education but would not endorse tax increases or any other means for raising revenues. In fact, that was precisely the strategy that Mr. Maier and the CRT Executive Committee had devised.

Key leaders within the CRT who advocated education reform had a difficult tightrope to walk, publicly and within the Roundtable. Governor Deukmejian opposed tax increases, as did many CRT members.[6] The Jobs and Education Task Force wisely decided *not* to push for a unified organizational position that would threaten the CRT's fragile consensus. Instead, more than 50 corporate executives wrote to the Governor as individuals to press for more money. In addition, at Superintendent Honig's request, 15 or more large companies testified that they would be willing to pay more taxes for educational reform.

These disputes and partisan maneuverings continued for another month. The Governor delayed signing SB 813, and postponed welfare, unemployment, and Medicare benefits to signal his unwillingness to exceed budget limits. A state supreme court ruling found the Governor's action unconstitutional. In the end, the Governor closed some tax loopholes (which was a thinly disguised means of raising taxes), and Democrats agreed to his proposal to reallocate some resources from other areas of the budget to K–12 education.

With this final compromise, California passed the most significant school reform bill in the state's history.

Stage 4: Continuing the Involvement

How successful was the Roundtable's foray into statewide education reform? Of course, many individuals and groups deserve credit for effecting the reforms. But CRT undoubtedly made a significant, perhaps pivotal, difference in both the passage and the substance of SB 813.

As the new kid on the block, the Roundtable had entered California's contentious political battleground with a nonpartisan approach that enabled it to play a broker's role. The timing was right for change, and the political actors were in place. But a powerful yet responsible weight was needed to tip the balance. By committing prestige and resources and developing a clear agenda that was above the partisan skirmishing, the Roundtable may have provided the missing element that had been so conspicuously absent in past stalemated efforts to achieve education reform in California.[7]

Opinions about the long-term educational value of SB 813 are divided. Some commentators see it as insignificant; others call it a money bill and nothing more; still others view it as an unwarranted and dangerous centralization of education; finally, some analysts hold that SB 813 broke a political logjam, began the infusion of new funding into a system in dire straits, and introduced some innovations and a spirit of reform.

There was still work to be done, however. The initiatives relating to the structure and operation of the teaching profession had not passed, and these were major concerns for CRT. Task Force members knew the business community would need to continue its active involvement to promote SB 813's implementation and to push for deeper reforms.

In addition, the Roundtable actively pursued nonlegislative measures to promote educational improvement, including:

• Development of a handbook to encourage business and community groups to get involved with their local schools, which offered concrete steps to guide this involvement. Copies were distributed to some 220,000 CRT member-company employees.

- Creation of a reference guide, which contained abstracts of more than 600 programs of business support for education.
- Work on defining the competencies needed for success in the business world.
- Establishment of a joint task force with California's education leadership to seek nongovernmental solutions to the crisis in mathematics and science.

In December 1983, the Roundtable decided to pursue its unfinished legislative agenda. It wrote to the Governor expressing the belief that SB 813 needed to be strengthened and that the issue of teacher credentialing should be addressed. In January 1984, CRT organized meetings with legislators and the Governor's staff to push these issues, and then continued low-level efforts throughout the 1984 and 1985 legislative sessions. But the legislature was not yet ready for more battles over K–12 reform. The concern and momentum that remained were channeled into a new commission, called the California Commission on the Teaching Profession, chaired by a CRT member.

The story of California's struggle to renew its once outstanding system of public education is not complete. The Roundtable played a distinguished role in its early chapters, so that now the CRT is a legitimate actor in the education policy system. But more must be done over a long period of time. The Roundtable's success depended on the energy, sophistication, and dedication of several prominent CEOs, particularly Cornell Maier. Yet, CRT has not institutionalized this commitment. As leaders and events change, the question remains whether the Roundtable's unique record of service to improving education will continue to be written.

REFORM IN MINNESOTA

About half of Minnesota's 4.6 million people live in the Twin Cities of Minneapolis and St. Paul and their surrounding suburbs. Aside from these and several smaller urban centers, the state's population is scattered in small towns and rural settlements. Other than a small minority population (about 3 percent of the state's total) mostly located in the Twin Cities area, Minnesotans are white and of predominantly Protestant Northern European ancestry.[8]

The most vigorous sectors of Minnesota's economy are in the manufacturing of high value-to-weight products and, not coincidentally, in the cultivation of entrepreneurs and small businesses. This emphasis led to Minnesota's early entry into high technology and related industries. The state is now a national center for high tech manufacturing and corporate headquarters (seventh in the nation). Minnesotans consider a strong education system an important element in the state's past economic success.

The state has a history of rural cooperatives and a vigorous labor movement.[9] Politically this has translated into progressive populism, represented in part by the Democratic Farmer-Labor Party. Despite its traditional willingness to support relatively high spending on education, environmental concerns, and other social programs, the state is fiscally conservative, strong in favor of local control, and inclined toward a pragmatic approach in tackling new ventures. There is also a rural/urban political schism that is often played out in the state legislature.

Minnesota's business leaders have a long record of involvement in social policy issues. Corporate giving in Minnesota has consistently been 50 percent above the national average, and business leaders belong to a variety of organizations that deal with public affairs. Indeed, it is common for high- and middle-level managers to have held either elected or appointed public office and therefore to have an enlightened view of the civic responsibility of business. According to knowledgeable observers in Minnesota, the civic involvement of business leaders exerts considerable peer pressure on one another to participate in public affairs.

All these characteristics of Minnesota—a small size and relatively homogeneous population, one major urban area that contains the state capital, a progressive and pragmatic political tradition, and an economy based on a higher percentage of innovative businesses, which feature creative managers, highly skilled professionals, and a competent work force—combine to create an intimate and participatory policy system in which the actors know each other and frequently meet to share in the formulation of public policy.

Stage 1: Getting Involved

Founded in 1977, the Minnesota Business Partnership (MBP) is a membership organization of the CEOs of 80 of Minnesota's largest companies, most of them based in the Twin Cities. MBP has a full-time staff (composed of a director, a research director, and two administrative support personnel) that conducts research and formulates policy positions for the CEO membership. The Partnership raises money for its standard operations by charging each corporate member a fee based on the corporation's revenues. Special projects, such as the education study described below, are paid for not by membership fees but by voluntary donations. This means that MBP can launch new initiatives only if most members agree to take action.

Like the California Roundtable, the Partnership generally deals with broad policy issues rather than the specific interests of particular businesses. Until 1982, it concentrated largely on state tax issues, seeking primarily to improve the business climate in the state by lowering taxes. Reasoning that high taxes were the result of legislative spending decisions, MBP decided to examine the state budget to see if spending priorities needed to be changed and public funds used more cost-effectively. Since education accounts for over half of the state's budget, MBP concluded that it should focus on K–12 education issues.

But the Partnership's interest in education was broader than concerns about efficiency. In 1982, MBP formed the Educational Quality Task Force, under the leadership of Lewis W. Lehr, Chairman and CEO of Minnesota Mining and Manufacturing (3M), to determine what business leaders could do to improve the *quality* of education in Minnesota. Of particular concern was the relationship between quality and cost, for most members believed that improvements in quality did not necessarily imply increased costs. The Task Force, which included CEOs and deputies from 14 companies, questioned whether public school students were receiving the kind of education that would enable them to thrive and prosper in an increasingly competitive world. In addition to having a general sense of civic concern and responsibility, the Task Force believed that the state's ability to attract and retain the type of business necessary for Minnesota's innovative economy depended on a high quality education system.

For the most part, members of the Task Force were well informed about education policy issues. They felt that the education system was not keeping pace with the state's needs, and suspected that the criticism leveled against education by the national commission's reports was essentially accurate when applied to Minnesota. Moreover, some deputies were involved in the development of a controversial 1982 report by Minnesota's Citizens' League, an organization of 3,000 individual and 600 corporate members. This report was sharply critical of Minnesota public schools and proposed a general voucher system.

Although most MBP Task Force members generally believed that there were problems in the education system, they knew neither exactly what was wrong nor what should be done. For one thing, the education community did not agree that reform was needed. The years from 1972 to 1982 had been relatively lean times for education in Minnesota. Enrollment decreases of 21 percent, increasing federal regulations, rising costs, and revenue shortfalls resulted in some teacher layoffs and a slowdown in hiring. During that period, Minnesota's per pupil expenditure as a percentage of per capita income dropped from sixth to eighteenth nationally. The professional education associations conveyed a simple message to business, the media, and the public: Minnesota schools were outstanding, and whatever problems existed lay in inadequate funding.

The Minnesota Business Partnership's Educational Quality Task Force realized that it needed more information to understand the condition of Minnesota's K–12 education system and to propose practical solutions if its suspicions proved well founded. Though the MBP staff could do policy analysis, they were not experts in education and knew that their studies would be viewed with skepticism. The Partnership therefore commissioned Berman, Weiler Associates (BW) to conduct an independent study to sort out the conflicting messages about the quality of Minnesota public education.[10]

The consultants were given one year (July 1983 to August 1984) to produce reports on student performance and the costs of education and to offer concrete recommendations for improvement *if* it was indeed necessary. By contractual agreement, MBP maintained an arm's-length relationship with the consultants throughout the study. BW reported frequently on the study's progress, but the Partnership neither interfered with nor tried to influence the study's findings or recommendations.

Stage 2: Developing a Reform Agenda

From the outset, the Partnership consulted with key representatives of the education policy community. The Education Quality Task Force established a Liaison Committee, which included representatives of all major actors with an interest in K–12 education. This group held formal meetings with the Task Force about once every three months from the beginning of 1983 until after the study had been completed and MBP had presented its recommendations.

The Liaison Committee provided an arena for the business community to inform education representatives, key legislators, and the media about the progress of the study. Its very existence sent a clear message to the policy community that MBP was serious about dealing with education issues statewide. Not incidentally, the meetings helped to establish an expectation that the study would not be a symbolic effort that could be easily dismissed. When the various study reports were made public, the Liaison Committee was among the first groups to be given a presentation. This process of extensive interaction with members of the education community was consistent with the norms of behavior in Minnesota's close-knit, consultative policy system.

In addition to standard data collection and statistical analysis, eight panels composed of key education policy makers and educators were convened to help diagnose the strengths and weaknesses of public education.

In this period, MBP worked to keep the education issue alive within the state while trying to defer any major decision. Other reform-minded individuals in the state were, of course, developing their own agendas. For example, the Commissioner of Education was formulating reform ideas, and so were a variety of organizations, including Public School Incentives and the Citizens' League. But it was understood that major reform efforts would await the winter 1985 legislative session.

Analysis and Recommendations. The Minnesota Business Partnership's reports were made public in three stages: in February 1984, three volumes on student performance; in June 1984, a single volume on the cost of public education; and in November 1984, two volumes diagnosing problems with the system and making recommendations for improvement. The Partnership believed that this staged procedure would help establish the legitimacy of the study by providing solid analysis and data before offering possibly controversial recommendations. It was also consistent with the Minnesota consultative approach.

The first reports drew three conclusions. First, the data on student performance were incomplete, meaning that Minnesotans had no definitive means of assessing their education system. Second, the existing data, though incomplete, suggested that Minnesota students performed at about the national average. This finding was disturbing to those in the education community who had believed that Minnesota education was better than average. Third, and most important, the evidence available from the state's testing program indicated that Minnesota, like the rest of the nation, was experiencing serious difficulty in educating students in the higher-order skills (reasoning, creative thinking, and problem solving) essential for a full and productive life in the future. The analysis suggested, in short, that Minnesota had had a relatively good education system, which was now in decline, and that its students were not being adequately prepared for the twenty-first century.

The final reports went beyond student performance data to identify basic structural flaws in the K–12 system that, it was argued, prevented Minnesota's educators from helping students to realize their potential.

In these deficiencies, the Minnesota system was similar to education systems throughout the nation. For example, the reports argued that

- Minnesota schools often had student tracking, an unfocused curriculum, and low expectations for students.
- The organization of instruction and the working conditions of teachers made it difficult to teach higher-order skills.
- The nature of the knowledge base of teaching, the organization of the occupation, and the lack of incentives for change within the system made it difficult for the education system to be responsive to changing learning needs.

The final reports also contained recommendations (summarized in Figure 2) for a distinct departure from present practice and presented a 10-year plan for implementing the reforms.

The deputies on the Educational Quality Task Force supported the general thrust of the report, but they realized that they would face major resistance to a change of this magnitude. From their initial exposure to the proposed reforms to their final endorsement, the deputies wrestled with the issue of exactly what and how much to support and how MBP should position itself relative to the recommendations. This organizational decision process lasted four months (July to November 1984). In addition to internal analysis, extended discussion and consensus-building activities occurred among the deputies and CEOs on the Task Force, and finally among the general MBP membership.[11]

Stage 3: Working to Enact the Agenda

The final report, *The Minnesota Plan*, was released on November 12, a week after the general election.[12] The Partnership developed a brochure, *Educating Students for the 21st Century*, which summarized its position and was widely distributed.

The reform proposals received considerable press coverage, both pro and con. Spokespeople for several key organized elements in education, particularly the larger teachers' union, the school boards' association, and the superintendents' association, reacted negatively despite MBP communications efforts. Some critics asserted that business sought to cut education spending, not to improve its effectiveness. Others disagreed strongly with MBP's position that public education in Minnesota had reached the limits of its effectiveness and needed restructuring, insisting instead that the system was sound and could be improved if it received more money. In contrast, some editorial opinion

FIGURE 2. Major Elements of *The Minnesota Plan*

K–12 Schooling Should Be Restructured

- Junior and senior high schools should be realigned so that students would be expected to complete a core academic program by grade ten and then be free to choose any public or private school for two years.
- Students should be required to take knowledge-based statewide tests during grades six and ten before graduation from elementary and secondary school, respectively.
- The state should no longer require a distribution of courses for graduation, but should rely on the statewide examinations to establish performance goals for education.
- Secondary students should be provided the choice to take at least one elective course each semester outside their school.

Teaching Should Be Reorganized

- Teachers should be trained and supported to learn and use teaching approaches that assume that all students can master required subjects, with enough time and help from teachers and peers.
- The state should require that each student have an individualized learning program administered by teachers.
- The state should provide assistance to encourage the use of teacher teams consisting of a master teacher, three teachers, and three assistant teachers.

Authority Should Be Redistributed

- The state should encourage school-site management and establish mini boards of education at the school level.

Reforms Should Be Implemented from the Grass Roots

- The state should establish state mechanisms to assist local implementation of the Plan by supporting a research, development, and training network; establishing a program to deal with critical teacher shortages; raising teacher salaries; modifying teacher seniority and administrator tenure; and creating an entrepreneurial development fund and an education investment fund.

---

in the major newspapers as well as many individuals and groups already in the reform movement offered favorable opinions about the spirit of the plan and its recommendations.

MBP had clearly succeeded in focusing the education debate on a fundamental issue: namely, whether there should be deep structural reform of public education. The Partnership was now in the center of a storm of controversy, much to the surprise of some of its members. The stage was set for what was to be a divisive legislative struggle.

Operating in the Political Arena. During the 1984 session, the legislature had reviewed reform issues in light of the national ferment over education and had concluded that Minnesota had no need to parrot national reform proposals such as an increase in the length of the school day or year. Governor Rudy Perpich had not indicated any plans to make education reform a major issue, and his appointed Commissioner of Education was moving cautiously. The reform proposals from the Partnership, combined with other efforts already under way, changed the political climate and moved the education issue to center stage.

Although the Governor did not embrace the details and implementation proposals in *The Minnesota Plan*, he agreed with many of its basic principles: student choice after the tenth grade, competitive incentives for schools, increased accountability, and a move toward state deregulation. He and his staff began meeting in November 1984 with MBP representatives and others who were supporting such principles to explore possibilities for his education initiative.

A month and a half later, on January 4, Governor Perpich announced his Access to Excellence program, which proposed significant programmatic and financing reforms. The component that received the most attention was the open-enrollment provision, whereby eleventh and twelfth graders would be able to enroll in any school district in the state that would accept them. The legislative debate centered on this issue of letting parents choose where to enroll their children.

The Governor's proposal was very positively received by MBP. It meant that the state's major political agenda setter had made restructuring education his top priority. But Access to Excellence and *The Minnesota Plan* were different in detail—the latter was more comprehensive. Many who had endorsed the Plan were in a quandary as to whether to support the Governor's plan, which focused on immediately establishing student choice but without laying a prior foundation of changes in curriculum, testing, and instruction, as had been proposed in *The Minnesota Plan*. The tension was resolved when MBP decided to support the Governor's proposals as a practical first step to realizing key features of *The Minnesota Plan*.

This support was channeled through the formation of an umbrella organization, the Brainpower Compact, whose board consisted of former governors, educators, school board members, business leaders, and others who backed both Governor Perpich's Access to Excellence *and* the thrust of *The Minnesota Plan.* The key actors in this coalition, including representatives from MBP, met throughout the legislative session with representatives from the Governor's staff and the Department of Education to coordinate efforts to win support for the Governor's proposal. The accompanying organizational effort took shape gradually through January and February, and a part-time communications coordinator and lobbyist was hired by early March. MBP thereafter channeled its financial support and education reform efforts into the Brainpower Compact.[13]

On February 26, the Commissioner of Education presented the Access to Excellence bill to the legislators, spelling out the details and financing of the Governor's proposal. The Minnesota Business Partnership helped persuade Republican and Democratic legislators to give bipartisan support to the Democratic Governor's plan, and the bill passed significant preliminary hurdles in the legislature.[14]

Key education groups (the two teachers' unions and the school boards' and school administrators' associations) vehemently opposed the Governor's plan for open enrollment for eleventh- and twelfth-grade students, as they had MBP's reform proposals. They lobbied vigorously to stop the reform efforts, mobilizing large and politically powerful organizations that were particularly effective in rural areas. The letters and phone calls to legislators far outweighed the lobbying activities of the coalition supporting the reforms. Although the Parent-Teachers Association and the League of Women Voters supported resolutions backing open enrollment, they did so at the eleventh hour and could not mobilize any significant lobbying effort. The two school principals' associations also supported the reforms, albeit in a low-key fashion.

At the beginning of April, the larger teachers' union, MEA, the Minnesota affiliate of the National Education Association, issued a videotape portraying open enrollment as antifamily. On April 3, on a 14–to–13 vote, the House Education Committee removed the open-enrollment provision (but not the postsecondary option) from the omnibus education aid bill. On April 24, the Senate Finance Committee deleted the open-enrollment provision from the bill, and Senator Tom Nelson, the Senate author of the Governor's bill, publicly denounced MEA for its videotapes.

The drama was almost over, except for a last critical act. In a Conference Committee, a bill, the Postsecondary Enrollment Options Act, was passed providing for a limited form of student choice for the last two years of high school. In addition, other legislation was enacted that took initial steps toward some reforms suggested in *The Minnesota Plan*.

Stage 4: Continuing the Involvement

The Minnesota Business Partnership had developed an agenda in November 1984 that called for a dramatic restructuring of Minnesota education. The Partnership did not believe that these reforms would, or *should*, happen at once. Indeed, *The Minnesota Plan* had proposed a 10-year period in which reforms would be introduced slowly and systematically to minimize disruption and to determine what changes would work best in the state's 437 school districts.

In the larger view of progress toward a 10-year program of change, the legislation that passed in 1985 represented several surprisingly large steps forward, though not in the sequence or manner explicitly proposed in *The Minnesota Plan*. Implementation of the Postsecondary Enrollment Options Act began in September 1985, 10 months after MBP had published its initial agenda. The act does not allow open enrollment in any school district, but it does provide high school juniors and seniors with a choice, and it gives school districts some real competition. If the program works, a strong case could be made to make the options for students more comprehensive.

Other elements of the Partnership's agenda have begun to be addressed: for example, legislation authorizing 10 demonstration sites for mastery learning, some experimentation in differentiated staffing, and a stronger student testing program (though not as complete as MBP had urged). Furthermore, there appears to be a growing consensus about the need for school-site management and individualized learning plans, both of which were recommended in *The Minnesota Plan*. These steps are very much in line with the unfolding of a longer-term change process whose direction MBP favors.

However, there is no guarantee that progress will continue toward the structural change envisioned by the Partnership. Some deputies feel that their agenda has been displaced because of the attention paid to the Governor's program. The student choice issue, which dominated the legislative session, obscured many equally important or more important issues.

All participants would agree that the Partnership's activities shifted the debate and changed the education policy-making equation. The business community is now recognized as a stakeholder, though its legitimacy is still challenged by many in organized education circles.

The question for the future is whether MBP can use this hard-earned influence to continue progress toward reform. The Partnership is now regularly consulted on matters of educational policy and has become part of the statewide discussions. The Governor's [Education] Discussion Group, chaired by the Commissioner of Education and charged with developing a vision for the future of education, includes members of MBP and the Brainpower Compact (as well as members of various other reform groups). The Partnership continues to work through the Brainpower Compact; throughout the 1986 session its steering group met biweekly and concentrated on protecting the Post-secondary Enrollment Options Act. The Partnership's deputies and staff also meet often with representatives of education interest groups.

Despite these activities, several thoughtful observers and allies of MBP question whether the business community will maintain its long-run involvement in the reform process. As one experienced legislator commented, "The resisters to change are in for the long-run, but are the CEOs?" The future of reform in Minnesota may rest on the answer to this question.

COMMON FACTORS

California and Minnesota are very different in size, population diversity, and political climate. These differences account in part for the dissimilarity in how their business communities typically related to public policy making before the education reform movement. Minnesota's corporate leaders had long been an integral part of the state's consultative policy system, whereas California's corporate executives tended to focus on well-defined business issues. The perceived condition of public elementary and secondary education also was different. Almost all Californians considered the system to be in difficulty; Minnesota's education establishment, and probably the public, thought their system was outstanding, despite numerous danger signals and criticism from many civic leaders.

Such differences notwithstanding, both states' business communities played pivotal roles in stimulating and influencing major reform legislation. Both CRT and MBP succeeded in shifting the education debate, in placing their agendas in the center of the political arena, and in becoming recognized participants in education policy making. It is not the differences, therefore, that explain their success, but the many common points. The following sections examine common elements in the two cases.

Stage 1: Getting Involved

The Chief Executive Officer organizations in both states became involved gradually over several years before committing themselves to active efforts to help reform public education. They reached two major decisions that irrevocably committed them to the unfolding education reform drama.

The first decision was to focus their efforts on seeking *system-wide* reform at the *state policy level*. Though individual firms had previous involvement with local school districts, they had not had experience in education at the state level.

Complex reasons led CEOs to become so deeply involved:

1. A perception that public education was not graduating students who could handle basic entry-level positions (more a concern in California than in Minnesota) or enough students who could work cooperatively and creatively to fill managerial and technical positions.
2. A belief that U.S. education had fallen behind education in Japan and many European countries and that the success of the United States in the global economy required a strong education system.
3. A concern that a declining education system would adversely affect the business climate (more in Minnesota), might lead to social unrest (more in California), or would lessen the quality of life in the state (more in Minnesota).
4. A genuine desire to serve the community.
5. An objective of containing the costs of education (more a consensus view in Minnesota), limiting the overall state budget (most CEOs shared this goal in both states), and avoiding specific business tax increases (more of a concern in California).

The CEO organizations were loose collectives of executives who had diverse backgrounds and represented companies with different interests. To make decisions and take action required the leadership of at least one highly respected CEO, who had to form coalitions with like-minded CEOs to develop a consensus within the organization. Consensus did not require enthusiastic unanimity, but rather the lack of significant opposition. Moreover, actions taken on behalf of the organization had to implicitly operate within the limits of this working consensus. As conditions changed, the working consensus shifted. Thus, the leadership within the organizations had to be alert to concerns that arose among the membership and willing to adjust its position accordingly. The success of the CEO organizations' efforts therefore required highly skilled leadership both to develop and to maintain the necessary consensus within the organizations.

Similar political situations were present in California and Minnesota that helped create the conditions for the business decision to act. There was a feeling in both legislatures that the *timing* was ripe for considering education issues. (This belief was more pervasive in California than in Minnesota.) Corporate leaders recognized this window of opportunity, and the business organizations worked hard to reinforce the sense that major legislative action was needed. But another element formed part of the political picture: There was a belief that the political process would not produce significant reforms without *outside* pressure from the business community. (In California, the legislature had a reputation for not being able to act; in Minnesota, various commentators maintained that the teachers' unions held a veto over legislative action.) When CRT and MBP entered their respective policy arenas, there was a vacuum of strong political leadership committed to reform. If such leadership had been present in either state, it is doubtful that the business community would have taken the initiative.

The second decision in this initial stage was more formative than the corporate leaders may have realized. The Roundtable and the Partnership had to decide how to develop a substantive reform agenda. Business executives neither pretended to be experts in education nor knew which specific reforms they favored. They realized that they could not be influential without taking concrete positions, but CRT and MBP lacked in-house capabilities to formulate reform agendas. The business communities in both states therefore decided to hire a consulting firm to do the necessary work.

In both states, the job of monitoring and evaluating the work of the consultants was left to task forces composed of deputies and guided by committed CEOs.

Stage 2: Developing a Reform Agenda

During this stage, the CEO organizations had to decide how to relate to the education establishment while their positions were being developed. They also had to evaluate the consultants' reports on the status of education and determine their reform agenda in light of the consultants' recommendations. The critical process for this stage involved *learning* about the nature of the reforms, their justification, and their implications, and *evaluating* the soundness of the consultants' conclusions.

These processes were iterative in both states: The consultants presented material and arguments, CEOs and deputies asked questions, and there were additional rounds of presentation and questioning.[15] This intense process required a substantial commitment of time on the part of the deputies and, to a lesser extent, on the part of key CEOs. Business organizations considering engaging in this deep level of involvement should plan to budget time and resources for these essential learning and evaluation activities.

The CEOs and deputies finally had to reach decisions on the basis of whatever learning and evaluation had occurred. In both California and Minnesota, they basically had to choose between rejecting the recommendations or supporting their general thrust. In both states, the latter option was selected.

The complex matter of forming an agenda for education reform thus was ultimately reduced to a choice between simple options. This process of CEOs selecting one option from a limited range may seem unusual. However, high-level business decisions in investments and R&D are often distilled in the last analysis to just such a simple choice. It is standard operating procedure in the business world to rely on experts and to make informed but largely intuitive judgments from the alternatives presented. The effectiveness of this decision-making style depends almost entirely on the leadership abilities, good judgment, and risk-taking characteristics of the executives.

But deciding on a position in these types of CEO organizations was more complicated than the exercise of judgment by one individual. The California Roundtable and the Minnesota Business Partnership could act only if the leading CEOs could develop a consensus and avoid a significant, active opposition. This meant in practice that only those positions that already had broad agreement were ever put up for a vote. The key CEOs and their deputies had to build consensus and frame positions that minimized divisiveness, which was precisely what happened in California and Minnesota.

Because maintaining cohesion was necessary in both CRT and MBP, the public positions adopted consisted of the articulation of general principles of reform *plus* an insistence on political action. The consultants' recommendations were put forward as a means of realizing these principles, and CRT and MBP expressed flexibility in negotiating with all parties about specifics. Aside from the advantage that such a position had in the public arena, the generality of the principles allowed the organizations to reach and maintain internal consensus.

Stage 3: Working to Enact the Agenda

In this stage, business leaders had to react to events over which they had little control and to interact with the public, the education establishment, politicians, and others who had quite different agendas, interests and beliefs. Furthermore, the public activities of the representatives of the CEO organizations were constrained by the need to maintain consensus within their organizations.

In both states, a key decision at this stage involved the formulation of a strategy for release of the consultants' work and the dissemination of the CEO organizations' agendas. CRT and MBP used a two-pronged strategy of public presentations and private meetings with key legislators, the Governors' staffs, and representatives of interest groups. Both organizations also employed professional public relations firms in their outreach efforts. These intensive initial efforts were crucial because they established the agenda to which other actors had to react.

Three elements were essential at the stage of working for adoption: *lobbying, ongoing analysis,* and *CEO commitment.* Both the Roundtable and the Partnership underestimated the human and financial resources necessary to see their agendas adopted. (MBP's underestimate was much greater than CRT's and was further compounded by key staff personnel changes.)

In particular, lobbying needs to be done by professionals who know the legislative arena. The education establishment and other interest groups had a distinct advantage over the CEO organizations because the former were used to working in the trenches, where so many of the final legislative decisions were ultimately made. CRT's efforts were handicapped by not having a professional education lobbyist.

The need for ongoing analysis arises because no one interest can control or foresee the results of political negotiations. In both states, specific education reform alternatives had to be formulated and reformulated quickly, as legislative positions evolved. Without the capability to analyze education alternatives, MBP found it difficult to develop detailed new positions as negotiations unfolded.

The commitment of CEOs to push actively for their reform agendas was particularly crucial as legislative politics became intense. The ultimate influence that a CEO organization has in the political arena is to convince political actors that the business community is united behind a reform agenda. Commitment must be made visible—for example, through public appearances or private letters by Chief Executive Officers. This commitment will be constantly tested as issues of taxes and education reform come together in the legislature. Without such commitment, the internal cohesion of the CEO organization can erode; if that becomes known to the various political actors, the political currency of the organization is weakened. The Roundtable and the Partnership each had difficulties in mobilizing and maintaining CEO unity and commitment.

Stage 4: Continuing the Involvement

It would be easy for business to underestimate the staying power required to change education. The cases clearly show that reform is not a one-shot proposition. From the outset of CRT's and MBP's involvement, professionals in the education policy community asked whether business involvement would be short lived.

The California Roundtable has, in fact, continued its involvement, despite a slowdown in the state's reform process. But the organization has not institutionalized its commitment to education reform by, for example, creating a permanent policy-research staff or funding a freestanding, allied policy unit.

The Minnesota Business Partnership's efforts after the initial reform legislation still have to be played out. The Partnership does have a small permanent staff that can monitor reform efforts, and continues to make education reform a top priority. This degree of institutionalization may be sufficient to continue a strong, long-term effort. However, MBP must overcome its problems of maintaining internal consensus to support special activities in education. Some observers question whether the leadership within MBP will continue to be able to elicit such support from its members.

LESSONS FOR BUSINESS INVOLVEMENT

Business organizations like the California Roundtable and the Minnesota Business Partnership should consider the following lessons before becoming involved in statewide education reform:

1. *Internal Consensus Must Be Created and Maintained.* Business organizations should ensure that a consensus exists or can be created within the organization on the need for education reform. This consensus will have to be maintained continuously as political involvement becomes intense and potentially divisive decisions have to be made.
2. *CEO Leadership Is Crucial.* One or more CEOs must take a strong

personal interest in education issues and must be willing to commit time, energy, and personal prestige to the undertaking. These CEOs should hold the respect of the business community and the public.

3. *Effective Involvement Requires Competent Deputies.* Competent and dedicated deputies are essential at every stage of the process. Their full participation should be viewed as enhancing their positions in their home companies and not be considered as a distraction.

4. *Timing Must Be Right.* The business community can be influential only if there is a widely held view that reform is necessary and might not happen without business involvement. The organization should assess its ability to create a climate for reform by public or private political activities.

5. *Business Intervention Should Not Be Based on Narrow Business Interests.* Business organizations should stay above partisan battles or narrowly defined self-interest, and should formulate concrete proposals to maximize their impact on the education policy process. Under these conditions, corporate leaders can provide an external shock to education systems that resist change, and can thus be a catalyst for reform.

6. *Business Must Use Education Experts.* Because business organizations generally do not have expertise in education, they must work with people in the education establishment, build an in-house capability, or hire an outside consultant. Recommendations developed from any of these sources need to be evaluated carefully. As in many business decisions, the technical people will have much influence over the substance of alternatives presented to the CEOs.

7. *Lobbyists Are Needed.* Legislation is often won or lost in the trenches. Skilled lobbyists and public relations experts are needed at the outset and throughout the effort.

8. *External Coalition Building Is Important.* Coalitions with educators, citizen groups, and politicians will need to be built.

9. *A Long-run View Is Necessary.* Changing education takes time, and the first legislation passed is unlikely to result in all the improvements that are needed. A three-year to five-year commitment is probably required to maintain pressure on the policy system.

The final lesson is perhaps the most obvious. Business leaders can expect conflict and uncertainty when they enter the education policy domain. But business stands in a unique position in our society. The California and Minnesota stories demonstrate that business involvement in education reform, if exercised wisely, can be the difference between continuance of the status quo and constructive change.

NOTES

1. J. Guthrie and M. W. Kirst, *Conditions of Education in California*, Berkeley, Calif.: Policy Analysis for California Education, April 1984.
2. The entire business community encompasses more than the corporations belonging to the Roundtable. For example, many small businesses are members of the Chamber of Commerce, an organization that also seeks to influence public policy. For the purposes of this chapter, we will use the term "business community" to refer to the Roundtable (or to the Minnesota Business Partnership).
3. The Superintendent of Public Instruction is a nonpartisan elective office. The Superintendent is in charge of the State Department of Education, but otherwise does not have authority for programs without legislative approval.
4. Hart's election was bitterly contested. He lost the endorsement of the teachers' unions because he had had been the author of a bill that required newly hired teachers to take a basic competency test. His appointment as Chair of the Education Committee bypassed several other candidates who were less committed to reform, thereby signaling to the teachers' unions and others that the Democratic leadership in the State Senate was determined to pass significant reforms.
5. BW had privately tested these proposals with many key interest groups before recommending them to the Task Force, in order to find out where compromise (if any) might be possible and to avoid surprising major political actors.
6. The Chairman of the Roundtable sent a letter to the Governor during this period, indicating CRT's support for the Governor while suggesting a compromise on the funding issue. However, some individual Roundtable member companies felt the Jobs and Education Task Force was not adequately supporting the Governor and had gone beyond its charter. Letters stating these dissenting positions were circulated among Roundtable members and sent to the Governor.
7. The Roundtable's own evaluation of its efforts was positive, although some CEOs felt that without the Governor's stand taxes would have been raised to pay for the "Roundtable's reforms." On August 5, 1983, the chair of the CRT sent a memo to the membership summing up CRT's evaluation of SB 813 in comparison with its legislative agenda. The memo stated that a major portion, though not all, of CRT's agenda had been realized; that SB 813 was landmark legislation that would promote substantial improvement of student performance; and that its passage was in no small part due to the efforts of the Roundtable.
8. In 1981–1982, approximately 6.2% of public school enrollments were minorities, with 1.5% American Indian, 2.1% black, 1.8% Asian, and 0.7% Hispanic.
9. Minnesota has one of the strongest state laws supporting the rights of

public employee labor unions. The teachers' unions, the Minnesota Education Association (MEA) and the Minnesota Federation of Teachers (MFT), are particularly influential in state politics.

10. The Minnesota Business Partnership believed that the education analysts in Minnesota's close-knit policy community were already identified with some position. Consequently, the Partnership decided to go outside the state to seek a fresh and independent perspective. However, MBP knew that consultants based in another state would be viewed as people without a place in the Minnesota policy network and hence that some critics might judge the outsiders as unqualified to "pass judgment on the state."

11. For example, consensus building was necessary concerning the implication of BW's plan for state spending. The Minnesota Business Partnership had independently developed a tax plan that called for a 2 percent across-the-board cut in all areas of government spending. In contrast, BW's education plan proposed stable spending in real dollars for education, which implied increases to take inflation into account. It was agreed that MBP's tax plan could be interpreted to mean a 2 percent reduction in *overall* state spending, thus making MBP's tax agenda compatible with its education agenda.

12. The Partnership deliberately decided not to make the material public before the election in order to avoid a possible partisan polarization of the education debate.

13. Though this coalition strategy maximized the leverage of the Partnership, several MBP allies told us they were disappointed at what they perceived to be a limited effort. One proponent of Access to Excellence stated that the Governor had taken the lead in education reform at the beginning of January, expecting the Partnership to be right behind him, and yet when "the Governor turned around he couldn't see them." In fact, it did take some time for MBP to work through the details of the fit between its agenda and the Governor's. Moreover, the MBP executive staff left for other employment in this same period. In short, MBP had to mobilize a new organizational effort, raise additional money, and build consensus among its members.

14. In addition to direct lobbying efforts, MBP engaged in some public activities. For example, deputies, but not CEOs, continued to make presentations about *The Minnesota Plan*. In addition, Mr. Lehr, the CEO of 3M and a highly respected figure in Minnesota, traveled with Governor Perpich to locations around the state to address education issues.

15. In both states, the contracts assumed that the consultants' recommendations would be made public, regardless of whether the business community supported them.

Part II

MINI CASES: STRATEGIES FOR BUSINESS INVOLVEMENT WITH PUBLIC SCHOOLS

Introduction

ROBERTA TRACHTMAN

The mini cases were developed from interviews with corporate representatives and school people about the problems and promise of today's activities and the prospects for the future. Where possible, the processes and programs that they described were expanded through secondary interviews with other participants. In addition, all participants were asked to forward any documents that were pertinent to the partnership programs.

The mini cases have been organized according to the three broad categories of funding, programmatic, and policy initiatives. These three kinds of involvements are quite different from each other, although they are not mutually exclusive. It is altogether possible, as will be clearly demonstrated in some of the mini case studies that follow, that a corporation may simultaneously engage in a broad spectrum of collaborative activities. Naturally, such diverse and far-reaching involvement is not possible or desired by all partners.

8 A Focus on Funding

ROBERTA TRACHTMAN
City University of New York

There is little indication that large amounts of corporate money have been forthcoming to the public sector as a result of the private sector's recently renewed interest in education.[1] A report issued by the Council for Financial Aid to Education in 1986 indicated that corporations gave $1.7 billion to education in 1984; 5.2 percent of that is reported to be elementary and secondary school funding.[2]

Some of the more traditional ways in which the business community directly provides limited kinds of financial support include: paid work-study programs for students, teacher training at business locations, small grants to teachers for the creation and/or implementation of innovative programs, donations of scholarship monies for graduating high school seniors, the provision of equipment and materials, and the donation of small amounts to be used for the purchase of trophies, advertisements, and prizes.

Local Education Funds. The local education fund "is a third party non-profit entity whose agenda, at least in part, consists in developing supportive community and private sector relationships with a public school system."[3] Local education funds attempt to better link schools and their communities by providing a vehicle for private-sector donations. Since this form of support is usually limited, most of the money donated to these funds is used for small grants.[4]

Based on the success of two local education fund efforts, one in Pittsburgh and the other in San Francisco, a national nonprofit organization was founded in 1983 called the Public Education Fund. The Public Education Fund's goal is to strengthen public/private collaborations that now exist throughout the country by providing technical assistance and allocating financial resources through a matching-grant program. The Public Education Fund is described and discussed at length in the case study by Valerie Lies and David Bergholz in Chapter 5.

Supporting Research. In some communities, notably in California, Minnesota, and Washington, members of the private sector have financed education research to help formulate positions on policies relating to educational change and improvement. In other instances, as in the case of Metropolitan Life Insurance Company, business has made it possible for the research community to find out more about teacher needs and satisfactions.

Financial participation continues to be limited, and there is no indication that the private sector is willing or even interested in making up for the deficits in education resulting from federal cutbacks. As reported in a nationwide study of corporate America, the business community consistently responded that the funding of education is the responsibility and the obligation of federal, state, and local governments.[5] The mini case studies that follow describe some of the ways in which the private sector has chosen to participate financially in the schools.

THE BOSTON PLAN FOR EXCELLENCE

The Boston school system, the nation's oldest, has struggled with the same difficulties faced by schools in other large urban centers throughout the country. In 1981 and 1982, the Scholastic Aptitude Test (SAT) scores of Boston students were at least 60 points below the national average.[6] In its review of statistics published by a number of federal and state sources, the Boston Private Industry Council discovered that after adjustments for inflation were made, the average Boston family's income declined in the past decade.[7] Thus, although the city has generally fared well recently, many of its residents have not.

The Bank of Boston's Initiative

In February 1984, the Bank of Boston celebrated its 200th anniversary. To mark this occasion, the bank's leadership sought to publicly acknowledge its appreciation for the community's support in a way that would be consistent with its history of corporate social responsibility. The decision to establish the first community endowment for public school education came as a result of long discussions between leading Bostonians and bank officials. Because the bank was already engaged in programmatic activities with the public schools, it was sensitized to the system's needs. The establishment of a community-based endowment fund rather than a one-time grant seemed to provide a way in which the bank's gift could have a long-term effect.

With its initial gift of $1.5 million, the Bank of Boston established the Boston Plan for Excellence in the Public Schools. The bank's Chairman, William L. Brown, became the first Chairman of the Plan's Board of Trustees. The other trustees were drawn from among the leaders of business, education, and the Boston community at large. They were carefully selected to ensure adequate representation from both the public and the private sectors. The Boston Foundation (formerly known as the Permanent Charity Fund of Boston) provided staff support and some funding.

The creation of this umbrella organization offered a mechanism through which private money could be dispersed to the public schools. The Board of Trustees became the final review committee, thereby providing a nonpartisan, highly responsible group to distribute the donations. Although any donor could require that funds be used for a particular kind of project, the Board would provide oversight and be accountable for all Plan activities. In addition, this group became a forum for disparate but interrelated parts of the community. It was hoped that this might facilitate greater understanding and decrease the isolation of some of the city's most significant institutions.

The Endowment Model

By making donations to an endowment fund, corporations receive additional tax benefits while maintaining control over the ways in which the money is used. The interest income generated by each initial contribution is dispersed for programmatic use, leaving the original grant intact. This method makes it unnecessary for the fund to look for new sources of income each year and enables it to concentrate efforts where they can be most effective: on funding good proposals that will improve teaching and learning in the Boston schools.

Dr. Daniel Cheever, President of Wheelock College and a Plan trustee, explains that this model of public/private interaction is guided by three important premises:

1. Although a relatively small amount of money is distributed to each school, these discretionary funds can be used to meet local needs. In the world of K–12 education, this kind of control is rare and cherished by those able to obtain it.
2. The private sector's participation symbolizes its commitment to the public schools. This expression of commitment is important to those

in education who feel that their task needs to be shared with other members of the community. The private sector's assistance is seen as an expression of mutuality and common interest.

3. The establishment of the Boston Plan provides for the leveraging of more private-sector resources through the network of friends and acquaintances that exists among the members of the business community. Dr. Cheever hopes that additional contributions will be used to reach more schools, rather than provide for larger grants. He believes that this program is effective because it helps the schools to define their needs and create programs that will help them to meet those needs.

So far, the Boston Plan has led to four endowment grants.

The School Initiatives Grant Program. The first program to be sponsored under the Boston Plan was initiated by the Bank of Boston. The School Initiatives Grant Program provides competitive grants of up to $10,000 for school-based projects designed to help individual schools achieve excellence. The first call for proposals elicited responses from 77 of Boston's 123 schools. Eleven grants were awarded in January 1985, ranging from $2,045 to $7,530 and totaling more than $51,000. Before the proposals were submitted, they were reviewed by local panels composed of teachers, administrators, parents, and representatives from the business community, higher education, cultural institutions, and community organizations. The final review committee was the Plan's Board of Trustees.

A second round of competition during 1985 resulted in the distribution of $48,692 to 13 schools, bringing the total for 1985 to $100,000. By the fall of 1986, more than $200,000 had been dispersed through the School Initiatives Grant Program. William Brown, chairman and CEO of the Bank of Boston, expressed his appreciation for the efforts of school personnel who created plans that helped their schools move toward excellence. The need to plan for improvement from within is critical, and the grant program enabled the teachers and administrators to assume an active role in the improvement of their schools, rather than waiting for change to be imposed on them. The funds provided by the bank offered both an incentive for creativity and the assurance that good ideas would not die because of lack of money.

Teacher Fellowships. A few months after the first endowment was established, the Bank of New England donated a five-year, $300,000 grant to Boston teachers. It was designed to enable up to 350 teachers to renew their teaching skills in the areas of science, writing, mathematics, and computers. According to Peter McCormick, the bank's Chairman, "We believe . . . that the enhancement of teachers' skills is one of the most critical factors in the success of our public schools in the future."[8]

To increase the effectiveness of this approach to staff development, teachers accepted as fellows are required to attend an eight- to ten-day summer session at a local host university and periodic follow-up evening or Saturday sessions during the fall. Fellows receive two stipends, one of $600 at the completion of the summer session and an additional $200 upon presentation of an in-service workshop in their schools, at which they share some of the benefits and lessons learned at the Institute during the summer program. This second stipend is intended to encourage the wider dissemination of ideas and to create a network among school staffs.

ACCESS. In April 1985, the New England Mutual Life Insurance Company marked its 150th anniversary by creating a $1 million endowment fund to assist graduates of the Boston schools in their pursuit of postsecondary education. Unlike the other programs that operate under the aegis of the Boston Plan, ACCESS focuses on the student who needs financial aid and advice. The ACCESS program was developed by a broad-based committee of education and business interests under the leadership of the Greater Boston Chamber of Commerce. The Boston Foundation provided a start-up grant of $130,000 and subsequently gave a $1 million challenge grant. By the fall of 1986, more than $5 million had been contributed to the fund by dozens of Boston businesses.

Given the limited number of school guidance personnel in the Boston public schools (estimated at one counselor for every thirty-six students) and the sometimes overwhelming number of students who need help in selecting a higher education institution, the ACCESS program pays the salaries of additional financial aid advisors, who help students identify sources of aid and fill out college aid application forms. ACCESS also provides "last dollar" scholarships to students who have not been able to secure all the aid they need. According to a recent study conducted by Boston University, "Neither individual performance nor demographics is the critical factor influencing college retention. What matters is money."[9]

HEART. The fourth endowment, provided by the John Hancock Mutual Life Insurance Company, is targeted at a group that has received little attention historically: the more than 10,600 Boston middle school students in grades 6 to 8. It is the largest grant ever donated to a middle school system.

The Hancock Endowment for Academics, Recreation and Teaching (HEART) has created a $1 million fund to be used in the improvement of educational and athletic programs, and it is estimated that the endowment will yield about $100,000 annually.

An equal sum will be devoted to reviving after-school intramural athletic programs for middle school students. The athletic programs will take place at community school facilities. Participation will depend on satisfactory attendance and academic performance.

According to Hancock Chairman and CEO John G. McElwee, "Although the ultimate responsibility for public education rests with the public and its officials, John Hancock is convinced that the corporate sector can and should make a significant contribution. . . . Hopefully, HEART will inspire other corporate support of middle school youngsters."[10]

Accomplishments and Prospects

The Bank of Boston's original endowment to the city's public schools has served as a catalyst, stimulating efforts by other corporations. The establishment of an umbrella organization has enabled the private sector to participate in a way that both satisfies its sense of commitment to the schools and the city and provides for accountability. The Boston business community has recognized the importance of the public school system as a supplier of both its future work force and its customer base. The historical importance of the private sector in Boston has made this renewed commitment heartily welcomed and appreciated by a school system anxious to return to its previous state of excellence.

As described by Jeffrey Graham, a Vice-President at the Bank of Boston, the corporate community is not interested in making policy decisions for the schools. He believes that the private sector wants to maintain the institutional role of the school as a public entity but that there is need for support from private sources. The Boston Plan, which received $80,000 from the Public Education Fund to pay for staffing costs, is an independent trust that allows for the maximization of corporate donations, without placing the enormous burdens of administration on each donor.

William Brown has stepped down as the Plan's Chairman so that other private-sector participants will be able to share in the development of the programs and their outcomes. The absence of a formal, structured mode of evaluation of programs after they have been funded reflects the Plan's belief that critical reviews are needed before funding rather than afterward. It is possible, however, that more formal evaluations may eventually be required by the Board of Trustees.

The Boston Plan for Excellence in the Public Schools is a model that may be appropriate for use in other communities. It requires the private sector's recognition that a sound system of public education is essential to the health of the economy and the welfare of the country. By its very nature, the Plan allows for mutual decision-making and the sharing of interests and resources. At the same time that it is based on the corporate sector's acknowledgment of general school need, it allows donors to establish guidelines and targets for their funds and encourages the development of specific, school-based responses. To all concerned, this constitutes a win-win situation.

BEST BET

A *Nation at Risk*, published in 1983, was the first of a series of recent reports calling for education reform throughout the nation.[11] To some, it was a virulent critique of an institution that needed to be changed from the outside. To others, it was a call to educators to reevaluate practices and procedures in their schools in order to determine how they could be improved. In a town in New England, one businessman read the report and decided that he could no longer ignore the critical needs of the schools in his community. Since the publication of *A Nation at Risk*, John Rennie, President of Pacer Systems, Inc., an aviation equipment manufacturer and provider of engineering services, has become a significant and visible friend to the schools, teachers, and students in Burlington, Massachusetts.

A Champion from Business

Mr. Rennie's decision to become involved with the public schools was based on his recognition of the importance of his own schooling. According to Paul Sirotkin, Pacer's Manager of Corporate Affairs, John Rennie believed that his education had enabled him to become a successful entrepreneur and that it was his responsibility to find a way to pay back the schools. His position as Chairman of the Small Business Association of New England had put him in contact with Paul Tsongas, then a U.S. Senator. The two men discussed the importance of school/business relationships, especially for high technology industries. As a result, John Rennie, with the assistance of Senator Tsongas's staff and the local Chamber of Commerce, contacted Burlington's Superintendent of Schools, Thomas Michael, and conversations began.

The result was Building Excellent Schools Through Business-Education Teamwork (BEST BET). This venture reflected Mr. Rennie's determination to avoid the pitfalls of other school/business partnerships he had investigated. He did not want to be seen as an outsider eager "to tell the schools how to do it better."[12] He was convinced that teachers and other school personnel were best equipped to determine their own needs and that the private sector's role should be to provide the necessary resources for programs that had been carefully considered and reviewed.

The BEST BET process reflects this philosophy. Proposals are submitted for review and consideration before resources are obtained. Only after a program has been approved is funding undertaken. There is no general fund to which the private sector is asked to contribute. John Rennie believes that this enables the private sector to feel much more confident about how money and other resources will be used. It provides for a level of accountability that is of great importance to those called upon to participate. Even though Pacer continues to be BEST BET's major funding source, this method is still considered the most viable.

A Champion from the Schools

Leadership of public/private ventures is often shared by representatives of both sectors. In Burlington, the Principal of the Marshall Simonds Middle School, Richard Connors, has had a leading role in the school system side of BEST BET. The middle schools have not usually been the beneficiaries of school/business interactions, but when Connors heard about BEST BET, he was one of the first to seize upon what he saw as an extraordinary opportunity for his school. His initial discussions with Mr. Rennie convinced him of the sincerity of the plan. He therefore asked Mr. Rennie to talk with the parents and teachers in his school about the program's possibilities.

According to both Mr. Connors and Mr. Sirotkin, the school community was suspicious of the offer at first. Past corporate-sector initiatives had never amounted to anything, so the reaction was understandable. But it posed a real impediment to the implementation of BEST BET. Mr. Connors understood that the attitude of school leaders would be critical to the effort, and he therefore became one of the program's principal advocates. He encouraged his teachers to create proposals focused on those needs that were most critical. He became a permanent member of BEST BET's Steering Committee so that he would be able to participate in the selection and approval of proposals throughout the district. In his view, BEST BET has succeeded in Burlington because it reflects a shared vision. But he also recognizes that it is a personal statement, which might not work in other places with other players.

How the Process Works

For the most part, the BEST BET program is managed by a Steering Committee that sets the rules, evaluates proposals, and serves as the primary liaison between the school system and industry. Several senior high school teachers and administrators, a representative from the Chamber of Commerce, and Mr. Rennie and his secretary are the standing members of the Committee.

During the program's first two years, Pacer contributed the majority of funds for approved projects, although several other area businesses also contributed. This has been partly because Mr. Rennie wanted to be sure of the program's success before approaching industry in a large way. However, greater participation from other businesses in the region is expected in the future.

The Goal: Better Schools for Burlington

The improvement of Burlington's schools is the overriding focus of the BEST BET proposals. A recent Situation Report described the program's specific objectives.

For the Students
Improve the educational program content
Increase interest in school/subjects
Improve relationships with teachers
Provide information on career options
Provide information on the general needs of industry
Promote teaching as a career choice
Provide insights on business as a vocation
Increase opportunities for compensation

For the Teachers
Improve status/self-image
Increase morale
Increase opportunities for compensation
Improve currency in profession

> Provide enrichment/support for class topics and help relate topics
> to the world of work

In General
Improve facilities and equipment
Make better use of excess space
Improve morale in the school system
Develop better ties between schools and industry[13]

The broad scope of these objectives reflects a primary goal of BEST BET: to respond to needs communicated by those who work and learn in the public schools. Mr. Rennie has not sought to establish another education policy group. Rather, he hopes to provide the school system with supplementary resources that will enable it to change itself.

The first proposal to be funded demonstrated that this program would not exclusively or primarily concern itself with activities related to technology. The Marshall Simonds Middle School hired a nationally known writing consultant from the University of New Hampshire to offer a one-day writing workshop to its English teachers. BEST BET paid the consulting fee of $500 and $800 to cover the cost of substitute teachers.

During BEST BET's first two years, 186 projects were completed. The cost was $87,000. In the second year, approximately three times as many proposals were funded and completed as in the first year, an increase to 139 from 47. This increase was important because it indicated that more teachers had become aware of the opportunity BEST BET offered and that their skepticism about the program had sharply decreased. They were able to see that Mr. Rennie's offer was genuine, and they were eager to use some of this newfound money and other resources in their pursuit of educational excellence.

A Look Toward the Future

It is hoped that within the next few years, BEST BET will "become somewhat 'institutionalized.'"[14] It is anticipated that "the projects undertaken will grow in complexity and scope (not necessarily requiring more funds) and the relationship with the school people will become stable and enduring."[15] Such a goal indicates a strong private-sector commitment to a long-term relationship with local schools. However, the program's funding is not to become successively greater. "A program of this type should not become so large that it intrudes on the normal budgeting process. It should not be considered an 'alternative budget.'"[16] This caveat reflects the very definite and prescribed role the Burlington private sector has chosen to play. BEST BET will continue to provide funds on the margin to encourage change in incremental but important ways.

IMPACT II

The renewed interest in education reform has often focused on the quality of American teachers and the schools of education that prepare them for their profession. One early reform program recognized the considerable talent and expertise of teachers and sought a way to harness and disseminate the good ideas they had already put into practice. In 1979, the Exxon Education Foundation funded a pilot program in New York City, which supported the beliefs that there is a significant amount of good teaching in schools, that teachers know which programs work well, and that other teachers are more likely to incorporate good practices that have been presented to them by their peers.

This last point is particularly important in light of some of the recent criticisms of staff development programs, which have been notoriously underfunded, underattended, and underutilized. The IMPACT II model (based on a previous project called IMPACT, a college and university program also funded and administered by the Exxon Education Foundation) seeks to identify classroom programs that have already proved successful. Theoretically effective but untried programs are avoided in favor of those that practitioners can describe as having worked for them. The public school teachers who apply for IMPACT II grants agree not only to stand behind their program, but also to stand before their peers and answer questions about efficacy, practicality, and adaptability. The belief in top-down efforts to promote system-wide educational innovation is exchanged for interactions based on notions of collegiality and self-motivated improvement.

Teachers who participate in this small-grant program have responded to their own needs, rather than those identified by superintendents or school boards. As such, they are, by definition, special. However, the national director of IMPACT II, Ellen Dempsey, emphasizes that this specialness is most assuredly not limited to the teachers who have already been recognized.

How the Process Works

In 1979, the Exxon Education Foundation made its first IMPACT II grant of about $250,000 to the New York City Board of Education. These funds were provided so that teachers, known as *developers*, could package and disseminate classroom programs to other teachers, who would be known as *replicators*. The name of this second category has since been changed to *adaptors* in order to more accurately reflect the process. Teachers who become aware of exemplary programs are more likely to take them on as their own and modify them to accommodate personal needs than they are to accept and unconditionally replicate them.

This personalization is more than cosmetic. For innovation to work, local conditions have to be appropriate. Those who scoff at this view need only research some of education's notorious failures—for example, the new math, open classrooms, teacher-proof curricula—to realize the strength of local differences. A systematic evaluation of the impact of IMPACT II in 1983 by Drs. Mann and Fenwick, professors at Teachers College, Columbia University, supports and underscores this view. Those teachers who adapted the developers' programs reported even greater changes in their teaching behaviors than the developers themselves had experienced. In addition, adaptors were more likely than developers to have tried to convince other teachers to use these strategies.[17] This suggests that enthusiasm for educational improvement cannot be mandated but needs to be nurtured through personal exposure and experience.

Who Is Chosen?

The original Exxon grant established an IMPACT II staff as part of the Division of Curriculum and Instruction at the Board of Education. To inform the school community of the existence of this program, the staff initially contacted superintendents, principals, and union chapter chairpeople in the hope that these individuals would be able to spread the word to teachers. At the same time, public service radio advertisements described the effort, and an ad was placed in the newspaper distributed by the New York teachers' union.

This process has been somewhat modified over time because teachers who have already received grants are now able to serve as ambassadors within their own districts. According to Ellen Dempsey, more than 60 percent of the schools in New York City have one or more teachers within their buildings who have received one of the 1,800 IMPACT II grants distributed in the city since 1979.

The *IMPACT II Handbook* notes that "the problem with other minigrants has always been that the effect stops when the money runs out."[18] To eliminate this weakness, the program was designed to offer two types of grants (one for developers and one for adaptors) and to establish and promote the creation of a network of teachers to sustain interest in effective instructional strategies. To provide for this network, teachers who submit programs that qualify them for developer grants are asked to present their programs at workshops for teachers interested in adapting them. A catalog of new developer programs is produced each year and distributed to all schools in the fall so that interested teachers will have the opportunity to select a program most appropriate to their needs.

Some teachers apply for adaptor grants after reading the catalog; others first become aware of the program possibilities after attending an IMPACT II workshop. Workshops are often held after school or on weekends; some are scheduled on a professional or staff development day during school hours. If a teacher would like to attend a workshop or visit a classroom where a program is being used, IMPACT II provides funds for a substitute teacher.

A Look at the Program's Success

Both Ms. Dempsey and Drs. Mann and Fenwick (who conducted a longitudinal, pretest, and post-test evaluation of the programs in New York and Houston) believe that the two-stage design of this program and the networking focus are the reasons for its success. IMPACT II has sought to lessen the isolation experienced by teachers and the lack of status and respect they feel. The $300 developer grant is an honorarium. The receipt of this grant or the $200 adaptor grant draws each teacher into a network of like-minded individuals anxious to initiate practices that will improve the instruction in their classrooms and thereby promote learning.

In a profession where financial rewards are few, IMPACT II money will do little to counterbalance fiscal inequities. These grants cannot be used to finance laboratories or make large-scale computer equipment purchases. They will not pay the salary of a classroom aide, nor are they intended to pay for university courses or the advice of expert consultants. IMPACT II dollars are provided for the dissemination of good teaching practices to other teachers who are interested in learning them. At the same time, they provide money for much needed classroom supplies.

To ensure the very special notion of peer review, as well as to provide for continuity and ongoing participation, the committees that select the winning applicants include former grant recipients. Those who once belong to this group of special educators find that they always belong; they are not the recipients of one-time recognition. Instead, they remain visible and active members of a teaching corps devoted to professional growth. Grant recipients reported significant changes in their instructional strategies after participation in this program.[19] The long-term effectiveness of these approaches may result in improved education within their classrooms as well as greater personal satisfaction for those teachers who measure their own success by how well their students learn. Although the focus of IMPACT II is the individual teacher, there is no limit to the program's ripple effect.

New Sites

The success of the IMPACT II pilot programs has led to the establishment of this model in 22 school districts throughout the country. Within each district, the basic model has been adapted to suit local needs. At most sites, program personnel are funded by the school system, with some outside assistance from the private sector and foundations. In Los Angeles and San Francisco, the public education funds administer the program as part of a larger effort to provide assistance to the public schools. In many cities, businesses and corporations have provided money for teacher grants, printing, receptions, and substitute teachers. The individual programs reflect the resources and resourcefulness of those involved. However, the program in New York is no longer funded exclusively by the Exxon Education Foundation. In 1982, the New York City Board of Education joined the Foundation as a partner in funding the program, and since then the program has been institutionalized within the system. However, the New York City program still depends on the support from Exxon and other foundations and corporations.

IMPACT II now is a national program that provides teachers within each network the opportunity to interact with teachers from other sites. As a result, the skills and creativity of teachers no longer have geographic limits. There is a national office located in New York City and funded by a consortium of foundations and corporations. Four times a year, IMPACT II publishes *The IMPACT II Star*, a newsletter that offers up-to-date information about programs throughout the country and enables teachers to keep in contact with each other. Every other year, grantees are invited to attend a national convention that brings teachers together for discussion and dissemination of program ideas.

This convention reflects the underlying premises of IMPACT II: Excellent teachers practice their craft throughout the country in ways that often go unrecognized and unrewarded. Because of the weight of the educational bureaucracy that surrounds them, or merely because they have never had the opportunity to offer their skills to others who would be interested, they often are unable to share their expertise. IMPACT II attempts to find these teachers so that their talents and skills can reach a wider audience and their creativity will not be restricted by time and place. Further, IMPACT II recognizes and rewards good teachers to encourage them to remain in teaching.

THE GENERAL ELECTRIC FOUNDATION

General Electric's precollegiate education program is targeted at students, teachers, and the general improvement of science and mathematics education. The General Electric Foundation currently spends $1 million a year to upgrade teaching skills, strengthen curriculum, and provide leadership support to inner city schools. Foundation money and support are given to national efforts, but many of the Foundation's approaches are more narrowly focused and tied to the communities where General Electric (GE) plants and offices are located. To maximize the effectiveness of its grants, the General Electric Foundation often works through existing local organizations, universities, and community-based public education funds. This approach ensures that knowledgeable professionals will provide continuing and appropriate oversight for local activities. At the same time, however, the Foundation expects to receive appropriate evaluations of the programs that it has supported. According to Phyllis McGrath, a Program Manager at the Foundation, "GE and the GE Foundation are strongly committed to strengthening the school systems of our nation. . . . There's little we can do to improve teacher salaries, but we can provide current and prospective teachers with incentives and professional recognition."[20]

The Teacher Focus

In 1985, the GE Foundation and the Association of Science-Technology Centers established a program called Science Teacher Education at Museums (STEAM). It was initiated in response to the severe shortage of qualified elementary and secondary school science teachers. As indicated by the National Science Board's report, "the potential of science museums as a site for teacher-training programs should be recognized, encouraged and supported."[21] A long-time supporter of individual museum efforts, the GE Foundation funded a 1984 survey of science museum directors to learn about their programs and future plans. As a result of the information obtained, GE created the STEAM program and awarded the Association of Science-Technology Centers $352,500 to establish a two-year grant competition. This money is being dispersed to science museums and other science centers (e.g., botanical gardens) in the form of planning and enrichment grants for the development and improvement of their science teacher-training programs.

A total of 100 science institutions applied for these grants; as of mid-1986, more than $217,000 had been earmarked to support the plans of 42 museums throughout the country.

Project to Increase Mastery of Math and Science (PIMMS). The Project to Increase Mastery of Mathematics was organized in 1979 by a group of education, business, and labor leaders. In 1983, the scope of the organization's activities was enlarged to include science as well as mathematics.

Early in 1984, the GE Foundation Fellowship Program for Mathematics Teachers was established, and a pilot phase was carried out during the second semester of the 1983–1984 school year. The program had two salient goals: By recognizing outstanding teachers, it hoped to reward instructional excellence; further, by offering other schools the opportunity to benefit from the advice, experience, and expertise of these outstanding educators, GE hoped that the many excellent practices and programs would be replicated to reach a larger number of students.

The 13 teachers who participated in the pilot were chosen because of their subject matter competence, teaching effectiveness, and successful involvement in statewide curriculum development. All the secondary schools in Connecticut (GE's home state) were notified of the pilot program, and all were invited to submit specific requests for help. Typical requests sought assistance with programs for remediation, for the noncollege bound, for the mathematically gifted, for implementing the use of the computer in K–12 mathematics classrooms, and for advice on how to introduce more mathematics teaching into the curriculum.[22] Recipient fellows were allotted five days to visit other teachers and school administrators across the state. It was reported that the total demand for fellow-days far exceeded the supply.

In the spring of 1984, the fellowship program was expanded to include science teachers. Financial support continues to be supplied by several Connecticut employers in addition to GE, at the cost of $7,000 per fellow. In the first year, the GE Foundation funded 21 mathematics fellows; support for the remaining 19 fellows was shared by several other corporations.

To provide the fellows with an opportunity to increase their knowledge and to develop a network of teachers, the program was expanded in the summer of 1984 to include a five-week institute held at Wesleyan

University. Fellows received a stipend of $2,000 for their participation at the Institute, which featured classes and seminars, and provided guest lectures; particular attention was given to how to transfer their new knowledge to classroom applications. Each fellow was awarded an additional $1,500 honorarium for providing workshops, professional development seminars, and consultative assistance to schools on request.

The PIMMS program has received national attention and has served as a model for other "master teacher" training efforts.

The Forgivable Loan Program for Prospective Secondary Mathematics Teachers. To encourage students of mathematics to obtain teaching credentials and then pursue careers as secondary school mathematics teachers, 16 northeast institutions of higher education put together a loan agreement with the GE Foundation in 1984. These institutions, including Dartmouth, Princeton, Brown, Brandeis, Smith, Vassar, Yale, Connecticut College, and Wesleyan, formed the "Consortium for Excellence in Teacher Education." This Consortium administers the funds provided by the GE Foundation, and reviews applications and awards loans on the basis of academic performance and faculty recommendations. These loans are interest-free until graduation. Recipients who go on to teach at least three years of secondary school mathematics are excused from repayment.

The General Electric Foundation Teacher Award Program. Realizing that instructional excellence often goes unrewarded, GE decided to provide for a teacher award program. The program is administered by existing community foundations and public education funds in several locations where GE has significant operations. The local foundation or fund establishes a community committee to review proposals from teachers for innovative approaches to mathematics education. It publicizes the program, provides necessary application forms, and makes the grant awards.

GE chose to provide the money through existing local foundations in an effort to make the process more responsive to local needs and variations. With the provision of additional funds from other corporate sponsors, the mini grant programs have expanded to reach more teachers and schools.

Attention to Students

Science, Math, and Relevant Technology (SMART) is an after-school recreational program that introduces science and mathematics in a club atmosphere. The program is currently being run in five cities through the local Girls Clubs of America. The leadership of the Girls Clubs initially approached the GE Foundation to provide support for a program that would encourage girls to become interested in science and mathematics as school subjects and as the basis for future careers. GE's primary role is that of funding; the program's organization and administration fall to the leaders of each Girls Club.

Minority Engineering Program. GE has made a major commitment to attracting minority youths to science and engineering careers. This concern is most clearly reflected in GE's support of summer institutes and weekend engineering orientation programs for minority youth. These programs are offered by universities and community-based organizations throughout the country in an effort to upgrade the skills of undereducated minority students. The youngsters receive specialized, intensive classroom instruction in science and mathematics. The money from GE is used for scholarships and stipends for students, as well as to reduce the overhead and administrative costs of the participating local organizations.

While most programs are held on the East Coast, GE, in collaboration with the American Indian Science and Engineering Society (AISES), funded a two-week summer program for high school students at the Colorado School of Mines.

The Manhattan Center for Science and Mathematics. The Manhattan Center for Science and Mathematics is a New York City high school founded in 1982 to provide intensive science and mathematics preparation for selected high school students. One of the center's goals is to address the serious underrepresentation of minorities in science and engineering. Having quickly recognized that additional resources and community support were vital to the program's success, Coleman Genn, the school's principal, approached a number of companies with a plan for their participation and support.

The GE Foundation staff learned about the Manhattan Center through several New York employees who were serving as school volunteers. Given the nature of the school and GE's desire to be responsive to those areas of need identified by its own employees, the Center's proposal received particular attention. In 1985, a three-year grant of $137,500 was made to fund the GE Scholars Program. During its first year, 27 juniors received special services and participated in activities aimed at college preparation. The program consists of after-school, weekend, and summer activities, including field trips to universities and museums, workshops to improve writing and research skills, and SAT preparation.

Each participant is assigned a GE mentor with a science and engineering background. The initial group of 27 scholars continued with the program in their senior year, and they were joined by 21 new juniors. A third group was to enter the program in the next year.

To supplement the Scholars Program and employee volunteer efforts at the Manhattan Center, GE provided a $15,000 grant to the school to pay for the services of two teacher/writers from a New York-based consortium called "The Teachers and Writers Collaborative." These specially trained teachers now work with students from the high school to improve their written communications skills.

GE and the GE Foundation are committed to quality science and mathematics education for reasons that combine a strong sense of corporate social responsibility with a large measure of enlightened self-interest. It may just be that such a combination is the requisite for success.

NOTES

1. R. Trachtman, *School/Business Collaborations: A Study of the Process and Product*, University Microfilms, Inc., 1985; D. Mann, *All That Glitters: Public School/Private Sector Interaction in Twenty-three U.S. Cities*, New York: Teachers College, Columbia University, 1984.
2. Council for Financial Aid to Education, *Corporate Support of Education 1985*, New York: Council for Financial Aid to Education, 1986.
3. Public Education Fund, *The First Two Years: The Public Education Fund, 1983–1985*, Pittsburgh: Public Education Fund, 1985.
4. Ibid.
5. C. Shakeshaft and R. Trachtman, "Corporate-School Partnerships: The Perspective of Business," presented at the annual meeting of the American Educational Research Association, San Francisco, 1986.
6. "$1.5 Million is Gift to Boston Schools," *New York Times*, February 8, 1984.
7. Boston Private Industry Council, "Poverty in Boston," in *Goals for Boston, II(2)*, June 1984, 2.
8. Included in a newsletter released by The School Committee of the City of Boston, June 28, 1984.
9. News release issued by the New England Life Insurance Company, April 2, 1985.
10. News release issued by the John Hancock Mutual Life Insurance Company, February 13, 1985.
11. National Commission on Excellence in Education, *A Nation at Risk: The Imperative for Educational Reform*, Washington, D.C.: U.S. Government Printing Office, 1983.
12. R. Trachtman interview with Paul Sirotkin, 1985.

13. *Burlington BEST BET Program*, Situation Report, October 1985.
14. Ibid, p. 11.
15. Ibid.
16. Ibid.
17. D. Mann and S. Fenwick, "The Impact of IMPACT II: 1982–1983," Teachers College, Columbia University, October 1983.
18. *IMPACT II Handbook: "Take an Idea and Go Creative,"* New York: IMPACT II, 1984.
19. D. Mann, "The Impact of IMPACT II," *Phi Delta Kappan, 63*(9), May 1982, 612–614.
20. Telephone interview with Phyllis McGrath, January 1986.
21. Cited in the *ASTC Newsletter, 13*(4), July/August 1985, 8.
22. PIMMS program description, September 1984.

9 Programmatic Participation

ROBERTA TRACHTMAN
City University of New York

Programmatic interactions between the public and private sectors reflect shared responsibilities, trust, and cooperation. The mini case studies that follow illustrate some of the new ways in which collaborative efforts can be realized. Included are examples of corporate involvement targeted at teacher training, some that focus on improving school management, some that address acknowledged deficits in science and mathematics education, and others that underscore the need for teacher reward and recognition.

Collaboration takes many forms: These case studies are provided as examples of what is possible, not prescriptions for any one best way. Since these mini cases describe nontraditional forms of involvement, before beginning them it may be useful to examine some of the more traditional forms of programmatic participation.

School Board Participation. Serving on school boards has traditionally been one of the most important ways of involving business with the schools. In fact, as described by Timpane, "For the first half of the twentieth century, business involvement in education was pervasive. Almost all school board members were business or professional men, and public school management was modeled on business management."[1]

Cooperative Education. Cooperative education is probably the oldest and most enduring form of partnership between business and education, dating back as far as 1906.[2]

In cooperative education programs, school coordinators supervise students while they are on the job, arrange for job opportunities with employers, and help to link work experience with classroom learning. Unlike other types of vocational education, cooperative programs pro-

175

voke little need for schools to purchase or update their equipment to keep pace with changes in technology. "Coop" students are able to gain hands-on experience in real settings.

Vocational Education. Vocational education is an "umbrella" term for many activities in which schools and businesses are jointly involved. Legislation related to vocational education began in 1917, with the Smith-Hughes Act, which appropriated funds to the states to promote agricultural, industrial, and home economics subjects.

The 1946 George-Barden Act and the 1963 Vocational Education Act revised earlier legislation that no longer met the needs of a greatly expanded industrialized nation.[3] The 1963 law substantially increased funding to the states to assist them to maintain, extend, and improve existing programs, and to develop new programs of vocational education.

In 1968 a National Advisory Council on Vocational Education was established, and was composed of Presidentially appointed representatives from labor, management, the general public, local school boards, and vocational and technical education.

The 1984 Carl D. Perkins Vocational Education Act extended the involvement of the business community in education at the federal, state, and local levels. It mandated that (1) private industry represent a majority on the National Advisory Council on Vocational Education, (2) at the state level, these councils have a majority representation by employers and union leaders, and (3) technical committees be established, composed almost entirely of employers, to advise state boards of education on various aspects of vocational education.[4]

As mandated by federal and state law, business involvement in vocational education takes the form of advisory committee participation. The purpose of these committees is to provide up-to-date information to educators regarding the needs of employers and the skills necessary for employability. This involvement usually includes meeting with the teachers to help them to devise curricula that are meaningful and appropriate to the business subject.

Recent research indicates that the vocational educators in the public schools continue to have the most opportunity to interact with the business community.[5] These teachers of "business subjects" express considerable interest in engaging business personnel as classroom speakers to provide "real-life" role models for their students, as well as to bring real-world expertise to the classroom.

Experience-Based Career Education (EBCE). In the early 1970s, four laboratories funded by the National Institute for Education (NIE) developed programs that tried to integrate work experience and education in high schools. Unlike cooperative education programs in which students receive wages, EBCE involves employers and other members of the community in an effort to improve the general learning and life skills of participants. EBCE provides an integrated work/education program for students. School people consult with employers, on site, about what students will do and learn in the work setting.

A recent analysis of the effects of EBCE found that students involved scored better on various measures of academic performance and that students at all socio-economic levels from all types of residential areas profited from their EBCE experiences.[6] Another analysis found that recent evaluations of EBCE projects demonstrated that personal development and academic performance can be improved through experiential activities.[7]

Collaborative Councils. One of the most important stimuli to the creation of collaborative councils was the publication of Willard Wirtz's *The Boundless Resource.* His principal recommendation was "that there be established, in at least twenty-five cities, Community Education-Work Councils through which school officials, employers, members of labor unions, and members of the public engage collaboratively in developing and administering education-work programs."[8]

A collaborative council is a mechanism for establishing communication across the business/education/labor sectors over an extended period of time.[9] Council membership is expected to be representative of major sectors of the community, with each serving as an equal partner in the effort. Improving the school-to-work transition as well as the more general upgrading of education is the avowed goal.

JTPA: A Federal Initiative. To train economically disadvantaged individuals, the federal government passed the Job Training Partnership Act (JTPA) of 1982 to replace CETA (Comprehensive Education and Training Act). This new law required that each state appoint a state Job Training Coordinating Council consisting of representatives from business/industry; the vocational education board (which is the state advisory council on vocational education); state postsecondary institutions; organized labor, and so on. The JTPA mandates that a collaborative council, the Private Industry Council (PIC), have a voice in program operations that is at least equal to that of local chief elected officials.

The Committee for Economic Development played a major role in the establishment of the Private Industry Councils, working for their establishment with a group of other business organizations. Today, more than 400 fully functioning Private Industry Councils throughout the country bring business thinking to the development and operation of employment and training programs.

A Helping Hand. In 1982, Michael Timpane published his overview of corporate activity in and attitudes toward public education.[10] He expressed the belief that since a principal role of public education was preparing people for work, corporate interest and involvement were inevitable. The assistance provided in this helping hand category is of several types: increased business participation in career-awareness or work-experience programs; managerial assistance, which includes the loan of personnel to the schools to help them manage their "business affairs" more expediently; and the adopt-a-school movement, in which individual businesses seek to involve themselves in some of the activities of specific schools, with the goal of improving their educational programs. This last form of involvement seems to have captured the hearts of many business executives and has received most attention in the media.

JOBS FOR AMERICA'S GRADUATES

In 1979, Delaware Governor Pete du Pont initiated Jobs for Delaware's Graduates (JDG), a forerunner of similar initiatives in seven other states. This program was designed to prepare "at-risk" high school seniors for unsubsidized employment in the private sector after graduation. Unlike many programs that preceded it, the JDG effort was not directed at securing part-time employment for youths during the school year or the summer months. As described by Sean Sullivan in his review of school-to-work programs, the procurement of part-time employment for the disadvantaged is not the same as making these young people more employable.[11] Although work-study and cooperative education programs bring some benefits to their participants, these activities are not often able to improve the long-term employment rates of young people traditionally recognized as hard to employ.[12] Given what was known about the needs of this group, JDG sought to avoid the pitfalls of other school-to-work transition programs.

The Local and National Programs

Due to the success of the original Delaware program, other states soon became interested in replicating this model. In each of the seven replication sites—Arizona, Massachusetts, Michigan, Missouri, Ohio,

Tennessee, and Virginia—a local Board of Directors was set up with representatives from the public and private sectors. In general, representation on each local Board approximates the following proportions:

Business	45–60%
Government	6–18%
Labor	6–18%
Community	6–18%
Education	6–12%

Although most of the money for each of Jobs for America's Graduates' (JAG) eight sites is from public sources, considerable contributions from the private sector have also been provided. This sharing of financial responsibility has increased the private-sector interest in making the program work; the private-sector members become concerned stakeholders, rather than mere observers. This literal and figurative "buy-in" is an important feature contributing to the success of the JAG school-to-work transition program.

In addition to the local sites, a nonprofit national JAG corporation exists in Washington, D.C. The national Board of Directors is a bipartisan, racially mixed group; its composition reflects JAG's need for broad-based community support. The office in Washington, D.C. operates entirely on private sector grants and donations totaling approximately $550,000 annually. The establishment of the national corporation has increased the program's credibility, improved its ability to provide for review and accountability, and facilitated the funding of its programs.

The Delivery of Services

Jobs for America's Graduates attempts to build on and remediate (where possible) those aspects of the students' education most directly related to gaining and retaining a job. The student participants are chosen by school administrators and teachers. According to JAG's *Five Year Research Report*, these students are high school seniors who do not anticipate enrolling full time in postsecondary education training; whose academic performance in high school has been average or below average; whose employment experience is limited or nonexistent; who are enrolled in general academic programs (90 percent), and who are members of low-income families (53 percent). Unlike the youngsters who are targeted for inclusion in Job Training Partnership Act (JTPA) programs, the level of family income is only one of the criteria used to determine eligibility for JAG. JAG participants are selected by school officials, not by narrow programmatic guidelines. Some consider this to be a plus; others believe that it results in "creaming" of the students who are the best prospects, rather than those who truly need the services. The decision to utilize school-based personnel in the selection helps bridge the gap between the external program and the site school. This has reduced some of the distance between school staff and the JAG Job Specialist who works at the school. It has also provided the Job Specialist with essential background information about the needs and aspirations of the students who are selected. The sharing of this information sometimes alleviates the difficulties encountered by other professionals who attempt to work with youngsters through agencies that are less knowledgeable about their specific needs. It also helps to integrate the program more directly into the daily activities of the students involved.

The Job Specialist

The Job Specialists are chosen by the JAG Board of Directors at each job site. Although they are not necessarily certified teachers, all have had at least some teaching and/or business experience. In some schools, the use of noncertified personnel posed a problem initially, but the JAG Board insisted on hiring its own employees in order to maintain direct control and to free them from the burden of other administrative duties. However, like other faculty members, the Job Specialists are subject to school rules and regulations.

Regional supervisors oversee the Job Specialists. In addition, an accreditation group is sent out by the national office in Washington to provide another layer of accountability. In instances where programs do not comply with JAG standards, assistance is provided by both the local JAG office and the national group.

The duties of the Job Specialist are specific: During the school semester, the Specialist is expected to instruct students in 33 competencies identified by the local employing community as important to job success. These include career planning and decision making, job search and job interviewing, job-holding and job-keeping skills, basic academic skills (to a limited degree), leadership and personal development skills, and personal survival skills. According to test scores before and after participation in the program, especially sharp gains are made in job search skills, job-holding skills, and work-relevant attitudes. In a recent nationwide study of both large and small businesses, these were among the skills identified as most critical to success on the job.[14]

The Job Specialist is expected to locate possible jobs for JAG students. One of the most important initial activities is to set up a job bank to facilitate the flow of information about opportunities in each community. Members of the Board of Directors serve as liaisons to the community, helping each Specialist gain access to the information needed. The personal introductions to the business community provided by the Board members significantly improve the quantity and quality of job opportunities. Thus, it has become obvious that the support of each community's leadership is essential for this program to succeed.

The placement of students in appropriate positions when they graduate is not the last step in the process. During the following nine months, students keep in close contact with their Job Specialist. The significance of this relationship is difficult to quantify. For some students, the JAG counselor may be the only adult who has been able to provide special attention and care. The importance of this support is magnified during the student's first few months of employment, when the problems of transition are most severe. JAG reported that this assistance has decreased the difficulties some of the young people might have otherwise experienced.

The Career Association

The Career Association is a club to which JAG students belong. Through its activities, students are offered opportunities for decision making and leadership. It sponsors contests testing job readiness skills, provides for civic and social activities, and holds fund-raising programs. Whether these activities have contributed to the employability of JAG students is difficult to assess, but the Association certainly offers some students another avenue for self-expression and a source of motivation.

The Outcomes

According to JAG's Director of Program Development, Carol Sheffer-Hartmann, a minimum of publicity was given to this program at the beginning so that it would have the time to improve itself. JAG was established to demonstrate, test, and evaluate a comprehensive program for school-to-work transition in diverse labor markets. It was specifically interested in whether participation would improve the rate of successful employment for "at-risk" students. The findings were reported in its *Five Year Research Report*, "JAG participants . . . [are] employed significantly more than comparison group members during the first three to nine months following high school graduation. Females, black and other racial minorities, youths with lower academic performance, and youths from low-income families tend to benefit the most from partici-pation in JAG programs."[15]

The Costs

The average cost of one JAG placement plus follow-up services is $1,400, which JAG reports to be half of the JTPA average and one-quarter of the CETA Title II average. Those who are concerned about this figure must consider the following, reported in the study entitled *Reconnecting Youth:* "Disconnected youth represent a $20 billion-a-year loss for corporate America and for state and local governments. . . . In major cities it is not unreasonable to assume that half of the youth population is at-risk. . . . Two-thirds drop out because they have given up on the school as a vehicle for their success."[16]

The Prospects

Having completed its research, the JAG national board hopes to introduce the JAG school-to-work transition model into five states each year in order to make the program truly national in scope. Although it has not yet attempted to operate in large cities, the JAG Board hopes to initiate that kind of expansion, possibly in a place such as Atlanta. Given the very different problems associated with large-city school sys-tems and urban business communities, outreach efforts to such large districts will have to be carefully considered and orchestrated.

According to *Crossroads*, the JAG newsletter, "The focus of the Board's plan . . . is to redirect existing funds from JTPA and Summer Youth Employment for maximum impact on the youth employment situ-ation. . . ."[17] Yet, the nationwide expansion of JAG will clearly depend on the availability of local funds, the local public schools' willingness to participate, the enthusiasm of local business and labor communities, and their commitment to identify and encourage appropriate job place-ments. Most needed of all is the participation of community leaders who approve of and support the program. JAG will not be successful in a vacuum; it requires the collaboration of all.

THE D.C. MANAGEMENT INSTITUTE

During the 1980s, the concept of the principal as professional man-ager has received considerable attention. The belief that school adminis-trators need to be managers and curricular leaders has prompted some educators to seek the management experience of the business community. In the 1985 Carnegie publication, *Corporate Classrooms*, the authors report that business and industry spend approximately $40 billion each year on the development, training, and retraining of their employees.[18] Over time, the private sector has learned which management practices best support the development of a company's human resources.

The Context

The Superintendent of the Washington, D.C., public schools, Floretta Dukes McKenzie, has long been associated with this school system. Before becoming district superintendent in 1982, she had been a teacher, a building principal, and a central office administrator in the Washington schools. Dr. McKenzie's multiple experiences enabled her to understand the school system from several perspectives. The decision to aggressively seek the participation of the business community was a direct consequence of her personal experiences as a school system insider.

Dr. McKenzie believed that an outreach to the business community should be directed by the following understanding: "It's time for managers of public resources to stop trying to pick corporate pockets; to start helping our private sector companies find cost-justified approaches to coupling the business interest of their shareholders with the educational interest of young people."[19] McKenzie approached the business community to offer its expertise, and not its funds, to both students and staff within the D.C. schools.

Most business entities in Washington are "small businesses"; although they are more likely to employ high school graduates than large companies are, it has been more difficult to involve them in school activities. Instead, the large D.C. corporations have become active partners with the public schools.

The Process

At Dr. McKenzie's direction, contact with the corporate community was channeled through her Executive Assistant for Corporate Affairs. The creation of this central-office position provided a manageable mechanism for private-sector participation with the public schools. D.C. businesses participate in a variety of program activities in the schools, with particular emphasis on employability and career programs. The "adoption" of a Washington elementary school by the White House received national media attention.

In 1983, Dr. McKenzie sought to involve the private sector in ways that would have a greater system-wide impact. Although neither the ongoing employability and career activities nor the efforts of the more than 13,000 school volunteers were abandoned, the Superintendent believed that the greatest source of private-sector expertise had yet to be tapped. Given the cuts in federal spending, a more careful and deliberate use had to be made of what resources would be available to the schools. Improved managerial planning and decision making in noneducational, noncurricular areas could be most easily and most advantageously supplied by those in the business community who had already learned how to do this well. In 1984, with the creation of the D.C. Management Institute, Floretta McKenzie's idea became a reality.

To establish the Institute, the American Society for Training and Development recommended a list of potential corporate participants. Eleven corporations from this list agreed to join the first advisory board. A university consultant was hired to help design a "needs assessment instrument" for the 24 school participants in the first management program. Teachers were not included in the pool of candidates, since the purpose of the Institute was to improve the skills of people who were managers already. One participant candidly remarked, "Those of us in this first group felt flattered to be included, but wondered whether we had been selected because our skills were deficient."[20]

The detailed needs assessment had to be completed in order to make future training sessions appropriate to the participants. Participants were asked to consider their own personal and professional needs. Principals were asked to identify those needs that they viewed as most significant in their respective buildings. School managers with system-wide responsibilities were asked to examine their larger areas of control. Dr. McKenzie and Dr. Robert Carlson, the Executive Assistant for Corporate Affairs, were determined to avoid the errors of other staff development efforts. They designed a program in which participants' needs would direct the activities.

Although responsibility for training was given to those with appropriate experience and skill, the needs of school personnel were central to the program. Without this built-in requirement for mutual ownership, the D.C. Management Institute would have suffered from the same ills that have beset many change efforts.

Type of Involvement

The Institute directors were equally concerned with making the most efficient use of the corporate trainers. Decisions relating to who would teach what and when were not determined until a clear understanding had been reached regarding the needs of the schools. Once this determination had been made, those corporations with specific knowledge in the identified areas of need worked with the Institute's directors to plan the times and places that would be mutually convenient.

The First Phase—Training Sessions. Some of the sessions required that participants leave their schools for two, three, or even five days at a time. This kind of participation could not have occurred without total support from the Superintendent, as well as a sincere and strong commitment from those corporate personnel who were directly and indirectly involved. Throughout the process, this keen sense of commitment was expressed by both the private- and public-sector leaders. School participants were made to feel that they were part of a special group that was being given a special opportunity. During each training session, the design of the program enabled school people to hear about the problems of other administrators in a nonadversarial environment. (All sessions were held away from the school district.) The sessions enabled school personnel who usually did not interact with each other regularly to gain a greater understanding of each other's difficulties and problems. A forum such as this is often not available to diverse sectors of the school community, and so the training sessions provided the opportunity for a network to grow within the district. Participants considered the creation of this network a valuable outcome of their experience.

The Second Phase—The Training of Trainers. One of the stated goals of the second stage of the process is the "training of trainers." Since the Washington, D.C., schools eventually hope to eliminate the need for corporate trainers, school personnel who complete the initial phase of the program are trained so that they will be able to teach the curriculum themselves. Accordingly, they participate in the training sessions held for the subsequent group of candidates in order to gain the necessary experience to conduct these sessions themselves.

The second stage also involves the design and implementation of a project within each administrator's area that reflects knowledge gained during the training sessions. This, of course, consists of an application of the theories to a real-life setting. The administrators formulate projects that best reflect their needs.

The Third Phase. As of 1986, plans for the third and final phase of this program were under way. During this last phase, school administrators and corporate CEOs and managers gathered at a local university to work together at trying to resolve the education problems presented in a series of case studies. Dr. Carlson felt that this third stage would help to "keep the mix going" between the public and private sectors.[21]

The Outcomes

Although at the time of this writing a formal evaluation has not yet been done, a considerable amount of anecdotal evidence indicates that the program has achieved many of its goals. One of the participating principals reported that the training improved her ability to maximize the talents of her teachers. Further, it has put her in touch with the perspectives and problems of other managers in the school system. She now feels part of a network of like-minded leaders.[22] According to Dr. Carlson, a more rigorous assessment was to take place, so that the real benefits would be highlighted and improvements could be made. Additionally, once the real-life projects have been undertaken and completed, much more evidence will be available regarding the program's success.

The D.C. Management Institute has enabled business participants and school administrators to "disabuse themselves of the notion that the school system is unique."[23] As a result of these cooperative efforts, a greater emphasis is now placed on the ways in which the public and private sectors are more similar than dissimilar, and how they have much to share with each other. Consequently, the "we–they" perspective has been decreased and replaced by a greater level of understanding.

The Motives

As described above, the business community in Washington, D.C., is predominantly small business; yet, because of the resources needed, only large corporations have participated in the program. They have chosen to participate because they are interested in the improvement of the schools in their community. At the same time, their trainers are offered an opportunity to practice their skills on a new group of people, and so they are able to upgrade their own performance as well.

The Future

In 1986, the second group of administrators was poised and ready to start its training, as the first group began to make practical use of what they had learned. Through the Management Institute, the Washington school system had made a commitment to its leadership. It was expected that as they became better managers, they would be better able to improve the teaching and learning in the schools.

AETNA LIFE & CASUALTY

In 1985, the Aetna Life & Casualty Foundation held a day-long meeting of its Board of Directors and senior management to discuss urban public education. To gain a broader, more accurate understanding of the issues, they invited a panel of experts to speak to them on the state of American schools. This panel, moderated by Fred Hechinger of *The New York Times,* included Diane Ravitch of Columbia University; Bill Honig, Superintendent of Instruction for California; Albert Shanker, President of the American Federation of Teachers; and Badi Foster, President of the Aetna Institute for Corporate Education and lecturer at the Harvard Graduate School of Education.

Alison Coolbrith, Vice President of Corporate Public Involvement at Aetna, defines the corporation's position on education this way: "Corporations, like the public, must begin to realize how complex the issues in education are, and how great the need is for commitment and creative investment of resources. . . . Aetna Life & Casualty sees the importance of education in our day-to-day operations. Our company hires, competes and conducts its business among people whose education affects our success. Education . . . determines the limits of a corporation's potential, influencing decisions about employees, office locations, investments and markets."[24]

Since the mid-1970s, Aetna has been transformed from a company that provided insurance to one that provides financial services. This shift has significantly affected the company's short- and long-term personnel needs, while creating a new and expanded customer base. Both changes have contributed to Aetna's interest in helping to improve public education and to the commitment by senior management to using company resources toward this end. Aetna is a people-intensive organization. It cannot ignore or deny the impact of a well-educated populace. The programs it supports reflect its philosophical and practical concerns with education and training, both internally and in collaboration with the community.

Aetna Institute for Corporate Education

Since 1984, the Aetna Institute for Corporate Education has offered programs to serve entry-level employees in need of remedial and basic skills training, and programs for corporate executives. The Institute's creation clearly reflected a company belief that its people are its most important resource. As Robert F. Phillips, a Vice President, puts it, "Our success depends largely on the quality and availability of people who are educated and trained."[25]

The Aetna Institute's primary purpose is to meet the business needs of the company through education. These needs, however, are not seen as limited to the education of the staff. The company's leadership believes that over time, its health is dependent on the well-being of the larger society. At the Institute, this perspective has been translated into the creation of the External Programs Unit, which works alongside the Aetna Life & Casualty Foundation and the company's long-standing Corporate Public Involvement Department. The External Programs Unit was designed to help build the educational capacity of the community, a role consistent with Aetna's goal of being a socially responsible member of the private sector. At the same time, involvement in public education is seen as tied to the corporate bottom line. That is, company participation can contribute to the development of an adequately and appropriately trained labor supply that will enable Aetna to fulfill its mission.

The Context Defines the Programs

The City of Hartford, Connecticut, where Aetna is headquartered, is beset by many of the same problems that afflict other urban areas: The schools report high dropout rates. The work force is aging. Employers report present and projected shortages of qualified entry- and middle-level workers. The culturally and racially different population groups in the city have few ties to each other and little access to the decision-making process. Although these groups constitute the majority in numbers, their power to effect change is limited.

The School/Business Collaborative Program

Under the auspices of the Greater Hartford Chamber of Commerce, a public/private advisory committee was created to provide a forum for developing a collaborative approach toward addressing the city's needs. Senior-level representatives of Aetna and of many other area businesses sit together with school and community leaders to define the critical issues, implement plans, and evaluate programs. Their goal is to stimulate and coordinate public/private activities for the improvement of the city's schools.

The Aetna Foundation's Programs

The Aetna Life & Casualty Foundation has participated in the Hartford public schools in many ways. According to former Program Officer Pamela Bartlett, "We're in the schools a lot . . . we interact with everyone . . . we meet on a regular basis. The 'people component' of this interaction is critical."[26]

Bartlett describes this strong commitment as a corporate priority. In Hartford and other major company locations, Aetna employees are encouraged to participate in their communities and are recognized for that participation. Similarly, Aetna executives are expected to be good corporate citizens, and they are held accountable for the programs undertaken and the results obtained.

In 1983, the Foundation gave a three-year grant of $712,000 to the Hartford public schools for the training of teachers and principals. The grant focused on helping educators to design and implement programs that would improve the learning, teaching, and managing in their school buildings. It was made so that the schools could help themselves to provide a better education for the youth of the city.

The Saturday Academy

To strengthen the connections among members of the community, Aetna, and the school system, a unique program was developed by the Education Committee of the Community Index Summit Conference. This group included many of the leaders of Hartford's black community; Badi Foster, President of the Aetna Institute for Corporate Education and a lecturer at the Harvard Graduate School of Education; and Catherine Jenkins of the Aetna Institute.

A decision was reached to offer a Saturday morning program for Hartford seventh graders. The Saturday Academy would be housed at the Aetna Institute for Corporate Education and funded by Aetna. The program would have two distinctive components: It would *not* be remedial, and each participating child would be required to bring a parent or other adult to the sessions.

Hartford teachers were asked to nominate students who were on grade in reading and mathematics. On nine consecutive Saturday mornings during the fall of 1984 and again during the spring of 1985, approximately fifty selected students participated in three different kinds of courses: computer literacy, mathematics and science, and oral communications. Parents were allowed to attend two classes with their children; then, at about 11:00 A.M., they moved off to participate in a work-shop designed especially for them. During these sessions, guest speak-ers provided parents with information about computer literacy, parent-teacher interactions, and other topics relevant to their needs.

Employees from Aetna participated on an Advisory Committee that spent a year planning the program. Catherine Jenkins was asked to be the Academy's Director. During her tenure, she was assisted by other Advisory Committee members from the community, the schools, and the corporation. The teachers in the program were selected by school administrators.

The program was an overwhelming success. The Saturday Academy was a program by, and for, the community. It worked because those involved were able to make it a collaborative venture that offered a way for all to be winners.[27]

The Long-Term Commitment

Aetna has also been involved with the city schools through an em-ployee released-time tutorial program, donations of equipment and fur-niture, a summer jobs program for young people, and youth employ-ment pilot projects. The company offers its facilities for tours and provides other, limited grants.

For the people of Aetna, the commitment to the public schools is strong and enduring. In the words of David Rippey, a former staff mem-ber of the Aetna Institute, "Because the purposes and effects of the public schools are diverse and pervasive, we are all stakeholders. . . . Public education is our sole collective expression of a democratic idea."[28]

HEWLETT–PACKARD

The industrial revolution has given way to an information revolu-tion, and the low-cost, high-powered computer is at its core. The great-est impact of this revolution is the effect that electronic products have had on the jobs performed by almost every employee, rather than the numbers of jobs created by the computer industry and its suppliers. It is

The Hewlett-Packard case study was written by R. Trachtman in collaboration with Gary Gubitz, who was working under NIE Grant No. Q–83–0061 at the time he conducted this research.

predicted that few businesses will remain untouched. The computer and other electronic devices have created a world of science-based engineering, automated manufacturing, professional services, and sophisticated maintenance; in this world, mental, social, and communications skills are more in demand than manual skills.

Yet, many people fear technology. They believe it will rob them of control over their lives instead of giving them greater control. Somehow, they have not learned to use technology to their advantage. This lack of technological know-how is especially acute among young people looking for jobs for the first time. High school can be the best place to learn to use new technologies, but few schools are equipped to teach them. Alarmingly high percentages of students, especially those not college bound, slip through school without the skills needed to get a satisfying job.

Hewlett-Packard has produced precision electronic equipment since 1939. Its profitability is linked to a technologically literate work force and a general populace of well-educated consumers. The company recognizes these needs and in 1986 contributed approximately $65 million in cash and equipment to support education worldwide. Although most of those recipients were institutions of higher education, corporate attention has recently been focused on precollegiate needs.

In the past, the very complexity of the company's equipment largely precluded giving it for instructional use below the college level. The company kept in contact with secondary schools mainly through local chapters of national programs such as Junior Achievement or Mathematics Engineering and Science Achievement (MESA). Today, however, Hewlett-Packard's machines, particularly its computers, can be used by high school students. As a result, the company's involvement with the public schools has increased considerably.

The Seventh Corporate Objective and the People Link

Good citizenship is one of Hewlett-Packard's seven stated corporate objectives. It requires that the "corporation be an economic, intellectual and social asset to each nation and each community in which it operates."[29] This strong sense of social responsibility accounts for the $65 million in cash and equipment donated by Hewlett-Packard during 1986, but this kind of giving is only one expression of the company's involvement. What John Young, President and Chief Executive Officer

(CEO), has nurtured and encouraged most is the *people link*. Teresa Roche, Educational Relations Manager, puts it this way: "We have tried to create a network of champions."[30]

This network includes individual employees, who are empowered to participate in their communities in ways that are locally determined. Support comes from the top, and participation in regional, state, and national groups is also common. But much of the activity is idiosyncratic and responds to local needs.

Peninsula Academies

In 1979, the Stanford Mid-Peninsula Urban Coalition (a community service agency funded by private foundations, businesses, and individuals) identified a group largely alienated from Silicon Valley's growing electronics industry: minority youths. Research showed that 15,000 jobs were open in the area, but that few minority youths were qualified for even semiskilled, entry-level openings.

To address this mismatch, in 1980 the Urban Coalition and the Superintendent of the Sequoia Union High School District in Redwood City-Menlo Park decided to involve the private sector. The Coalition's staff introduced educators to key business leaders, many of them CEOs. From the very beginning, top company leaders were included because they were in a position to commit the resources of their organizations and to attract money from private foundations. This select group agreed to start a program whose objectives were to reduce the high dropout rate among high school students, to help decrease youth and minority unemployment, and to reduce the number of unfilled entry-level jobs in local companies.

The industry leaders spread the word to their peers to provide additional support to the program. This task was made easier by a promotional videotape, "The Peninsula Academies: Contributing to Success," which was created by Hewlett-Packard.

As industry support was developing, a planning committee of top leaders from the school district and participating companies was formed. After defining the program, they turned implementation responsibilities over to a program director hired by the Coalition and paid by foundation gifts. A steering committee comprising principals, teachers, Coalition staff, and middle managers was organized to assist the director. Steering committee task forces also included representatives from the schools and local companies. Care was taken to involve industry people at all levels of policy and decision making.

To deliver a quality program and to best reach the youth at risk, the planning committee created two mini schools within existing high schools: the Electronics Academy to teach electronics test and assembly skills and the Computer Academy to teach computer operation and programming skills. Students were admitted to the program in the tenth grade.

In each academy, a core academic program of English, science, and mathematics was taught by specially selected teachers from the district. The drawing cards for the programs were the electronics and computer laboratories, which had been outfitted with equipment donated by industry. Hewlett-Packard contributed most of the equipment for the computer lab, including 10 personal computers and associated printers, plotters, disc drives, software, and training manuals.

To reinforce the link between classwork and the skills needed on the job, corporate employees were loaned to the schools to serve as instructors and to provide vital information to teachers and students. Industry people were also called on to be guest speakers in classrooms, arrange field trips to area manufacturing facilities, counsel school guidance personnel, help students in job searches, and serve as mentors. The mentoring program matched a volunteer from industry with each eleventh-grade student in the academy. These mentors served as role models and provided personal encouragement; they helped the students to believe that they could comprehend and apply complex technology.

The Academies program guaranteed students a summer job once they completed the eleventh grade, providing they met program requirements. In addition, they were offered jobs in the last semester of their senior year to ease the transition into the working world.

The American Institute for Research in the Behavioral Sciences reviewed the performance of the Peninsula Academies program from 1980 to 1983. Data on attendance, proficiency test scores, pass rates, grades, and attrition rates were collected for Academy students and for a comparison group of non-Academy students who had similar characteristics and who were enrolled in the Sequoia Union High School District. The findings indicated that Academy students missed fewer days of school than the non-Academy students and that their mean proficiency scores in written English, reading, and mathematics were also consistently higher. A very significant finding was that only 1 percent of Academy tenth-grade students dropped out of school in the year under scrutiny. Moreover, the instructors and parents reported that students had an improved self-image and a more positive attitude toward school after participating in the program.

As a result of this positive evaluation, the Academies concept has been replicated in eight sites. Hewlett-Packard participates in the three academies in the Bay Area, and a local employee is designated as the company's liaison to each school. The company continues to support the Academies concept because it works. Over time, the Academies have served the underserved and educated the hard-to-reach. Employees who have worked with these students have been richly rewarded for their activities in terms of both personal satisfaction and recognition from the company.

Institute of Computer Technology

The Institute of Computer Technology, located in Sunnyvale, California, has a different target audience. It seeks to interest high-achieving students in a career in engineering and computer design.

The program is conducted after regular school hours, and more than 1,000 students from third graders to high school seniors have participated. A director, an engineer, and an administrative support person were loaned from two companies, Hewlett-Packard and International Business Machines, to get the program started. Those companies also loaned management and administrative personnel to support the Institute, while part-time instructors were provided by more than 20 area companies, along with computer equipment worth more than $650,000.

Equipment Donations

Hewlett-Packard has donated equipment to schools throughout California through a number of different programs. During the 1983–1984 school year, 64 schools received Hewlett-Packard equipment worth $3.6 million. In addition to providing enough equipment for whole classrooms, the company trained teachers to make the most effective use of the machines. This staff development program included all-day meetings at company facilities and resulted in the creation of a curriculum guide to help teachers design computer programs to fit various subjects and teaching styles.

Another popular program enables company employees to provide equipment to the schools of their choice at a significantly reduced cost. Hewlett-Packard pays 75 percent of the list price (up to $20,000) of any piece of equipment, and the employee pays the remaining 25 percent. Because the corporation places no stipulations on the kind of educational institution chosen, public and private elementary, junior high, and senior high schools have benefited from this incentive plan.

Industry Initiatives for Science and Math Education

In 1985, 14 Bay Area companies, including Hewlett-Packard, launched the pilot program of the Industry Initiatives for Science and Math Education (IISME). The program's goals are to improve the quality of science and mathematics teachers, curricula, and tools, and consequently to raise the quality of education delivered to students and increase student motivation to study these subjects.

IISME brings high school teachers into industry during the summer to increase their knowledge of emerging technologies. Each of these Industry Fellows receives a weekly salary of $600 from participating employers. To facilitate the transfer of their summer work experience into classroom practices, Industry Fellows are assisted by professors at the Lawrence Hall of Science of the University of California at Berkeley. In addition, company mentors guide teachers in their work assignments and assist them in developing classroom applications. The long-range goal is to employ 25,000 American science and mathematics teachers nationwide each summer so that they will be better able to teach the 3.75 million students they meet when the school year begins.[31]

Purpose of Evaluations

The evaluations of the Peninsula Academies and IISME programs have provided Hewlett-Packard with important accountability data. The very positive results have helped to stimulate additional corporate involvement, while heightening the interest and commitment of business leaders who have participated from the beginning. Although it is often difficult to quantify the results of company involvement with the public schools, Hewlett-Packard supports evaluation as a way to determine its continued corporate presence in education partnerships.

Hewlett-Packard's involvement with the public schools is driven by the company's need for a technologically literate society and its desire to be a responsible corporate citizen.

THE NEW YORK CITY PARTNERSHIP

The New York City Partnership was formed in 1979 in the wake of the city's fiscal crisis. The immediate civic circumstances were clear, dramatic, and threatening; the response captured the spirit of cooperation in a real crisis. The Partnership was formed under the leadership of David Rockefeller for the purpose of bringing the private and public sectors together in the interest of "making New York City a better place in which to live, to work, and to conduct business."[32] Since its inception, the Partnership has directed its attention to such diverse areas as economic development, housing, public safety, transportation, youth employment, and education.

The New York City Context

New York's population has become poorer, older, and more heterogeneous than it was in the 1970s. The proportion of immigrants is the highest it has been in seventy-five years; one in four New York residents was not born in the United States.

Minorities make up the enrollment majority in public schools. Currently, 71 percent of the student population is black and Hispanic, and projections suggest that this proportion will increase. In the past, the public schools had a strong and vocal natural constituency, but they no longer do. The number of families with school-aged children has fallen, and this has taken a toll on parent and community involvement.

At a time when unemployment among New York City youth is higher than the national average, employers report that clerical, messenger, telemarketing, receptionist, secretarial, mailroom, and fast-food jobs remain unfilled.[33]

The Schools

In many ways, the New York City public school system reflects all that is New York. Within it, one can find the extremes of success and failure; it is enormous in size and has an infinite variety of clients; it encompasses the meanness of poverty and the promise of plenty.

As of 1985, the system employed 101,402 individuals, 58,672 of them teachers, to educate 931,768 students, at an approximate cost of $4.3 billion.[34] Although the high schools remain under the direct jurisdiction of the central Board of Education, the Decentralization Law of 1969 created 32 independent community school districts to serve the kindergarten through middle school population. Each district has its own school board elected by registered voters. This board hires the superintendent, principals, and all supervisory personnel for the district. As originally designed, the teacher pool from which staff would be hired by each district was to be governed by the Board of Education, but because of severe teacher shortages in 1984, districts were given the option of recruiting their own teachers, a practice that still occurs.

"The Mayor's Management Report" cites that for grades 2 to 9, 52.9 percent of pupils have been at or above grade level in reading scores since 1979, when only 40 percent read as well as other children in the United States at the same grade level.[35] However, the percentages change when grade-specific and district-specific results are examined.

Employability

Only about 23.1 percent of New York City's teen-agers are in the labor force, less than half the percentage in the rest of the country (47 percent as reported in the 1980 Census).[36] In 1982, the effective unemployment rate for young people between the ages of 16 and 21 was 40 percent (including those not in the labor force but available for work), and the rate for young blacks and Hispanics was considerably higher.

The financial costs associated with youth unemployment have been calculated,[37] but the personal costs in terms of quality of life cannot be. The direct costs to society include loss of goods and services that would have been produced by these people and tax revenues that their employment would have generated. New York City spends $62 million a year in direct public assistance benefits for these unemployed youths, not including federal- and state-funded benefits.

Employment during the summer months is a critical experience for at-risk New York teen-agers. Since 1981, the New York City Partnership's Youth Policy Group has helped to coordinate the provision of approximately 100,000 summer jobs to youth. Anecdotal reports have described the many benefits to both the businesses and the students.

The Partnership's Education Program:
A Cooperative Structure

The Partnership's initiatives on behalf of the schools are guided by its Education Committee. This Committee's goals and objectives are "to develop and express a shared definition of what constitutes a successful public school system, how that success can be achieved and transmitted throughout all schools in the system, and how that success will enable all the city's children to participate in and contribute to the social well being and economic future of the city."[38]

The Education Committee is composed of corporate CEOs, the New York City Schools' Chancellor, high-ranking university administrators, a representative from a significant community-based organization, and a chief officer of the teachers' union. These individuals are chosen to reflect all the groups in the city most interested in and concerned with educating young people. Corporate members of the Partnership's Board of Directors were approached to join this Committee, either because the profile of their corporations reflected educational interest or because they were personally interested in education.

To facilitate the activities of the Education Committee, two additional committees were created for the exchange of ideas among the city's various constituencies. In turn, these committees, the Policy Task Force and the Management Task Force, provide appropriate information to the Education Committee.

At the same time that these groups were established, the Board of Education created an office to coordinate activities relating to public sector/private sector interaction. In this way, oversight for the activities became a shared effort, with input provided by both the private sector, through the New York City Partnership, and the school system, through its central administration.

Given the enormity of both the problems and the potential in New York City, the Partnership has addressed itself to understanding and working toward the improvement of the schools by acting as a linking organization. It has sought to involve the private sector in the public schools through a series of programmatic interactions coordinated under the Join-A-School umbrella.

The History of Join-A-School

Join-A-School was born in 1982 as the result of a chance meeting between the city schools' Chancellor, Frank Macchiarola, now president of the New York City Partnership, and former Secretary of Health, Education, and Welfare, Joseph Califano, on a shuttle flight from Washington, D.C., to New York. At the time, Mr. Califano was writing a report on substance abuse in New York State. He believed that the private sector should be involved in any effort at reducing drug abuse among high school youths, and he proposed that this involvement be modeled on a program already operating in some cities, Adopt-A-School. Although Mr. Macchiarola rejected that name because of its paternalistic connotations, he believed that the idea had merit. He proposed the name Join-A-School to promote the notion of equality and mutuality.

Mr. Califano personally recruited the heads of Manufacturers Hanover Trust Company, American Can Company, and The Equitable Life Assurance Society to initiate the program with Mr. Macchiarola.[39]

The support of these influential CEOs was critical to the design and implementation of the program. The trust that existed among these leaders created an atmosphere ripe for experimentation and coalition building. In New York, institutions are large and bureaucratically burdened, and individualism and diversity are more the rule than the exception. Thus, the development of a collaborative effort that required the *personal* commitment of the participants was needed, and that is what emerged.

The Achievements of Join-A-School:
Everyone Benefits

The Join-A-School program has given the business community a firsthand look at what really goes on in the public schools. It has provided necessary visibility for New York City students who rarely reach the attention of the employing community. It has enabled the private sector to communicate important information to the schools about what students need to succeed in the workplace. These programs have brought school personnel into the workplace and businesspeople into the schools, thereby increasing communication between otherwise isolated groups and broadening the knowledge base upon which both sectors operate.

Teachers. Join-A-School links schools to external resources through pairings with businesses. For some members of the city's teaching force, the knowledge that others share their concern and involvement with the city's students has been a source of motivation and support. This is illustrated by a pairing that has existed since the beginning of the program: that between The Equitable Life Assurance Society and W.C. Bryant High School in Queens.

One of the most beneficial activities coordinated through this partnership has been the involvement of a third organization, the Foreign Policy Association, in the life of this high school. This nonprofit association aims to inform the American public on significant issues. Through a grant from The Equitable, the Association has been providing an American history teacher at Bryant with up-to-the-minute materials to use in classes. Amon Diggs, the teacher, reports that his classes have been invited to attend the Association's Public Forum Program. The students are thus able to listen to important speakers and even meet some dignitaries. Mr. Diggs points out that because most of these young people do not come from homes where this kind of activity would ever be commonplace, this experience is equally as important as listening to what the speakers have to say. The classroom activities that precede and follow each visit help to make the trips meaningful parts of the curriculum.

In a profession that offers few rewards, the involvement with the Foreign Policy Association has served to make this teacher feel special. He has been invited to attend dinner functions, where he has met and talked with people knowledgeable about foreign policy issues. This has provided for professional growth of the best kind, which could not have been gained by taking another university course. His involvement has "enriched and invigorated him."[40]

Principals. Join-A-School has given principals the opportunity to share management questions with private-sector managers, as well as to make maximum use of their corporate partners' resources of time, personnel, and some funding to improve their schools. A series of interviews with high school principals indicated some very positive outcomes associated with the program.[41] There was clear unanimity among the principals that the school/business collaboration was both a source of pride and a reflection of their own efforts and desires. Their involvement in the program stemmed from their belief that the business community could serve as a resource to the schools by providing both material donations and business expertise. The principals also spoke of the significance of bringing the real world to both students and faculty members, who are often isolated within the school environment.

The brokering role played by the New York City Partnership and the Join-A-School office of the Board of Education pairs the schools with appropriate corporate partners. But once the marriage is made, the principals develop their own relationships with their business partners. The activities thus reflect the needs of each school and the available resources of the business with which it is joined.

A Move toward Policy Involvement

Fifty-one high schools are currently joined to forty-eight New York City institutions, mostly to businesses but also to some universities and other nonprofit agencies. This programmatic involvement has been important not only because of the direct effects it has had on students, teachers, principals, and corporate participants, but also because it has developed a foundation of information for the corporate community about the schools and the people in them. Such a foundation is necessary if business is to move in the direction of policy initiatives. Policy initiatives are important because high dropout rates—about 40 percent in New York[42]—and high school students with weak basic skills are symptoms of systemic problems, whose solution requires extraordinary capabilities from very skillful, specially trained people. Those people need support to do their work well.

Programmatic involvement was the focus of the first phase of activities supported by the New York City Partnership. However, new leadership is taking these activities in a new direction. In October 1985, William Woodside, then Chairman and CEO of American Can Corporation, became Chairman of the Education Committee. Given Mr. Woodside's strong conviction that the business community has a definite, even critical role to play in the support of public education, the focus of Partnership efforts is shifting toward a greater policy role.

Several task forces have been created by the Education Committee for the purpose of marshaling the resources and expertise of the private sector to assist the public school system in its own improvement. A policy task force was created to promote greater public support for public education on the city, state, and federal levels. Further, in a cooperative effort with public school officials for these activities, individuals from the private sector will be called on to provide assistance in several noninstructional areas, such as elementary school security, facilities management, food services, and the computerization of student data. In addition, given its vast experience in the area of human resource development, the private sector may soon provide help in improving the quality of employment for teachers and school personnel.

In an era of reform and change, the New York City Partnership is in a unique position to help define the direction of education in New York City. Although the educational needs of the city are formidable, the resources and talents of those who live and work in it are equally vast. The Partnership will not waste this opportunity.

JOINT COUNCIL ON ECONOMIC EDUCATION

In some places, the rush to reform education has actually increased the number of districts finding themselves with staffs inadequately trained to teach what is being mandated. Much has been written about the present and predicted shortfalls among mathematics and science teachers, but less attention has been given to the insufficient number of economics teachers in K–12 classrooms. Given the present state of precollegiate economic education, this future insufficiency could be severe. In a 1985 study of elementary school teachers, Walstad and Watts discovered that about half had had no course work in economics and that another 25 percent had taken only one course. Secondary school social studies teachers who specialized in teaching courses or units in economics were sometimes no better prepared; 15 percent reported no course work, 25 percent had taken only one course, and 30 percent had taken two courses.[43]

Today, 27 states require that students receive some form of instruction in economics. At a time when efforts are being made to upgrade teacher education and tighten licensing requirements across-the-board, will it also be possible to address the problem of a teaching corps that has historically been undereducated in economics?

A Creative Answer

The Joint Council on Economic Education was created in 1949 by the Committee for Economic Development (and in 1955 was joined by the American Economic Association) to increase the quantity and enhance the quality of economic education throughout the country. Given the diversity of local educational needs, a decision was made to establish a decentralized network of State Councils that would receive technical assistance and some financing from and be coordinated by the national organization. Local affiliates pay no dues or fees to the Joint Council. A Board of Trustees was created to oversee the efforts of the Joint Council and its member groups. In a parallel effort, each State Council selected a Board whose membership was to reflect all sectors of the state economy.

The purpose of economic education is clearly defined in a Joint Council publication: "[The strength of the American system depends upon] approaching economics as a discipline, not as a form of indoctrination. Economic education is not rote learning of abstract rules any more than it is advocacy. The goal is understanding how the economic system works and developing the capacity to make informed choices."[44]

How the Joint Council Works

The 50 State Councils are made up of leaders from local colleges and universities; the state departments of education; business, labor, and agriculture; trade associations, and chambers of commerce. This broad cross section is intentional. All the represented groups will be affected by the future direction of economic education and therefore have been included to participate in its development. Michael MacDowell, President of the Joint Council, believes that the involvement of the total community is a prerequisite for helping young people to understand this country's economic system, and that without this understanding the country cannot prosper.

The State Councils have joined with more than 275 universities and colleges to create Centers for Economic Education. Faculties at these Centers include professors of education and economics, who work together to design appropriate, accurate, state-of-the-art preservice and in-service courses for teachers, using Joint Council materials, which include over one hundred print items, four film series, and microcomputer modules. This collaboration between education and economics departments has been critical to the creation of relevant and timely courses. The Centers are also involved in the development of curricula that can be used to facilitate teaching and learning in classrooms.

Teacher Training

The Joint Council believes that, in the final analysis, the teacher is the most important gatekeeper in economic education.[45] Given this philosophy, it has launched a two-pronged effort to encourage classroom teachers to update their skills in economics. The first prong is summer institutes offered at the Centers to provide teachers with sufficient training time. Many of these courses are financed by local businesses or through the Joint Council, thereby eliminating the need for teachers to make substantial cash outlays for graduate education. The second, more far-reaching, prong is the Developmental Economic Education Program (DEEP).

The Program assists school districts in improving their economic education curricula. Districts that affiliate with DEEP make a commitment to use quality educational materials at strategic points in their curricula and to participate in teacher-training and evaluation programs. Participation in DEEP is free, but the district must provide a teacher to serve as DEEP coordinator, who works directly with the local Center for Economic Education. These teachers are awarded fellowships to attend DEEP leadership training workshops, where they are instructed by outstanding economic educators in the most current techniques and procedures for making school children literate in economics. After training, these teachers fan out to local schools and, with their State Councils and local Centers, help spread the word.

In 1986, 1,057 school districts in 47 states were formally affiliated with a State Council and were actively participating in DEEP. They enroll 12.7 million students—about 32 percent of all students in the country; an additional 1,349 school systems had informal working relationships with the Joint Council's network. Considering that DEEP began in 1965 with 20 school systems, its growth has been enormous.

School systems participating in DEEP are provided with materials designed to improve their economic education programs. However, these materials are adapted to suit the needs of the local school systems. Recent research reported that students in DEEP schools outperformed their counterparts in non-DEEP schools by two grades on nationally normed tests of economic understanding. This finding motivated the Joint Council to inaugurate a major expansion of DEEP, which it hopes will provide economic education to 70 percent of K–12 students by the end of the decade.

Role of the Private Sector

The private sector has a clearly defined role to play in the improvement of economic education. Its representatives serve on State Councils, where they offer their practical knowledge and expertise directly. In some instances, they also serve as advisors, teacher trainers, classroom speakers, and field trip liaisons, bringing the real world into schools.

The State Councils and the Joint Council provide private-sector individuals an opportunity to participate with their schools in defined and structured ways. For interested businesspeople, this eliminates some of the difficulty in beginning a relationship with a school. Council activities also enable private-sector people to choose between working with a school on a one-to-one basis and working in conjunction with other business representatives. Over time, participation in State or Joint Council programs helps the private sector to determine an appropriate role for itself that will be beneficial to all.

A Clear Direction

The Joint Council believes that economic instruction needs to be integrated with other subjects and offered to students from the time they enter elementary school. To expand its DEEP program, it will need approximately $7 million to cover anticipated costs through the end of the decade. The merger in 1985 of the Joint Council with the National Center of Economic Education for Children has created an expanded materials and resource base and increased the Council's ability to achieve its goals.

NOTES

1. P. M. Timpane, "Business Has Rediscovered the Public Schools," *Phi Delta Kappan*, 65(6), 1984, 389.
2. P. E. Barton, *Partnerships between Corporations and Schools*, Washington, DC: National Commission for Employment Policy, RR–83–29, 1983.
3. J. W. Hillesheim and G. D. Merrill, eds., *Theory and Practice in the History of American Education*, Pacific Palisades, CA: Goodyear Publishing Co. Inc., 1971.
4. Committee for Economic Development, *Investing in Our Children: Business and the Public Schools*, Washington, DC: Committee for Economic Development, 1985.
5. R. Trachtman, *School/Business Collaborations: A Study of the Process and Product*, University Microfilms, Inc., 1985; and L. Miller, "Organizational and Political Dimensions of Private Sector/Public School Interaction: Focus on Urban Schools." Unpublished paper, New York: Teachers College, Columbia University, 1984.
6. R. E. Bucknam and S. G. Brand, "A Meta-Analysis of Experience Based Career Education," *Educational Leadership*, 40(6), 1983, 66–71.
7. W. W. Wilms, "Vocational Education and Job Success: The Employer's View," *Phi Delta Kappan*, 65(5), 1984, 347–350.
8. W. W. Wirtz, *The Boundless Resource: A Perspective for an Education/Work Policy*, Washington, D.C.: New Republic Book Co., 1975, p. 170.
9. G. Gold, "Public Education and the Private Sector," *Education Leadership*, 40(2), 1982, 4.
10. P. M. Timpane, *Corporations and Public Education in the Cities*, New York: Teachers College, Columbia University, 1982.
11. S. Sullivan, "Youth Employment," in *Meeting Human Needs*, Washington, DC: American Enterprise Institute, 1982.
12. Ibid., pp. 215–257.
13. Hudson Institute, *School-to-Work Transition Programs: A Policy Analysis*, prepared for Jobs for America's Graduates, Inc., January 1984.
14. M. Levine, "Committee for Economic Development: Selected Survey Results," New York: Committee for Economic Development, 1984.
15. Jobs for America's Graduates, *Five Year Research Report*, 1985.
16. Education Commission of the States, *Reconnecting Youth: The Next Stage of Reform*, A Report from the Business Advisory Committee, October 1985.
17. "JAG Launches a New Course after Five Years of Success," *Crossroads*, 1(4), 1985, 1,3.
18. N. Eurich, *Corporate Classrooms*, New York: Carnegie Foundation for the Advancement of Teaching, 1985.
19. F. Rosenau, "Beyond Philanthropy," *Educational Leadership*, 40(2), 1982, 5–7.
20. Personal interview conducted by R. Trachtman, Winter 1986.
21. Personal interview conducted by R. Trachtman with Robert Carlson, Winter 1986.

22. Personal interview conducted by R. Trachtman, Winter 1986.
23. Personal interview conducted by R. Trachtman with Robert Carlson, Winter 1986.
24. Aetna Life & Casualty Foundation, Inc., *Contemporary Issues in Public Education and Opportunities for Cooperative Initiatives*, Hartford, CT: Aetna Life & Casualty, Inc., 1985.
25. Aetna Life & Casualty, *Aetna Institute for Corporate Education*, Aetna Life & Casualty Foundation, Inc., n.d.
26. Personal interview conducted by R. Trachtman with Pamela Bartlett, 1985.
27. W. E. Cross, Jr., and L. Wallace, Jr., *The Saturday Academy: The First Year*, Hartford, CT: Aetna Life and Casualty, 1985.
28. Personal interview conducted by R. Trachtman with David Rippey, 1985.
29. Telephone interview conducted by R. Trachtman with Teresa Roche, Educational Relations Manager for Hewlett-Packard, 1986.
30. Ibid.
31. *A Proposal to Provide Continued Growth of Industry Initiatives for Science and Math Education*, submitted by the Industry Advisory Board of the Industry Initiatives for Science and Math Education Program in coordination with Lawrence Hall of Science, Berkeley, California, October 1985, photocopied.
32. The New York City Partnership, *The Partnership*, New York: New York City Partnership, Inc., undated.
33. Interface, *Youth Unemployment in New York City: The Cost of Doing Nothing*, New York: Interface, 1983.
34. New York City Board of Education, *The Chancellor's Report Card*, New York, 1985.
35. Office of the Mayor of New York City, "The Mayor's Management Report," February 1985.
36. *Dropouts from New York City Public Schools: 1982–1983*, New York City Board of Education, 1983.
37. Interface, *Youth Unemployment*.
38. Original Partnership mission statement.
39. R. A. Lacey, *Becoming Partners: How Schools and Companies Meet Mutual Needs*, Washington, DC: National Commission for Employment Policy Research Report Series, RR–83–33, 1983.
40. Personal interview conducted by R. Trachtman with Amon Diggs, June 1985.
41. *Join-A-School* interviews conducted by M. Levine and R. Trachtman during the spring of 1985.
42. New York City Board of Education, *The Chancellor's Report Card*, New York, 1985.
43. W. Walstad and M. Watts, "Teaching Economics in the Schools: A Review of Survey Findings," *Journal of Economic Education*, Spring 1985, 139.
44. M. L. Frank, *The History of the Joint Council on Economic Education* (Third Ed.), New York: Joint Council on Economic Education, 1984.
45. Ibid.

10 The Policy Arena

ROBERTA TRACHTMAN
City University of New York

Taking a historical view of policy involvement in public schools, it must be noted that the early years of corporate activity consisted largely of participation on local school boards, with representatives of local business acting in what were clearly policy-making roles. The withdrawal of business from participation on these local boards can be traced to the late 1960s and 1970s, when the issues with which boards were dealing changed from the traditional considerations of curriculum, costs, and keeping up with burgeoning school populations to the far more contentious issues related to equity, school closings, and civil rights. It was also a time in which school boards became both the site of fierce battles among various community groups and springboards for local politicians or those with political aspirations. Serving on school boards meant dealing with politically volatile issues and often demanded enormous outlays of time and considerable personal commitment. Business generally did not want to play this role and hence withdrew. (See Timpane, 1982, for a discussion of this period of involvement.)

It was not until the early 1980s that there was a renewal of activity on the part of business. (One important exception has been the continuous participation of companies in vocational, cooperative, and career education.) Much of that activity has been either through funding of programs or, more important, the development of various kinds of programmatic involvement.

Through participation in the public policy arena on behalf of the public schools, business has the opportunity to play a powerful role in ensuring quality education. The case, "A Tale of Two States: The Business Community and Education Reform in California and Minnesota," provides a detailed picture of what happens when business makes a commitment to such participation. In both states, the story is far from over, and neither the benefits nor the costs are clearly known yet. These two cases are meant to be instructive rather than models for others to follow. This chapter includes two other examples of such policy-oriented participation: one in the state of Washington, and one in Philadelphia. They represent alternative ways in which business has organized itself to have some impact on state or local education policy.

William Woodside, retired Chairman of the Primerica Corporation (formerly American Can Company), is an outspoken advocate for more business involvement at this level. His own company has had a long, successful involvement in New York City's Join-A-School program, and the American Can Foundation has supported a number of education programs aimed at systemic reform in public schools. One such effort is a pilot project with the American Federation of Teachers and focuses on recruiting liberal arts college students into teaching and supporting their professional development through internships and mentor programs. That project will be developed in a number of cities in collaboration with local colleges and universities.

It is not clear that the business community can and will sustain its level of active participation in education policy issues at the local, state, and national level. The business community's participation may, in large part, depend on the ability of the education community to uphold its half of the partnership. To do this, the various interests in the education sector will have to commit themselves to working collaboratively.

THE BOEING COMPANY, THE WASHINGTON ROUNDTABLE, AND STATEWIDE REFORM

Because the Boeing Company is a major employer in the state of Washington, its commitment to quality education is a reflection of its business needs as well as its understanding of the critical importance of education to the health and welfare of every community. In a summary report issued by the Washington Roundtable in 1985, T. A. Wilson, the company's Chairman and Chief Executive Officer (CEO), remarked: "We need a superior education system both to develop and to attract the skilled work force that will assure our state's continued prosperity. The talented people we try to attract want the best for their children, and a good education system is one of the significant factors in their decisions about where to live."[1]

A Tradition in Involvement
and Change in Direction

The Boeing Company has long been interested in education. It has traditionally supported colleges and universities through scholarship programs, direct grants and endowments, donations of equipment, and an industrial affiliates program. However, with the renewed national interest in public school education sparked by the publication of *A Nation at Risk*,[2] the breadth and depth of Boeing's involvement changed considerably. In 1984, with the creation of its first corporate Management Advisory Committee on Education, the leadership of the Boeing Company clearly proclaimed its concern for the state of K–12 education and announced that the time had come for Boeing (and others in the private sector) to participate in the reform of the public schools.

To accommodate this new direction, the Committee designed and implemented a formal program of precollegiate education assistance. In order to allow for these efforts, it was first necessary to revise some corporate policies and practices that had long governed Boeing's interactions in education: To stimulate awareness and to gain a better understanding of those who work in K–12 schools, a corporate policy was changed to allow for company membership and participation in educational organizations and associations; to provide limited funding for some precollegiate programs, Boeing had to change its company contributions regulations; and to encourage employee voluntarism, a new policy provided leave with pay for participation in certain school activities.

These changes *allowed* for new relationships, but did not *guarantee* them. Thus, to facilitate their development, an Education Manager at each Boeing facility was identified as the corporation's local representative to the schools. This identification process underscored senior management's commitment to these new efforts and provided for greater accountability. With one individual at each site given this charge, the Advisory Committee would be better able to monitor the progress of the diverse community programs.

To spread the word, formal presentations were made to managers at all levels, describing the realigned emphasis on education and encouraging their promotion of public/private relationships. *The Boeing News*, an in-house publication, was asked to provide articles describing the company's support of education voluntarism and the general state of education in Washington. A nationwide education hot line for employees needing information on Boeing education support made access to information easy and fast.

The Boeing Involvement in Washington

Boeing's activities in the state of Washington are varied. Some are targeted at teachers, some at students. Some are undertaken unilaterally; others are part of joint private-sector efforts. Much of Boeing's activity is in response to locally determined needs. Local managers are encouraged to define their programs with school leaders. Carver C. Gayton, Manager of Educational Relations and Training, explains that Boeing is not interested in telling teachers what to do. Instead, he believes that the participation of Boeing employees in school activities will reinforce the interdependence of the business and education sectors of the state.

For Students. Boeing has produced brief videotapes on entry-level careers for use as counseling tools in the high schools. The company discovered that relatively few guidance personnel are available to assist students with career selection (the ratio of guidance staff to students is approximately 1 to 400). Consequently, it created these films to fill in some of the critical missing information students sorely need. They offer up-to-date data on various career options, required skills, necessary high school courses and follow-up education, salary expectations, and career growth potential.

A "Computer for Kids Contest" is held for fifth-grade classes in five different school districts; personal computers are awarded as prizes to the winning classes.

The company offers internships to qualified high school students.

For Teachers. Boeing participates in Technology in Education (TIE), a collaborative venture by schools, industry, and colleges and universities to upgrade the skills of current mathematics and science teachers and to increase the pool of qualified applicants.

Teachers are given access to the company's management and skill-training courses. Boeing employees serve as instructors in vocational classes.

The corporation funds a mini grant program for teachers to support innovative classroom projects. Teachers are nominated by students, parents, administrators, or their peers. A citizens' group comprising primarily businesspeople provides oversight for this program and is responsible for making the final selections.

For Programs. The company donates equipment, material, and some funds to support other activities and programs in the Washington public schools. Boeing employees serve as classroom speakers and offer career-day presentations throughout the state.

Boeing is an important participant in Private Initiatives in Public Education (PIPE) and LINK, two public/private collaborations created to pool the resources of Washington's business and education communities.

The Business Roundtable and Its Recommendations: Another Aspect of Boeing's Involvement

The participation of Boeing's CEO in the Washington Roundtable has been critical to the success of this business group. Mr. Wilson headed the Education Committee of the Washington Roundtable from 1983 to 1984 and served as the Roundtable's Chairman from 1984 to 1985. His decision to serve in these capacities was deliberate: Because of his position as CEO of one of the two most significant corporations in the state (the other is Weyerhauser), his participation was essential to the success of a business group that hoped to effect statewide education reform.

In 1983, the Washington Roundtable funded a major study of education. The membership of the Roundtable (thirty-two corporate leaders and two citizens-at-large) also funded a full-time loaned executive director to provide general oversight for the study. In addition, other private-sector executives were asked to participate in the study of single issues. When the Roundtable's recommendations were made known to the state's legislative leaders, it was clear that the private sector had identified discrete areas of need. The Roundtable concluded that a reallocation of money in the state education budget would make the implementation of its recommendations possible.

As of March 1986, five of the Roundtable's major recommendations had been passed by the legislature.[3] The highest-priority recommendation, the implementation of a preschool program for at-risk children, received strong support from Governor Gardner and is now law throughout the state. The legislature earmarked $3 million to implement a pilot program.

As a result of the Roundtable's findings, a special legislative subcommittee has been created to look at the question of career ladders for teachers. The Roundtable's study raised serious concern about inequities in the salaries offered to teachers at the middle of their careers. It questioned the national rush to increase *starting* salaries, while ignoring the compensation offered to teachers later in their careers. The Roundtable issued this finding after comparing teacher salaries with those of professional workers in industry who had similar education and experience. The comparison showed that after approximately 15 years of service, teacher salaries reach a plateau, whereas industry salaries continue to rise.

The Roundtable recommended that a statewide tenth-grade test be added to the existing fourth- and eighth-grade tests to improve the evaluation of student progress and needs. In March 1986, the state legislature voted to implement this recommendation.

The Roundtable found that too much nonproductive ("off task") time was being spent in classrooms throughout the state. Its recommendation that this deficiency could be remedied through staff-training workshops for all state educators was approved during the 1986 legislative session, and the State Education Department began devising an appropriate training program.

The recommendation concerning school financing was of great significance. In 1976, Washington had instituted a local levy "phase-down law," which required that by 1990 the state government would finance education almost exclusively, with localities being allowed to provide only up to 10 percent of the education budget. As a result of its study, the Roundtable membership concluded that this plan could damage important programs. It suggested that the mandatory phase-down in local levies should be frozen for two years, during which time a committee representing all sectors of the state could study the potential ramifications. This recommendation, too, has been made law.

Like other private-sector state groups, "the Washington Roundtable exists to apply the knowledge, creativity and leadership resources of its members and their business organizations to the most serious challenges facing the state of Washington."[4] The members have turned their education agenda toward a study of higher education in the state, but they continue to press for implementation of the programs and policies suggested in their first set of recommendations.

The Future Is Now

Support of K–12 education will continue to be a Boeing priority. Through its employees, who are also parents and community members, the company intends to assist the state of Washington in its pursuit of excellence in education.

THE PHILADELPHIA STORY

In 1982, Dr. Constance Clayton became Superintendent of the Philadelphia public schools. At the time of her appointment, the school system was faced with enormous problems and a limited number of prospects. The vast resources of the city were being largely ignored by a system struggling to maintain itself. School outreach efforts toward the private sector were few and unsystematic: The last major private initiative had occurred during the late 1950s, when the business community had become involved in selecting the members of the Board of Education. According to Richard DeLone, a critical observer of the Philadelphia scene and the senior consultant to a group of CEOs who now make up the Committee to Support the Philadelphia Public Schools (CSPPS), the business community had historically supported economic development and cultural activities but had not been involved in the public schools.

A Context for Change

Perhaps the climate was right. Perhaps the combination of the need for a better qualified work force and predictions that there would be fewer high school students sparked a renewal of interest, or perhaps it was the need to establish Philadelphia as a regional corporate headquarters that provided the motivation. Perhaps, instead, it should be traced to the appointment of Dr. Clayton, who saw a role for the private sector and invited its participation.

A civic umbrella organization called The Greater Philadelphia First Corporation created the CSPPS. Through the efforts of Sheldon Hackney, President of the University of Pennsylvania, and Ralph Saul, Chairman of CIGNA Corporation, the heads of major Philadelphia private-sector organizations agreed to serve as members and to contribute $50,000 a year to fund the CSPPS.

The Committee to Support
the Philadelphia Public Schools

Nine corporate CEOs, six college and university presidents, and two foundation presidents constitute the membership of this Committee, which is chaired by Mr. Saul. Conspicuously absent from the group is any public school representative. This was a deliberate omission and one that was supported by Dr. Clayton. According to Mr. DeLone, because the representation is completely private, CSPPS can act as a stronger lobbying group when searching for increased public school funding.

The Committee's mission is to "stimulate, coordinate, and focus private-sector assistance to the public schools."[5] The rationale for involvement is clear: (1) Public education is vital to the future economy and to the community's way of life; (2) the challenges facing the schools will not be met without broad community support; and (3) the private sector has expertise, resources, and prestige that can help make the difference.[6]

To facilitate the activities of the Committee and to make the best use of available resources, six task forces were established, each chaired by a participating corporate or university CEO, with representatives from the Committee's member organizations as well as nonmember institutions. This structure has helped CSPPS to accomplish its objectives because activities are more clearly defined and focused. The task forces are semiautonomous, which makes communication much less cumbersome. However, final policy decisions are not made independently by the members of a task force.

The six task forces focus on four priority issues: financial planning, management assistance, educational initiatives, and recognition of excellence. Furthermore, through its task forces, CSPPS sought to build a structure for stimulating and focusing assistance to the schools from a multitude of private-sector groups, not just the business community. Thus, the participation of foundations, cultural organizations, and institutions of higher learning was planned from the start. Those who created CSPPS intended to bring all the city's resources to bear in addressing the schools' needs. This outreach program was designed to include all who sought to participate. Since its inception, over 40 corporations, 15 higher education institutions, and 80 cultural organizations have participated in CSPPS programs.

The Task Forces:
Activities and Accomplishments

Financial Planning. Since its inception, the Task Force on Financial Resources, chaired by Edwin Tuttle of Pennwalt Corporation, has developed a five-year plan for the school district to provide for a balanced and stable budget through fiscal 1989. This plan was developed in close cooperation with officials of the school district. It supports many of Superintendent Clayton's educational initiatives, including desegregation, new testing programs, implementation of a standardized curriculum, development of promotion standards, remedial support for students failing to meet those standards, and computer education. It offers support for an expanded capital improvements program, modest salary increases for teachers, and increased spending on textbooks and educational materials. It has outlined procedures for saving the school district some $60 million through management efficiencies and controlled medical benefits costs.

In order to accomplish its objectives, the task force concluded that a modest local tax increase would be required. Tied to the Committee's support for this tax increase is the district's ability to realize financial savings through increased management efficiencies.

Management Assistance. In a report to The Greater Philadelphia First Corporation, CSPPS took the following position: "Fundamentally, the Committee believes the School District has dollars sufficient to the job. Effective management of those dollars is the critical issue. Since 85 percent of the School District's budget is people, improved human resource management is the top priority."[7]

To accomplish this goal, the Management Assistance Task Force's activities have been considerable.

- It provided oversight and guidance to a Hay Associates' study of the resource management needs of the school system.[8]
- It played an important role in developing a new procedure for the selection of principals, which has been adopted by the district. In a pilot project, it arranged for some principals to receive management training through CIGNA's Training Department. At the start of the 1986–1987 school year, the pilot was expanded to include management training at five CSPPS member companies—Sun Company, SmithKline Beckman Corporation, Rohm and Haas Corporation, ARCO Chemical Company, and CIGNA. The hope is that this project will be the foundation for a formal principals' management institute. Members of the Management Assistance Task Force are also developing an internship program for prospective principals.
- The Committee commissioned MSL, an executive search firm, to recruit an outstanding public administrator as a successor to Frederick Wookey, the Deputy Superintendent for Administration, who was on loan from Sun Company for one year.
- CSPPS helped the school district obtain the services of several other private-sector firms at reduced rates to review its legal department, its public relations activities, and its fringe benefits packages. Those and

other services have improved the cost-effectiveness of noninstructional programs.

Educational Initiatives. Additional task forces were assembled to promote educational initiatives in the humanities and the sciences, and to provide student employment as an incentive for academic achievement.

PATHS

The third task force initiated the Philadelphia Alliance for Teaching Humanities in the Schools (PATHS). This program was begun in the spring of 1984 to strengthen instruction in reading, writing, and the humanities. It was initially funded by, and continues to receive support from, the Rockefeller Foundation. PATHS also receives funds directly from the corporate community via The Greater Philadelphia First Corporation, and the balance is provided by the Pew Memorial Trust. Its original goal was to focus on the professional development of teachers as a way to improve humanities instruction in the classroom. This goal has been attained through a variety of approaches.

Building on initiatives that were already in place in a number of Philadelphia schools, the first PATHS program in 1984 was directed toward improving writing throughout the district. Practitioners and academics were brought together to determine the activities that would promote and improve writing for the youth of Philadelphia. The PATHS Writing Across the Curriculum project now involves over half of the public schools in the city.

The next major PATHS project will focus on the social studies curriculum. Like the writing project, this area was first proposed by Superintendent Clayton as one of her priorities.

In an effort to acquaint teachers and administrators with new techniques and approaches in teaching the humanities, series of one-day and year-long symposia are sponsored by PATHS and held at area colleges. In addition to offering educators a survey of new ideas, these symposia serve as forums for discussion and for the critical exchange of ideas.

The Summer Institutes were developed for Philadelphia teachers interested in participating in intensive, month-long programs of study. Participating teachers, called Institute Fellows, are encouraged to present their newly acquired knowledge to colleagues during the following school year.

The PATHS mini grant program supports projects to strengthen the humanities curriculum. Since its inception, it has offered two levels of awards: grants to individual teachers, which have a $300 maximum, and grants to groups, which are eligible to receive awards of up to $3,000.

MATHEMATICS AND SCIENCE INITIATIVES

A separate task force was created in the spring of 1985 to address problems associated with instruction in science and mathematics. Philadelphia Renaissance in Science and Mathematics (PRISM) was developed to strengthen these instructional areas; it is funded by a three-year $1.2 million grant from the Pew Memorial Trust and $300,000 pledged from Philadelphia area corporations.

PRISM has several major thrusts that require the collaboration of private-sector corporations, public school personnel, regional colleges and universities, and other organizations. Its major objectives are to introduce teaching of science in all elementary school classrooms, to enhance the professionalism of science and mathematics teachers, and to double the numbers of minority students taking advanced science and mathematics courses in high school.

To help accomplish these goals, the business community pledged funds for mini grants to teachers and for the establishment of two summer institutes, where teachers are able to refresh their mathematics fluency and gain greater insights into the sciences. In the fall of 1986, these teachers worked with university faculty on projects aimed at converting their summer experiences into useful teaching tools and methods. Further, interested teachers are able to secure summer internships in research and other professional positions in seven area companies with strong science or mathematics components. This internship serves to initiate a nine-month program that continues through the year in activities on college campuses, and culminates in the development of materials for use in classrooms.

The other thrust of this initiative will be the expansion of a ten-year-old partnership of schools, businesses, and universities, Philadelphia Regional Introduction for Minorities to Engineering (PRIME), which was created to enrich the mathematics and science program for secondary school minority students. In addition, a clearinghouse has been established to increase the use of corporate, museum, and community facilities in connection with the district's science and mathematics curricula.

EDUCATION FOR EMPLOYMENT

The most recent education initiative relates to both the high dropout rate in Philadelphia (reported by some to be 44 percent) and the need for a better-trained work force. As of 1986, the Task Force on Education for Employment was developing a program to provide summer and school-year employment for youths who met attendance and achievement standards. It proposed "The Two Percent Solution" to the problem of unemployment among high school students. The Private Industry Council took the lead role in marketing the plan to employers, who were asked to establish one part-time, work-study job for every fifty regular, full-time employees. The jobs were offered to students as an incentive for meeting basic skills and attendance requirements. As in the Boston Compact plan, positions were provided only for those students who were competent, and the development of these competencies was the responsibility of the public schools.

The task force also recommended a major reorganization of the vocational education program. It suggested the establishment of new programs that more clearly reflect the demands and requirements of area employers. It believed that these programs should be offered in satellite facilities rather than in the schools.

Recognition of Excellence. The private sector realizes that school personnel work in a world that offers few rewards or incentives for excellence. Consequently, the goal of the sixth task force, Schools on Parade/Celebration of Excellence, is to increase community awareness and support for the very outstanding people and programs in the public schools. Identified teachers receive awards and cash prizes and are honored at a dinner funded by CSPPS. Outstanding administrators, alumni, and friends of the public schools are also recognized and rewarded. During the past two years, $83,000 in cash has been awarded.

A Multifaceted, Carefully Considered Approach

A preliminary budget for the 1985–1986 school year indicated that about $1.75 million would be needed to support the CSPPS programs. It was anticipated that these revenues would be provided by foundation support, direct corporate contributions, and money supplied by The Greater Philadelphia First Corporation. The amount is certainly significant, but it does not tell the real story.

The programs have been devised with great care and at a cost that would be hard to measure. It is not possible to place a value on the time and expertise provided by the private- sector people who have served on these task forces. Nor is it possible to estimate the worth of the goodwill that has been stockpiled as a result of the interest in the community's public schools. How can the leveraging of more private assistance as a result of past friendships be quantified? What is the dollar value of a CEO's interest and concern?

At the time of this writing, the CSPPS program has been in existence for about three full years. The private sector is clearly involved in programs with students, teachers, and administrators. In other ways, CSPPS has helped to build recognition for the schools within the community. Through its development of a five-year financial plan, it has acknowledged the need for additional school funds and has made known its support for a modest tax increase. Yet, the private sector does not believe that this kind of involvement should continue forever. Mr. Saul describes it as "a temporary, bridging activity."[9] It is hoped that the programs, activities, and inter-organizational collaborations established through the efforts of CSPPS will continue long after the Committee itself goes out of existence. Thus, it is the responsibility of the school district to maximize this critical moment of engagement and to institutionalize the best programs and policies that emerge.

BUSINESS IN EDUCATION: HOW GOOD A GRADE?

The following is a transcription of a speech presented by William S. Woodside, Chairman and Chief Executive Officer, American Can Company (now Primerica), at The Conference Board's New Business Initiatives in Education Conference, in New York City on March 27, 1985.

These have been momentous years for school/business partnerships. All across this country, in cities both large and small, partnership programs are flourishing.

Nobody is keeping records, but the number of corporations involved in partnership programs must exceed several hundred. And not all of them are Fortune 500 companies.*

The Join-A-School or Adopt-A-School programs have received the most public attention. But other types of programs abound as well.

There are loaned-executive programs, in which senior corporate executives work in a specialized area such as administration, staff development, or resource management.

There are curriculum renewal programs, in which corporate specialists work with educators to develop course curricula that reflect private-sector technology, standards, and practices that students will encounter when they leave school.

There are mentor programs, in which teams of professionals conduct seminars for small groups of students interested in their particular field. This program has been particularly popular with law firms.

---

*Editor's note: A variety of such programs are described in this book.

There are programs in which business helps develop magnet schools to attract students in fields such as science or communications. There are programs in which computers or other expensive equipment are donated or loaned to the schools. And there are programs in which business works with intermediary organizations, such as the Joint Council on Economic Education, or Young Audiences, to improve particular courses.

Each program is important. Together, they demonstrate that the business community and the schools have come together for the benefit of public education. They demonstrate that in community after community, business is working with the schools to provide assistance, opportunity, and support that the schools and their students might not receive otherwise.

All of us can take great pride in what has been accomplished. In fact, if any of us involved in a partnership program were asked to grade ourselves at this point, we probably would not be too far off the mark if we gave ourselves at least a B +.

I think, however, that we are deceiving ourselves if we believe that these types of school/business partnerships can dramatically improve the majority of our nation's public schools. Each of us can cite examples where, with considerable private-sector involvement, we can turn around one school, perhaps a number of schools. But there are thousands of children who are not being touched by our efforts and who will not be touched by our efforts.

What about them?

That is why I believe that we are now at the stage where we need to look beyond our own individual partnership programs. We now need to focus on system-wide issues, because there are vast and fundamental improvements that must be made within our public schools. And we need to focus on the political arena, because that is where the major decisions are going to be made about the funds, priorities, and programs that will make or break our system of public education.

Some corporate communities already are moving in this direction. The Committee to Support the Philadelphia Public Schools has completed a major study of the school system's personnel management programs and currently is reviewing school resources and expenditures.

The Boston Compact is another program that has been organized to stimulate system-wide improvements in the public schools. A specific set of reciprocal obligations binds the schools and the corporations that participate in the Compact.

In the political arena, corporations involved in the Memphis, Tennessee, Adopt-A-School program organized a public relations campaign that helped produce an overwhelming vote in favor of a tax increase that provided additional money for that city's school system. Memphis voters had rejected the tax increase in an earlier election.

Business groups in New Orleans and Cincinnati also have worked to help raise tax revenue for the public schools.

These are important examples of corporate communities that are involved in education issues that reach beyond a single school. We need more of them.

But in the long run, the eventual success of today's business/school partnerships—the grade that is accorded us—will depend on something else. It will depend on the impact we have on the decisions that are made in our state capitals and in Washington, as well as in our city halls.

For us to be effective will mean more than telling our lobbyists to put in a good word for public education every now and then. It will mean more than sending a corporate executive to Washington or Albany for an occasional goodwill visit. It will mean organizing ourselves into an active, sustained support mechanism on behalf of public education.

It will mean building coalitions that seek major and permanent improvements in such areas as teacher training and certification, salaries, educational standards for students, and special programs for the disadvantaged. It will mean actively acknowledging that good public schools, good school buildings, good school libraries, and good school teachers will require more of our time, take more effort, and cost more of our money.

It will mean providing our system of public education with something it does not enjoy at the present time: a base of public support that is strong, secure, and generous; one in which our schools receive—because our children deserve it—the wholehearted and unqualified support they have every right to expect from every level of government, including the federal government.

Some business groups in Minnesota and Florida are making efforts to bring the business community together on statewide education issues. On the West Coast, the California Business Roundtable recently agreed to campaign on behalf of an $800 million tax increase—provided the funds were spent entirely on education. The tax bill passed.

These are promising signs. We need to become active at the state level. But we also must develop strategies that will enable us to have an impact on education policy at the national level.

One alternative is to institutionalize our concerns by working through our corporate legislative representatives. That, however, would place an additional responsibility on people already hard pressed for time and resources.

A second alternative is to work through our trade associations. The problem here is that trade associations assign their highest priority to issues that directly affect the daily business of their members. Social issues, when they are put on the trade association agenda, tend to take second or even third billing.

A third alternative is to form ad hoc corporate coalitions in Washington and our state capitals.

Corporations organize these ad hoc, or special-purpose, coalitions because there are times in the public policy process when more can be achieved by highly focused collective actions than by the uncoordinated efforts of individual companies acting on their own.

Ad hoc coalitions exist, and are effective, in such areas as health care, industrial growth, tax reform, and international trade. Why not action coalitions for public education?

Such coalitions could help bring to life some of the recommendations of existing study and advisory groups to which corporations already belong, such as the recommendations in the Committee for Economic Development's recent policy statement on business and the schools.

Action coalitions could, for example, begin working on an adequate system of educational funding. I do not mean simply more funding; I mean equitable funding—funds that are targeted to those school districts where the needs are greatest.

They also could take action on issues relating to the professionalization of teachers. Despite the lip service we give to teaching in this country, it still ranks near the bottom of the list among potential career paths for our most able college graduates. It is no wonder, because there are few material rewards for good teachers. Ernest Boyer, former U.S. Commissioner of Education, hit the nail on the head when he said, "Young lawyers if they work hard become partners in the firm. Young doctors if they work hard get a second yacht. Young teachers if they work hard get old."

In suggesting this broader, more organized effort on behalf of public education, I do not mean to minimize what we have achieved in the past or to trivialize the effort that has gone into establishing the partnerships we now have.

The one-on-one institutional relationships that marked the initial phase of the partnerships provided us with a window on the world of public education.

They made it possible for corporations to learn, on a firsthand basis, the problems the public schools face day in and day out. And the schools, though somewhat skeptical at the beginning, came to recognize that corporations had some important resources and skills that could benefit them.

These initial programs generated a remarkable outpouring of personal involvement and commitment. In my own company, as a result of our Join-A-School program experiences with Martin Luther King Jr. High School, I can identify people who two years ago never thought twice about the public schools but who now are among their most articulate and effective advocates—both within the company and within their own communities.

School/business partnerships, though, have reached an important turning point. Some of you may know about a recent study conducted by Dale Mann, a professor at Teachers College, Columbia University. Professor Mann studied partnerships in 23 large cities and determined that the dollar value of the grants, goods, and services the private sector provided in those cities was about $25 million a year. While that may sound like a lot of money, it is in fact only a small fraction of the annual costs of operating these school systems.

Since private-sector financial contributions could only be marginal at best, Professor Mann advised school leaders to be far more systematic and thoughtful in developing programs that could leverage these marginal resources in order to achieve the widest possible results. And partnership programs as a whole, he said, could only achieve maximum results if they matured into long-term programs of political support.

"The most helpful results of school/business partnerships," Professor Mann wrote, "are those political coalitions aimed at major, permanent increases in financial support for public schools."

Although Professor Mann addressed his comments primarily to school superintendents, business needs to hear his message as well. We are not only partners in this venture; we are the powerful partner. If the partnership program achieves substantial results over the long haul, we may deserve more than half the blame.

We need to take a careful look at ourselves. Many of us in the corporate world have vigorously supported school/business partnerships. But, have we been as vigorous in opposing public policy decisions we knew would harm the public schools? We have repeatedly said our partnerships were much more than supersteps and actions that could help provide the broader political and public policy support our schools so desperately need.

Fred Hechinger, education columnist for *The New York Times*, wrote about this dilemma forthrightly in the *Harvard Business Review* (Jan.–Feb. 1985, 64, 1). " . . . In the end," Hechinger concluded, "all these cooperative ventures will amount to little more than public relations unless the business community abandons its frequently schizophrenic posture; supporting the local schools while simultaneously instructing, or at least permitting, its lobbyists to support cuts in state and federal expenditures for public education and such legislation as tax credits for parents whose children attend private schools. Common sense should show the futility of any corporate policy that gives to the local schools with one hand and yet takes away funds with the other."

That's not the way it was supposed to happen.

When corporations once again became involved with public schools we said we did not become involved in public education to let government off the hook. We said we did not want government using our involvement as an excuse to ignore its own responsibilities. We said we did not want our programs to become a screen of voluntarism behind which an entire generation of young people, too many of them underprivileged, would be denied basic opportunity and justice.

It is time to make good on those promises.

There is no question the job can be done. We need to play an activist role in Washington, because the decisions of Congress and the Executive Branch will set the tone for the nation as a whole. And we need to play an activist role in the state capitals, because they are becoming new centers of power in determining the level of financial and programmatic support our public school systems will enjoy.

There is only one more question we need to ask ourselves: Why should we do it? Everyone needs to form his or her own answer to this question. Let me give you mine.

In this era of specialization, with its demand for short-term payoffs, there is a powerful temptation for a corporation or any other organization to shut its eyes and ears to any event, situation, institution, or person that does not relate to the immediate business at hand. Frankly, that's an awful lot of people, situations, and institutions to ignore.

I have long believed that our nation's long-term success, our very survival even, depends not so much on the business decisions we make today or tomorrow but on the social policy we develop for the next decade and the next century.

We need to remember that we are not just a pluralistic society; we also are an interdependent society. And no society, no matter how strong or secure it feels at a specific moment, can survive if its institutions and people lose sight of each other, if they live and work apart from one another and fail to see the goals they share in common both as a people and as a nation.

A first-rate system of public education is every bit as important to our future as our national defense system. There simply is no more valuable down payment we as a nation can make in our future than to invest in efforts that strengthen our elementary and secondary public schools.

NOTES

1. *Washington Roundtable: 1984 in Review.* Seattle: Washington Roundtable, 1985.
2. National Commission on Excellence in Education, *A Nation at Risk: The Imperative for Educational Reform*, Washington, DC: U.S. Government Printing Office, 1983.
3. Telephone interview conducted by R. Trachtman with Martha Darling, Executive Director of the Washington Roundtable, March 1986.
4. *Washington Roundtable: 1984 in Review.*
5. Policy Statement prepared by the Committee to Support the Philadelphia Public Schools, March 4, 1985.
6. Ibid.
7. *Progress and Plans*, issued by the Committee to Support the Philadelphia Public Schools, January 25, 1985.
8. Policy Statement, Philadelphia Public Schools.
9. *The Future of Inner City High Schools: The Public-Private Contribution*, proceedings of a conference held June 21–22, 1984, sponsored by the Federal Reserve Bank of Boston and Harvard University, Center for Business and Government, p. 22.

Afterword

P. MICHAEL TIMPANE
Teachers College, Columbia University

A book like *American Business and the Public School* could not have been written before the 1980s. This is not simply because the case studies set forth here had not yet occurred. More significantly, no one could have imagined that the varieties of business/education relationships described here would soon appear. Business had been conspicuously absent from the education policy world for two decades at least, having been a minor player, at best, in the desperate educational difficulties of the 1960s and 1970s. Moreover, by the late 1970s, the fortunes of education policy were at a low ebb. No one was foolhardy enough to imagine or predict that education would soon return to the top of the nation's agenda as a preeminent issue.

The recitation of subsequent events is all too familiar: *A Nation at Risk*, the flood of national-level reports and studies that have followed it, and the unprecedented array of state legislative and policy-making activity still going on. Education has become one of the highest items on everyone's agenda in the development of national economic health. The participation of the business community has developed so widely and deeply that now it is almost assumed, and the policies adopted bear the mark of business interests in clear standards and accountability.

The studies presented here offer some of the first detailed accounts of prominent business/education initiatives taken during the mid-1980s; until these studies were drafted, most participants were too busy organizing activities to reflect upon them. The studies, moreover, were written by participants from all sectors—from corporations themselves, from the world of educational practice, and from the community of policy analysis—and thus present different perspectives on the causes, significance, and impact of business involvement.

The case studies also illustrate most clearly the swift development of an unprecedented range of business engagement with education. There has never been so forceful an expression of this, with the possible exception of the launching of vocational education in the first decades of this century (but vocational education is most certainly *not* the major focus of the current business interest). Business participation in education throughout the nation has widened systematically since the early 1980s. It moved first from the periphery of local education policy activities—in the form of career awareness days, work experience programs, and so forth—to the very center of local education policy making, namely, the curriculum, the qualifications and performance of teachers, and the management of the schools. Inevitably, it moved also from a focus on projects to an active interest in policy making. This shift led to another, from an initial concentration on local activities to a focus on the states as the most vigorous agents of education reform in our time.

Finally, the business interest has extended from its original narrow concern with skills needed to produce employable citizens to wide-ranging concerns for the preparation, recruitment, pay, and treatment of teachers, and for improvement in the ways in which schools are organized and managed, and to a deep concern with how the schools are financed. In the most recent reports embodying this trend, those produced by the Carnegie Forum and the National Governors Association, this interest extends to yet another level—explicit concern for restructuring of the schools and reorganization of education systems.

As surprising as anything else, and a most hopeful sign for the future, has been the persistent nature of the business interest. It was widely predicted at the outset that the business community would be here today and gone tomorrow. This has not yet been the case. In the fifth year of the new business involvement, interest does not yet show signs of abating or disappearing. The Committee for Economic Development, from whose initial interest these case studies sprang, remains actively engaged in the analysis of education problems and the development of recommendations for business activities. The United States Chamber of Commerce and its local affiliates have kept education improvement high on their agenda. Regional economic development groups, such as the Southern Growth Policy Board and, most recently, the Northeast Midwest Congressional Coalition, have continued to put political influence behind further education improvement for the sake of our economic prosperity. The most current federal plans to develop trade legislation to deal with the "competitiveness" problem have significant educational components, and, indeed, contemporary proposals to reform the nation's welfare programs propose to end dependency through education and employment programs for the great majority of welfare recipients. Both developments seem to enjoy the same broad, nonpartisan, public and private basis of support that has characterized education reform since the early 1980s.

Clearly, there are at least as many case studies still in the making as are reported in this book, and as much promise of consequent educational progress as these instances truly report. This literature is just beginning to appear. There are thousands of school districts, business leaders, and interested citizens who have not yet heard or believed developments like those recounted here. Hopefully, this book will be the first step in their necessary education.

Appendix A

School/Business Partnerships:
Their Impact on Teachers
in Small Urban and Rural Districts

ROBERTA TRACHTMAN
City University of New York

To examine both the process and product of school/business interactions through the perceptions of school participants, a nationwide, indepth telephone study was designed and implemented during the first six months of 1985. In each of 85 randomly selected small urban and rural school districts throughout the United States, four school participants were interviewed: the superintendent, a school board member, a teachers' organization leader, and the teacher who was nominated by each superintendent as being the most involved in activities with the private sector.*

To include the full range of possible economic circumstances and activities, the sample was drawn from five regions throughout the United States, the Northeast, the Southeast, the Midwest, the Southwest, and the Northwest. Twelve states within these five regions were selected, using as cluster points those big cities that had previously been included in Mann's "Glitters" study.[1] The selected states were Massachusetts, New Jersey, Georgia, Mississippi, Florida, Wisconsin, Michigan, Ohio, Texas, California, Montana, and Washington. Decisions regarding which of the states to include were based on evidence provided by Mann's study regarding the significance and amount of each state's participation (or lack thereof) in private-sector initiatives in education. The total public school enrollment within these states represented approximately 43 percent of all students enrolled in public schools in the United States in 1978.[2] Eighty-five sites were selected from within those twelve states, stratified according to available school enrollment figures and the estimated total population figures of those places.

Using the Rand McNally 1983 population estimates for counties and cities over 25,000, and the 1980 census for latest available estimates

---

*Dale Mann collected and analyzed the data on the superintendants and school board members.

for other cities and towns, a random sample was drawn from each state so that each stratum of population would be appropriately represented.

Three hundred and thirty respondents from twelve states throughout five geographic regions of the country composed the final sample. They were interviewed at length, by telephone, using four separate protocols that sought to discover their perceptions and perspectives regarding school/business activities. This researcher was most keenly interested in the perceptions provided by the teachers who were involved in these activities.

CONCLUSIONS

The renewed interest in education by the private sector is welcomed by some and is a cause for concern to others. The findings of this study provide important new information on the impact of these partnerships on teachers and therefore on the education process. Furthermore, data were gathered on the types of involvement in these smaller school districts, supplementing information already existing on business/school relationships in large urban districts.[3]

The literature on school/business partnerships reports that the education community is concerned that business participation might be tied to "strings." Some believe that the business community may attempt to trade the promise of its vast resources for greater control over education policy. Like Joel Spring, some educators regard the private sector as having aims that are merely self-serving, and motives that reflect only self-interest.[4] They worry that the business sector is interested only in supporting the "sorting" function of education;[5] they fear that there will be demands for a particular *quid pro quo* from the private interests that choose to participate.

These concerns have been voiced by those who fear that the input of corporate money will result in the redirection of education. With regard to cash donations, the study indicates that the amount of money coming into the schools from outside is minimal. In the districts included in this study, the business community has not attempted to fill the gaps left by cuts in federal spending; in addition, according to most of the teachers, this is not the role that they hope business will play.

Greater "vocationalizing" of the school curriculum is another significant concern voiced by educators with regard to the involvement of the private sector. Participants in this study did not find this fear justified. Although the participation of the private sector is certainly greatest in business education courses, through work-study programs, classroom speakers, and the impact on curricula provided by advisory committees, teachers did not define this participation as attempting to control or direct their instruction. Teachers who were involved with business partners reported that decision making is a joint effort in which both partners are actively engaged. Although the majority of public/private interactions continue to occur within the "vocational" classes, the perspective offered by these teachers, as well as that provided by the findings of the study by the Committee for Economic Development (1985), indicates that the business community is interested in "employability skills," which are defined as "problem-solving skills, command of the English language, self-discipline, and the ability to acquire and apply new knowledge."[6] The teachers in this study pointed to the value to both themselves and their students resulting from the suggestions and kinds of experiences provided by these representatives of the "real world." The teachers welcome this level of involvement and hope for its continuation, since they believe it positively affects student performance.

School/business interactions are initiated by the public sector, generally as a result of the interest and resourcefulness of an individual teacher. Teachers reported little institutionalization of these interactions. The teachers who are involved are not casual about their own efforts, but most were unable to point to any formal structure that plans for and implements the participation of the business community. The nature of the involvement seems to be at the programmatic level, with the benefits accruing to the direct participants—the teachers and students—rather than to the school or system as a whole.

The teacher participants reported greater personal satisfaction in the involvement of other adults in their daily professional lives. They indicated that these interactions provided them with increased feelings of self-worth; their business partners provided them with both recognition and rewards, which are especially important to those who occupy a system in which these two "honorifics" are often absent.[7] School/business collaboratives have made teachers more aware of the needs of the corporate community in ways that are acceptable and meaningful to them. These partnerships have helped to decrease the isolation and insularity of teachers; they have also enabled teachers to feel more directly connected to the larger world. As a result, teachers have broadened their sights as well as their own personal and professional goals. Teachers report that they will continue to seek the participation of the private sector in order to show their students that the school is not the only place for learning and that what they learn in class is relevant to life outside.

The limited interaction between schools and communities illustrates the limited interactions among school personnel. The superintendents and the school board members in this study, as well as the leaders of the teachers' organizations, seem not to be fully aware of the unique effects that these interactions have had on teachers. The kind of participation described by nonteaching school personnel is focused on how, or if, the private sector should be approached for greater involvement in education *policy* decisions. As described in the literature, an expanded role for the private sector might include lobbying for increased educational funds, as well as becoming an advocate and supporter of state and federal legislation directed at education improvement.[8] Although there are several examples of this kind of participation in big cities like Boston and Minneapolis, and throughout much of California,[9] school personnel interviewed for this study were less able to indicate its presence.

Support for greater funding of education and increased political involvement were potential benefits described by some of the superintendents, school board members, and teacher leaders; however, the superintendents in this study reported that the involvement of the private sector has continued to be of the "traditional kind," with little effect on funding or taxes in their districts. The teachers' organization leaders indicated that the involvement of the private sector has had little impact on teachers in general, since direct donations to staff development have been minimal, and there have been almost no political reverberations resulting from business interest and participation in their districts. However, they too believe that these involvements should be encouraged and expanded so that more teachers will become aware of the potential benefits.

Throughout the United States, there are examples of interesting, effective, and rewarding school/business interactions. Whether these collaborations will result in systemic change does not seem to be important to these teachers—they care most strongly about what works for their students and what will make their hours in school more significant and meaningful.

IMPLICATIONS

The participation of teachers in public/private collaboratives has expanded their roles, increased their self-esteem, and provided for professional growth. For some, these relationships offered an opportunity for "entrepreneurship" that was not available to them through other teacher activities. This study found that interaction with the private sector improved teacher morale and the quality of a teacher's work life. This finding needs to be shared with others. Teachers need to report on what they have experienced in order for this innovation to reach all of those who might gain from it.

School/business interactions may be another way in which schools can become more effective places for learning. This study suggests that these interactions are being sought at the local level by individual teachers, with the encouragement of their immediate supervisors. This survey indicates that the role of the principal in these interactions seems to be largely ceremonial; this kind of participation should change, since support from first-line administrators is both necessary and desirable. Their greater participation might result in more community involvement as well as in the participation of more teachers and students.

In some communities, gaining the support and respect of the business community will require little effort, since that support has been historically forthcoming. In other places, there is little support for education. In districts where there has been dissatisfaction with the product of schools, significant racial tension, or a seriously diminished school-aged population, the "wooing" of the business community will be a much more arduous process, requiring more time and many more small steps.

School/business partnerships are often easier to forge at the secondary school level, since it is easier for both partners to understand the mutual advantages. However, recent early childhood interventions indicate that good preschool programs are very effective for low-income youngsters.[10] There is reason to believe that greater involvement of the business community in elementary school classes might also provide additional opportunities for growth and learning among youngsters, as well as promote the same kinds of increased feelings of self-worth among the teachers who are involved. Since there were so few school/business interactions reported at the elementary school and middle school levels in this study, it seems that their potential at these levels is truly underdeveloped.

A great deal of speculative information exists about which industries are employing high school graduates and what level of success and failure they encounter at each job. Teachers in this study reported that if they were more informed about job-related issues, they would be better able to provide appropriate learning experiences for high school youth, as well as devise better strategies for counseling and guiding them as they make the difficult transition from school to work. The involvement of local employers would help to inform guidance counselors and other school personnel in ways that could increase the employability of their graduates.

The burn-out experienced by teachers cannot be solved by the business community. However, the expertise that the business community has in areas of staff and human resource development could be used as a model for education. Although the teachers and teacher leaders in this study reported that this expertise has yet to be tapped, it has the potential for addressing a systemic problem that is nationwide.

SOME FINAL SPECULATIONS

During the interview and discussion process, several themes emerged that point to issues of consequence for teachers as well as for American education in general. Since these "reverberations" are not directly supported by the data collected, I have chosen to describe them as speculations.

The Teachers' Role

Teachers who have participated in these school/business interactions feel they are better able to design courses and activities to meet the individual needs of their students. The *business partners* have been asked to participate in many ways, but throughout this participation they *are guided by teachers*, rather than by state-mandated curricula or tests. According to some teachers, this response to local need has been a great deal more effective than other kinds of additional services and/or funds provided by external governmental agencies. The business community at each site is being asked to help improve the education of students in a way that is closely related to the students' needs.

The effectiveness of this effort could be used to garner greater support for the decentralization of authority throughout the schools, so that classroom teachers would have more decision-making power and control over which curricula and materials are used with their students. Since they have most direct knowledge of their students' weaknesses and strengths, teachers should be given a greater role in deciding what should be taught. It is also likely that this change in the distribution of authority would go a long way toward increasing the professionalism and self-esteem of the teaching corps.

The Specter of Big Business

There are some who think that the business community's participation in education is self-serving and of little real value. The teachers in this study did not concur with this view; in fact, many believed that even if business is motivated by the need for an improved work force, this should not be considered an inherent evil. *Teachers were more likely to cite the mutuality of interest* rather than to condemn the underlying motivations of their business partners.

It may be that more educators need to realize that the private sector need not be kept at arm's length. While schools and businesses do not have the same goals, their futures are closely aligned.

Teachers, however, are critical to the future of education. Those who continue to ignore this will find themselves seeking change by chasing windmills. In an era of scarce resources and heightened competition, such a pastime is more than merely foolish; it is a guarantee of failure.

NOTES

1. D. Mann, *All That Glitters: Public School/Private Sector Interaction in Twenty-three U.S. Cities*, New York: Teachers College, Columbia University, 1984.
2. Ibid.
3. Ibid.
4. J. Spring, *Education and the Rise of the Corporate State*, Boston: Beacon Press, 1972.
5. J. Spring, *The Sorting Machine*, New York: David McKay Co., Inc., 1976, p. 3.
6. Committee for Economic Development, *Investing in Our Children: Business and the Public Schools*, Washington, DC: Committee for Economic Development, 1985.
7. D. Lortie, *Schoolteacher*, Chicago: University of Chicago Press, 1975.
8. M. Levine, "Barriers to Private Sector/Public School Collaboration: A Conceptual Framework," in *Barriers to Private Sector/Public School Collaboration*, Washington, DC: American Enterprise Institute for Public Policy Research in collaboration with the National Institute of Education, 1983; M. Levine, Ed., *The Private Sector in the Public School: Can It Improve Education?*, Washington, DC: American Enterprise Institute for Public Policy Research, 1985; and D. Mann, *All That Glitters*.
9. Committee for Economic Development, *Investing in Our Children: Business and the Public Schools*, Washington, DC: Committee for Economic Development, 1985.
10. L. J. Schweinhart and D. P. Weikert, "Evidence That Good Early Childhood Programs Work," *Phi Delta Kappan*, 66(8), 545–548 (1985).

Appendix B
Committee for Economic Development Survey Results

Case studies of specific companies' activities in education provide important insights into the process and outcomes of collaboration. The range and scope of business involvement is provided in data collected in a survey conducted by the Committee for Economic Development in 1984. A written survey was sent to 500 large businesses and 6,000 small businesses. In addition to questions concerning attributes for employability, respondents were asked about their companies' involvement with public schools.

An analysis of these responses provides some insights into how businesses view the role of schools in preparing students for work, as well as factors that appear to be related to a company's involvement.

Company size is an important factor in business/education collaboration. The large companies (selected from among the Fortune 500) were more involved in collaborative activity with the schools and were more able to identify exemplary programs. Over half of the large companies responding had business/education programs. Fewer than 20 percent of the small companies identified such programs. A review of the comments suggests a difference in perception of the roles of schools in preparing students for work. Large companies seemed to think more in terms of generic skills and abilities. Small companies focused more on job-specific skills, commenting that schools do not equip students with these skills. It was not clear whether they believed the schools should do that.

Survey findings also suggest that collaborative involvement is related to knowledge of exemplary schools programs. Just as Gallup polls indicate that parents with children in public schools rate schools higher than does the general population, companies with active involvement can identify quality programs more often. No causal relationship can be inferred, but the two factors seem to go together. Knowledge of a well-functioning school program may inspire confidence to enter formal collaborative arrangements, or the experience of working with a school or school district may afford the opportunity to learn about good schools.

Where Are the Partnerships?   Although no statistical relationship existed between regions of the country and school/business partnerships among survey respondents, partnerships were more in evidence in the East and Midwest.

What Kinds of Companies Are Most Involved?   Among our respondents, companies in the utilities; electronic/high technology; and banking, insurance, and financial services sectors were significantly more likely to indicate involvement in partnerships with schools or school districts.

What Kind of Involvement Is Most Prevalent?   Respondents more often identified programmatic involvement focused on student development of employability skills and/or specific job skills and experience; for example, cooperative education, internships, and work-study. Such programs were more often related to office and clerical preparation than to any other category of employment. Collaborative programs identified in technical and semiskilled areas were frequently at the postsecondary level.

In addition, large companies identified involvement in more general programs, including Adopt-A-School, career awareness days, Junior Achievement, and Project Basic; advisory board participation; and serving as advisors on curriculum development.

Small Businesses.   Small businesses in the transportation, agriculture, and retail industries were significantly more likely to report involvement in business/school programs. Their involvement, in contrast to that of the large companies, was noticeably limited to occupational training and the school-to-work transition. Among the programs identified by these businesses were cooperative education, work-study programs, career counseling, youth job exploration, vocational-agricultural programs, and on-the-job training.

Survey Update.   In January 1986, each of the respondents in the large company category was contacted to update the information provided in the survey.

The following information is presented with the consent of the respondents. It offers both a picture of the range of education activity in the corporate community and a resource to the reader. Inclusion is on the basis of response to the survey.

SELECTED SURVEY RESPONSES

Aetna Life & Casualty Insurance, Co.*, Hartford, CT. Summer jobs; work-study; participation in the Greater Hartford Chamber of Commerce Education Advisory Committee; grants to the Hartford public schools for retraining educational personnel; The Saturday Academy for seventh graders and their parents; employees released time tutorial program; equipment and furniture donations; field trips.

Air Products & Chemicals, Inc.*, Allentown, PA. Adopt-A-School; guest speakers; job shadowing; sponsors; explorers programs; field trips; Junior Achievement; teacher training; equipment donations; business-education day for teachers; underwrites performing arts programs; student science awards; film and library interloan program; matching funds for curriculum project; education roundtable participation.

Alcoa*, Pittsburgh, PA. Junior Achievement; Partnerships-In-Education (similar to Adopt-A-School); pre-engineering program sponsors science fair projects, guest speakers, career day participation; scholarships for employees' children; service on local school boards encouraged; teacher training; funds various educational programs.

American Can Co.*, Greenwich, CT. Join-A-School with Martin Luther King School; sponsorship of SUNY/Purchase Westchester Partnership; provision of grants for school improvement programs to national and local groups (e.g., dropout prevention, teacher internships, junior high school project); leadership role in the education committee of the NYC Partnership, Inc.

American Express Co.*, New York, NY. Academy of Finance and Academy of Travel & Tourism programs, encompassing special courses for students, internships, job opportunities, extensive curriculum development, and teacher training; dropout prevention program; guest speakers; service on local school boards encouraged; cooperative education.

Amoco Corp., Chicago, IL. Cooperative education; work-study; internships; equipment donations; advisory boards; scholarship programs; career day participation; guest speakers.

ARCO (Atlantic Richfield Co.)*, Los Angeles, CA. Junior Achievement; Joint Education Project (under Volunteer Service Program), consisting of employee volunteers in schools (tutoring, counseling); teacher

---

*An asterisk indicates a CED trustee company.

recognition program; Adopt-A-School; grants to teachers; guest speakers; career days; company tours; equipment donations; ARCO Foundation, which funds educational programs and supports employee volunteer activities with matching grants corresponding to time given.

American Telephone & Telegraph Co. (AT&T)*, New York, NY. Substantial grants given to university programs, some of which are targeted toward high school science students, particularly minorities and women.

Banco Popular de Puerto Rico*, San Juan, PR. Internships; service on local school boards encouraged; guest speakers; career counseling; career day participation; cooperative education.

Bank of America National Trust & Savings Assn.*, San Francisco, CA. Created the California Educational Initiatives Fund in 1979, which provides funding for school improvement grants (seven other corporations now participate in its funding); Adopt-A-School; Junior Achievement; participation on California Business Roundtable; member of Tripartite Consortium for math/science; provided a grant for the creation of a summer institute for math teachers; field trips.

Bethlehem Steel Corp.*, Bethlehem, PA. Cooperative education; equipment donations; service on local school boards encouraged.

The Boeing Co.*, Seattle, WA. Series of partnerships with various school districts (e.g., plant tours, guest speakers, career day participation); service on local school boards encouraged; equipment donations; Computers for Kids (fifth-grade level; winning classes given computers); participates in Technology in Education (local science/math cooperative training program); Directions, which developed and produced videotapes for high schools; Junior Achievement; supports MESA (Mathematics, Engineering, Science Achievement), which encourages minority students to enter these fields; participates in Integrated Registry of Achieving Students, a multifaceted minorities program involving mentorships, employment, and scholarships; SENSE (Scholarships for Engineering Students' Education), which awards high school students scholarships for academic achievement; internships, summer jobs program; summer internships for teachers; one of the corporate founders of Seattle Committee for Excellence in Education, a program of teacher recognition cash awards; mini grants to teachers for special projects; sponsors Early Childhood Education course for employees; gift matching program; extensive funding of other local and national programs.

Boston Edison Co.*, Boston, MA. Adopt-A-School; cooperative education; work-study; internships for students; equipment donations; service on local school boards; scholarship programs; tutoring; career day participation; management assistance; guest speakers; field trips; advisory committees for vocational education.

Cabot Corp.*, Boston, MA. Enrichment program for gifted children sponsored by Boston's Museum of Science; employee matching grants programs to precollegiate schools; funding provided to Harvard School of Education for "brush-up" math courses for area teachers; support for the delivery of a program on safety in the science laboratory.

California Federal Savings & Loan Assn.*, Los Angeles, CA. Youth opportunity days; youth task force participation; advisory boards for secretarial skills; Adopt-A-School; funds teacher recognition program through the California Department of Commerce; service on local school boards encouraged; scholarships; career day participation; guest speakers; field trips; advisory committee.

Caterpillar Tractor Co.*, Peoria, IL. Plant tours; guest speakers; career day participation; Office Occupation contests in high schools.

Champion International Corp.*, Stamford, CT. Curriculum development in public schools; work-study; high school trainee program; internships for students; equipment donations for public schools; service on local school boards encouraged; scholarships; tutoring; speakers; service on state advisory boards; cooperative education; summer internships for students; tutoring; career day participation; field trips.

Chase Manhattan Bank NA*, New York, NY. Adopt-A-School; internships for students; research in projects for teacher training; equipment donations; service on school boards; scholarships; tutoring (after work hours); guest speakers; funded a Principals' Institute in NYC.

Chemical Bank*, New York, NY. Internship programs; work-study programs covering all of NYC; Lincoln-Douglas Debates (city-wide high school program in which the Bank provides personnel, support, and cash awards to student winners and their schools); Join-A-School program with a New York City high school and middle school.

CIGNA Corp.*, Philadelphia, PA. Cooperative education; curriculum development; work-study programs; internships for students and teachers; equipment donations; service on local school boards (released time for employees); participation on task forces; career day participation; guest speakers; field trips; vocational education; created a management program for principals of public high schools; CEO, Ralph S. Saul, is the Chairman of the Committee to Support the Philadelphia Public Schools; member of the Greater Philadelphia First Corporation; participant in Philadelphia Alliance for Teaching the Humanities in the Schools (PATHS); arts grants for youngsters to attend dramatic performances; museum grants for projects with public school youngsters; scholarship programs.

Citizens & Southern National Bank of South Carolina*, Columbia, SC. Serves on employment board for vocational schools; internships for high school students; equipment donations; scholarships for children of employees; school volunteers; career day participation; guest speakers; field trips; six or seven students are trained every six months (under the Job Training Act Partnership).

Colorado National Bank*, Denver, CO. Adopt-A-School elementary, high school; cooperative education; tours; Junior Achievement; Project Business.

Commonwealth Edison Co.*, Chicago, IL. Adopt-A-School; cooperative education; service on local school boards; contributions to the United Negro Fund; career day participation; guest speakers; field trips; participation in the Board of Education pre-engineering program.

Consolidated Edison Co. of New York, Inc.*, New York, NY. Join-A-School/New York City Partnership; advisory committees for business education; sex equity programs; marketing and distributive education; career exploration; vocational internship program for students who become teachers.

Consolidated Natural Gas Co.*, Pittsburgh, PA. Curriculum guidance; service on local task forces encouraged; employee volunteers teach business classes.

Dart & Kraft Inc.*, Glenview, IL. Junior Achievement; Adopt-A-School; management assistance to schools; scholarship program geared toward minorities; Employee Matching Gifts program; internships; summer jobs program.

Dayton Power & Light Co.*, Dayton, OH. Participates in Partners in Education (similar to Adopt-A-School); The Engineer Club of the Dayton Foundation (summer jobs and teacher training); charter member of Public Education Fund; Junior Achievement; sponsors science fairs; career day participation; teacher recognition; advisory committees; guest speakers.

Deere & Co.*, East Moline, IL. Cooperative education; work-study; internships for students; equipment donations; service on local school boards encouraged; scholarship program for employees' children; Project Business; Junior Achievement; guest speakers; field trips.

Detroit Edison Co., Detroit, MI. Adopt-A-School; curriculum advisory committees; cooperative education; career fair participation; employees teach business courses; serves on the pre-engineering college placement council; college scholarships for minorities and women in engineering; field trips; guest speakers.

Dow Chemical Co.*, Midland, MI. Cooperative education; donation of funds to implement the recommendations of the 1983 National

Task Force on Education for Economic Growth; participation in the Education Commission of the States (ECS); chair of the Michigan Partnerships for Education Task Force; creation of a Michigan partnership handbook; retiree participation in local schools; teacher internships; Touch Tech, a science extravaganza for Detroit students; "Wonderful World of Chemistry," a one-hour traveling assembly program; cash awards for teacher excellence.

Eli Lilly & Co.*, Indianapolis, IN. Equipment donations; service on local school boards; scholarships; participation on statewide task force, Indiana Congress of Education; tutoring; Junior Achievement; foundation funding of specific programs; field trips; matching gifts program.

The Equitable Life Assurance Society of the U.S.*, New York, NY. Adopt-A-School; summer student interns; equipment donations; mini donations; helps with school's fund-raising efforts; participation in the NYC Partnership.

Federal-Mogul Corporation*, Detroit, MI. Cooperative education; internships for students; equipment donations; service on local school boards encouraged; scholarship program for high school students; participation in a statewide task force; Junior Achievement; field trips; speaker programs.

Federated Department Stores*, Cincinnati, OH. Cooperative education programs; service on local school boards strongly encouraged; investigating an employee volunteer program; advisory committees.

First Chicago Bank Corp.*, Chicago, IL. Office Occupation Program (work-study); Hire the Future Program: internships for economically disadvantaged students; career day participation; guest speakers.

First Mississippi Corp.*, Jackson, MS. Junior Achievement; Public Education Fund; funding for economics education; teacher and student recognition programs; scholarship program.

Ford Motor Co.*, Dearborn, MI. Seminars on job search techniques; recruits applicants for full-time positions; equipment donations to public schools; service on local school boards; tutoring; career day participation; mentoring programs; guest speakers; field trips; advisory committees.

General Electric Co.*, Fairfield, CT. Financial support of National Science Education Association; funds science museum grant competition; fellowships for exemplary mathematics and science teachers; forgivable loans program for prospective mathematics teachers; teacher awards program; minority engineering program; after-school recreational science/mathematics program; Join-A-School with Manhattan Center for Science and Mathematics.

General Mills Inc.*, Minneapolis, MN. Work-study; summer disadvantaged youth employment program; Public Education Fund; Adopt-A-

School; curriculum development; cooperative education; internships for students and teachers; teacher recognition programs; teacher training programs; equipment donations; service on local school boards; scholarship program; participation on task forces; tutoring; career day participation; mentoring programs; management assistance; guest speakers; field trips; advisory committees.

General Motors Corp.*, Warren, MI. Cooperative education; job/ science fairs; career day participation; internships; service on local school boards encouraged; regional Public Affairs Committees sponsor, and participates in Science Olympiad and Olympics of the Mind; equipment donations; guest speakers; plant tours; scholarship programs.

Goldman, Sachs & Co.*, New York, NY. Cooperative education; school board participation, with released time provided; guest speakers; scholarship program for employees' children; career day participation.

B.F. Goodrich Co.*, Akron, OH. Junior Achievement; equipment donations; service on local school boards encouraged (time provided); guest speakers; career day participation.

Goodyear Tire & Rubber Co.*, Akron, OH. Cooperative education; curriculum development; work-study; internships for students (investigating the possibility of internships for teachers); equipment donations; college scholarship program; service on local school boards (released time provided); tutoring; career day participation; guest speakers; field trips.

GTE Corp.*, Stamford, CT. Scholarships to children of employees; grants to exceptional teachers; equipment donations; tutoring; Junior Achievement; employee volunteers; career day participation; guest speakers.

Holiday Inns Inc., Memphis, TN. Equipment donations; scholarships; advisory committees; curriculum development (hotel management); career participation; field trips; guest speakers; cooperative education; $250,000 for scholarships; equipment donations; service on school boards encouraged (with time and travel money); advisory boards for curriculum development; career day participation; guest speakers.

Hospital Corporation of America, Nashville, TN. Adopt-A-School; teacher recognition programs; teachers receive grants to pursue summer projects; equipment donations; scholarships; career day participation; guest speakers; field trips.

IBM Corp.*, Armonk, NY. Cooperative education; Adopt-A-School; faculty loan program; lending of equipment and training materials; computer literacy programs; participation on local school boards and task forces encouraged; educational funding (focused particularly towards minorities and women), encouraging involvement in technical disciplines; career day participation; guest speakers; Junior Achievement; employee volunteers in schools.

International Paper Co., Jay, ME. Adopt-A-School; teacher training grants ($50,000 a year); cooperative education; equipment donations; career day participation; field trips; speaker programs.

HNG/InterNorth Inc.*, Omaha, NE. Adopt-A-School; funds to inner city private school to develop employability program; advisory committees; teacher training of public school economics teachers; service on local school boards encouraged; scholarship programs; career day participation; guest speakers.

Johnson & Johnson*, Raritan, NJ. Cooperative education; classroom teaching; service on local school boards encouraged; scholarship program; career day participation; guest speakers; field trips; advisory committees.

Kayo Oil Co.*, Chattanooga, TN. Adopt-A-School; funds teacher recognition program; scholarships for minority students interested in business; career day participation; guest speakers; advisory committees.

Lincoln National Life Insurance Co.*, Fort Wayne, IN. Junior Achievement; work-study; vocational program for data center operations; sponsors summer employment program for economically disadvantaged youth; Leadership Program for disadvantaged youth (seminars re: leadership); Explorers Program (classes at Lincoln National in computer programming); guest speakers; career day participation; field trips; curriculum development program.

Mariott Corp., Washington, DC. Service on local school boards encouraged; career day participation; guest speakers; financial support to the Council for Financial Aid to Education; Cities in the Schools program (provides resources to students to encourage them to stay in school); Higher Education program (helps high achievers excel).

McGraw-Hill, Inc.*, New York, NY. NYC Partnership; internships; designing a cooperative education work-study program; career day participation; guest speakers; field trips; advisory committees.

Mead Corp.*, Dayton, OH. Executive Secretarial Advisory Council; Adopt-A-School; cooperative education; service on school boards encouraged; minority scholarship program; career day participation; management assistance; guest speakers; field trips.

Mobil Corp.*, New York, NY. Double matching grants program; cooperative education; work-study program; student interns; equipment donations; service on school boards encouraged; tutoring (after work); guest speakers; field trips; education foundation funding.

National Steel Corp.*, Pittsburgh, PA. Junior Achievement; career orientation days; community fairs; plant tours; guest speakers; career day participation; service on local school boards encouraged.

New York Life Insurance Co.*, New York, NY. Adopt-A-School; cooperative education; work-study program; career day participation; guest speakers; donations of office furniture.

Northern Telecom Ltd.*, Nashville, TN. Public Education Fund; Adopt-A-School; cooperative education; developing a work-study program; student interns; teacher training; equipment donations; service on local school boards encouraged; tutoring (after work); career day participation; guest speakers; field trips.

Northwestern Mutual Life Insurance Co.*, Milwaukee, WI. Adopt-A-School; guest speakers; career day participation; sponsors medical fair; employee volunteers; teacher training; cooperative education; IN-ROADS, which is geared to prepare minorities for business careers (tutoring and summer courses); Explorers (students introduced to data and word processing); service on local task forces encouraged; sponsors educational programs.

Palmieri Co.*, Washington, DC. Advisory committees; service on local school boards encouraged.

Pfizer Inc.*, New York, NY. Scientists lecture at high schools; field trips; sponsors organizations that help promote science teaching; project to promote safe laboratory operations in schools; scholarship program.

Philip Morris Companies, Inc.*, New York, NY. Junior Achievement; current focus on college-level programs.

Phillips Petroleum Co.*, Bartlesville, OK. Distributes educational films to secondary schools; workshops for science teachers; tours for high school students; Phillips 66 Scholarship Program; scholarships to relatives of employees.

Procter & Gamble*, Cincinnati, OH. Extensive work on business advisory committees (e.g., curriculum development and teacher training); Partners in Education, which provides services as requested (e.g., guest speakers, tours, work-study); Junior Achievement; scholarship program for employees' children; employee and retiree volunteers (e.g., tutoring and goal setting); participation on local school boards and task forces encouraged (time provided); mentoring programs; funding of educational programs.

Prudential Insurance Co. of America*, Newark, NJ. Adopt-A-School; curriculum enrichment (advisory boards, courses on site); work-study; career day participation; guest speakers; plant tours; employee volunteers (tutoring); academic and artistic excellence programs; Junior Achievement; service on policy commissions; foundation funding of local and national programs.

Ralston Purina Co.*, St. Louis, MO. Cooperative education; work-study; Junior Achievement; conducts summer courses for students at community social service centers.

RCA Corp.*, Princeton, NJ. Community Scholarships Program (cash grant to high school senior who in turn chooses outstanding teacher to also receive grant); MITE Program, which is an introduction to engineering for minorities (grants to colleges to invite minority students for on-campus experience as encouragement to pursue engineering in college); LEAD, which is an introduction to business for minorities (structured like MITE); sponsors "A Better Chance" (disadvantaged students are placed in prep schools and suburban public high schools and in homes in the community); SPISE (Select Program in Science Engineering), which consists of supplementary weekend classes for minorities to encourage future science and engineering studies; VIP (Volunteer Incentive Program), in which grants are given to organizations when employees volunteer; service on local school boards and advisory committees encouraged; equipment donations; Junior Achievement; guest speakers; plant tours; cooperative education programs with local high schools.

Sears Roebuck & Co.*, Chicago, IL. Office Occupations Program (cooperative education); guest speakers; career day participation; initiated and runs Academic Olympics (rewards academic achievement in 18 Chicago inner city schools); employee volunteers; service on local school boards and task forces encouraged; summer hiring program based on financial need; extensive foundation funding of programs through/with national educational agencies.

Security Pacific National Bank*, Los Angeles, CA. Extensive regional occupation program, consisting of on-the-job training in entry-level banking careers; Project STEP (Skills Training Education Program), in which job skills classes are taught by bank employees; widespread Adopt-A-School program; Junior Achievement; Youth Motivation Task Force (minority mentorship program); cooperative education; teacher training; career day participation; guest speakers; field trips; participation on local school boards encouraged.

The Singer Co.*, Stamford, CT. Curriculum advisors; cooperative education, mini grant review committee; participation in the National Merit Scholarship program; career day participation; guest speakers; field trips.

Skidmore, Owings & Merrill*, Chicago, IL. Adopt-A-School; participated in youth motivation program sponsored by the Chicago Association of Commerce & Industry; tutoring; co-sponsors a model building competition for high school students: top three students employed in model shop for summer; equipment donations; scholarships; career day participation; guest speakers; field trips.

SmithKline Beckman Corp.*, Philadelphia, PA. Business Experience Education Programs (BEEP), in which students work part-time for two years and full time during the summer; guest speakers; career day participation; curriculum development; field trips; service on local school boards encouraged; service on advisory boards.

Southeast Bank NA*, Miami, FL. Junior Achievement; career fairs; guest speakers; summer internships for disadvantaged students; sponsors Inside Track summer internships for college-bound black students to span high school and college years as inducement to settle and work in Miami after college. Foundation: Sponsors Art Treasure Trunk (visual arts training program for grade schools); initiated funding for Expressive Art Centers (special classes for visual and performing arts students); sponsored Critical Thinking & the Creative Thought Process (philosophical colloquium for teachers, principals, school board personnel, and area supervisors); service on school board committees encouraged; tours of bank for elementary and junior high school students; service on state and local task forces.

The Southern Electric Generating Co.*, Birmingham, AL. Contributes to the Southeastern Consortium for Minorities in Engineering (helps high school students interested in engineering); service on local school boards encouraged; career day participation; guest speakers; field trips; advisory committees.

State Street Bank and Trust Co.*, Boston, MA. Leading participant of Boston Compact, an agreement between business community and Boston high schools to improve academic preparation (links students to job opportunities); participates in programs in dropout prevention, minority retention, remedial education, school-to-work transition, summer jobs.

Sun Company*, Radnor, PA. Equipment donations; service on local school boards encouraged; scholarship program for children of employees; career day participation and sponsorship; guest speakers; field trips.

Tenneco Inc.*, Houston, TX. Junior Achievement; Adopt-A-School; cooperative education; summer jobs program; scholarships for disadvantaged youth; summer leadership seminars; summer courses for credit toward college; mentoring program; teacher recognition program; funds Volunteers in Public Schools (volunteer recruiting program); employee volunteers (released time provided); funds teacher training program; scholarships; plant tours; guest speakers; funding of national programs.

Texas Instruments Inc.*, Dallas, TX. Curriculum development programs; cooperative education; equipment donations; service on local school boards encouraged; career day participation; field trips; contributions to the United Negro College Fund; advisory committees; membership in Help Our Public and Private Schools (HOPPS); serves on Dallas education committee.

Time Inc.*, New York, NY. Adopt-A-School; curriculum development; cooperative education; staff development program for teachers; equipment donations; scholarships; career day participation; guest speakers; field trips; Richard Monroe (CEO), former chairman of the New York City Partnership's Education Committee, serves on a Policy Task Force on school finance.

Touche Ross & Co.*, New York, NY. Cooperative education; Board of Education Internship Program: career day participation.

Travelers Corp.*, Hartford, CT. Work-study program; field trips; guest speakers; career day participation; equipment donations (donated $1 million worth of Apple computers to Hartford High School).

Trust Company Bank*, Atlanta, GA. Adopt-A-School; advisory committee for curriculum development; magnet school participation; 12-week internship followed by summer employment for high school students; employee volunteers; career day participation; guest speakers; field trips.

Union Pacific Corp.*, Omaha, NE. Curriculum development; equipment donations; scholarships; tutoring (released time provided); career day participation; guest speakers.

United Technologies Corp.*, Hartford, CT. Junior Achievement; work-study program (particular focus on inner city youth); summer jobs for disadvantaged youth; scholarships for dependents of employees; PEP (Pre-Engineering Program), including guest speakers, field trips, etc.; funds INROADS (national internship program for minorities); equipment donations; career day participation; curriculum development; service on local school boards and task forces encouraged.

U.S.X. Corp.*, Pittsburgh, PA. Goal Program (work-study); scholarships for dependents of employees; Junior Achievement; guest speakers; INROADS (national internship program for minorities).

U.S. Trust Co. of New York*, New York, NY. Cooperative education; summer internships; career recruitment of high school seniors; employee volunteers; matching gifts program; limited foundation funding of local programs (focus more on college level).

Virginia Power & Electric Co., Richmond, VA. New Horizons Program; Adopt-A-School; curriculum development projects; Project Math/Science (employees teach subjects); educational projects in conjunction with the Science Museum of Virginia; summer workshops for teachers; material donations; career day participation; field trips; guest speakers.

Warner Communications Inc., New York, NY. Adopt-A-School; curriculum development; scholarships; career day participation; guest speakers.

The Washington Post Co.*, Washington, DC. Agnes Meyer Outstanding Teachers Award ($2,000 award to 12 outstanding teachers); the Washington Post Grants in Education program (mini grants for teachers); Success in Reading and Writing program (encourages use of newspapers, magazines, and leisure books in addition to textbooks); Summer Journalism Scholarships awarded to 63 local public school students to attend summer journalism school; distribution of Job Hunter's Guide to help prepare students who are entering work force; tours; speakers bureau.

Westinghouse Electric Corp.*, Pittsburgh, PA. Adopt-A-School; curriculum development; science honors program held at company site; summer jobs; SWEEP Program (after school part-time jobs); equipment donations; Westinghouse Scholarship Program and Westinghouse Science Scholarship; career day participation; guest speakers; field trips.

Xerox Corp.*, Rochester, NY. Curriculum development projects; cooperative education; work-study programs; teacher internships to train teachers in business; summer student internships; equipment donations; technical scholarship program; participation in National Merit Scholarship program; career day participation; guest speakers; field trips.

Young & Rubicam Inc., New York, NY. Mentoring program for high school students; guest speakers; Skill Development Program (for young people in settlement houses); career day participation; advisory committees.

Annotated Bibliography

Adams, Donald. (1985). Effective School-Business Partnerships. *School Business Affairs, 51*(1), 18–19.

> This article discusses the benefits of school/business partnerships in helping school districts achieve reform goals and meet financial challenges. It emphasizes the need for mutual benefits.

Aetna Life & Casualty Foundation, Inc. (1985). *Contemporary Issues in Public Education and Opportunities for Corporate Initiatives.* Hartford, CT: Aetna Life & Casualty Foundation, Inc.

> A discussion of public education by Diane Ravitch, Albert Shanker, Fred Hechinger, Bill Honig, and Badi Foster, with a specific focus on corporate involvement.

Barriers to Private Sector/Public School Collaboration. (1983). Washington, DC: American Enterprise Institute in collaboration with the National Institute of Education.

> This is a theoretical work written by representatives of education, business, and industry, who reflect upon the philosophical and practical barriers to partnerships between the public and private sectors.

Barton, P. E. (1983). *Partnerships between Corporations and Schools.* Washington, DC: National Commission for Employment Policy, RR–83–29.

> This is a lengthy overview of the historical relationship between corporations and schools. It provides descriptions of activities and programs in place, brief summaries of some successful partnership efforts, and references for more intensive study.

Barton, P. E. (1977). Community Councils and the Transition between Education and Work. *Industry/Education Community Councils: NIE Papers in Education and Work: No. IX.* Washington, DC: National Institute of Education.

> This study discusses the use of community education and work councils as ways to improve school-to-work and work-to-school transitions for youth and adults.

Bobrow, S. B. (1977). Reasonable Expectations: Limits on the Promise of Community Councils. *Industry/Education Community Councils: NIE Papers in Education and Work: No. IX.* Washington, DC: National Institute of Education.

> This article discusses the effectiveness of industry/education community councils in the improvement of education.

Bossone, R. M. (Ed.). *Proceedings: The Conference of the University/Urban Schools National Task Force: What Works in Urban Schools.* (ERIC Document Reproduction Service No. ED 220 549).

This report includes conference papers by Superintendents Richard Green (Minneapolis Public Schools) and Ronald Stodghil (St. Louis Public Schools), in which they describe some of the ways in which business and labor are involved in their school districts' improvement programs.

Britt, L. A. (Ed.). (1985). *Exemplary Practice Series: School Business Partnerships.* Phi Delta Kappa Center for Evaluation, Development and Research.

This is a compilation of articles and papers on school/business partnerships.

Bucknam, R. E., & Brand, S. G. (1983). A Meta-Analysis of Experience Based Career Education. *Educational Leadership, 40*(6), 66–71.

The authors point to the ways in which experiential career education programs can benefit students.

Burt, S. M. *Strengthening Volunteer Industry Service to Public School Education.* (ERIC Document Reproduction Service No. 062 528).

This manual describes the need for long-range planning and commitment from both sectors in the process of partnership. It was prepared for individuals in industry and education who are interested in gaining an overview of the process.

Burt, S. M., & Lessinger, L. M. (1970). *Volunteer Industry Involvement in Public Education.* Lexington, MA: Heath Lexington Books.

The authors offer a broad perspective on private-sector involvement in education, with attention to some of the barriers that may prevent or delay collaboration. Case studies are also provided.

Calvin, A. D., & Keen, P. (1982). Community Foundations for Public Schools, *Phi Delta Kappan, 64*(2), 126–127.

In this article, the authors describe the success of the San Francisco Public Education Fund.

Chaffee, Jr., J. *Business-School Partnerships: A Plus for Kids.* (ERIC Document Reproduction Service No. ED 198 354).

This report describes a variety of successful programs between schools and the private sector. Sources of additional information about programs mentioned in the report are included.

Citizens, Businessmen, and Educators: The Elements to Better School-Community Relations. An Occasional Paper. (ERIC Document Reproduction Service No. 075 892).

Improved school/community relations may result from better identification of problems and courses of action. This report consists of three statements made by a citizen, a businessman, and an educator, and a summary of the ensuing discussions.

Coleman, J. (1985). Schools and the Communities They Serve. *Phi Delta Kappan, 66*(8), 527–532.

Coleman indicates that changes in life and work styles have seriously affected the functioning of the neighborhood school. He suggests that there is a real need for educators to seek the involvement of community members who are no longer actively engaged in the process of education.

Committee for Economic Development. (1985). *Investing in Our Children: Busi-*

ness and the Public Schools. New York: Committee for Economic Development.

This policy statement describes a strategy for education reform, with particular emphasis given to the ways in which the business community can participate in this effort.

Committee for Economic Development. (1983). *Business and the Schools*. New York: Committee for Economic Development.

This document includes the presentations made by noted private- and public-sector individuals regarding the future of collaboration.

Committee for Economic Development. (1982). *Public-Private Partnership: An Opportunity for Urban Communities*. New York: Committee for Economic Development.

This is a policy statement on public/private partnerships as a successful strategy for improving urban communities. This policy statement is based on in-depth case studies of partnerships in Atlanta, Baltimore, Chicago, Dallas, Minneapolis-St. Paul, Pittsburgh, and Portland, Oregon.

Crawford-Clark, Brenda. (1985). When Schools and Businesses Pair Off, Both Can Live Happily Ever After. *American School Board Journal, 72*(2), 36–37.

This article describes school districts in Dallas, Texas, and Tulsa, Oklahoma, that encourage corporations to adopt local public schools. The characteristics and benefits of successful programs are described, and suggestions for implementing similar programs are offered.

Cromer, J. L., & McKenzie, F. D. (1984). Schools and Business—A Partnership for Children. *Journal of Children in Contemporary Society, 16*(3–4), 133–145.

This article describes an Adopt-A-School program initiated by the White House encouraging federal agencies to join with Washington, D.C. public schools in partnerships. The District of Columbia career programs involve local industry participation.

Cuban, L. (1983). Corporate Involvement in Public Schools. *Teachers College Record, 85*(2), 183–203.

A brief historical perspective on the involvement of the private sector in public school education, with some major caveats that the author suggests should govern present involvements.

Cummings, J. R. *Alternate Learning: Sharing Innovative Programs and Practices.* (ERIC Document Reproduction Service No. ED 172 391).

The author provides descriptions and characteristics of programs that reflect the urban school district's commitment to the restoration of relevance in the education of American youth. To achieve this goal, the author charges that educators must bring about school/community collaboration, such as the Dallas Adopt-A-School Program, the Metro-Atlanta Skills Center, and others.

Danzberger, J. P., & Usdan, M. D. (1984). Building Partnerships: The Atlanta Experience. *Phi Delta Kappan, 65*(6), 393–396.

The authors describe the partnership process in Atlanta and offer their impressions of the key ingredients that have contributed to its success. They believe that the Atlanta partnership can be used as a model for other communities.

Doyle, D. P., & Levine, M. (1985). Business and the Public Schools: Observations on the Policy Statement of the Committee for Economic Development. *Phi Delta Kappan, 67*(2), 113–118.

> The authors were co-directors of the Committee for Economic Development study. They describe CED's interest in education and the rationale for recommending a bottom-up strategy for education reform, emphasizing liberal education and enriched preschool education for children at risk.

Elsman, M. *Industry-Education-Labor Collaboration: An Active Guide for Collaborative Councils.* (ERIC Document Reproduction Service No. ED 206 907).

> Based on actual experiences of 150 collaborative councils, this handbook presents issues, questions, and examples to consider in initiating collaborations between education and the private sector.

Eurich, N. (1985). *Corporate Classrooms.* New York: Carnegie Foundation for the Advancement of Teaching.

> The author estimates that $40 billion is being spent by the business community to train and retrain employees. The need for this training results from the rapid changes in technology as well as from the inadequate preparation of workers.

Felker, R. D. (1982). *The Education-Enterprise Relationship: Meeting the Needs of a Productive Society.* Washington, DC: National Association of State Boards of Education.

> The relationship between technological progress and education is explored from the perspectives of three authors representing corporate and educational concerns. Contributors were Robert P. Henderson, Chairman and CEO, ITEK Corporation; Michael Kirst, Professor, Stanford University; and Donna Knight, Executive Director, Minnesota Wellspring.

Finley, G. J. (1973). *Business and Education: A Fragile Partnership.* New York: The Conference Board.

> The author presents some of the barriers to public/private interaction, with special attention given to the "communications gap" that exists between these two sectors.

The First Two Years: The Public Education Fund, 1983–1985. (1985). Pittsburgh: Public Education Fund.

> This document describes the activities of the public education fund during its two-year history.

Fosler, S., & Berger, R. (1982). *Public-Private Partnership in American Cities: Seven Case Studies.* Lexington, MA: Lexington Books.

> An in-depth look at the collaborative efforts in place in seven cities. The authors believe that the key lesson to be learned is that approaches must be designed according to civic circumstances.

Franchine, P. C. (1982). Adoption, Chicago Style. *American Education, 18*(6), 23–28.

> This is a description of the Chicago Adopt-A-School program. Types of activities are discussed, and Franchine offers a brief description of the motivations of the public and private individuals participating in the program.

Fraser, Bryna Shore, et al. *Industry-Education-Labor Collaboration: The Literature of Collaborative Councils.* (ERIC Document Reproduction Service No. ED 206 906).

> An annotated bibliography of over 150 published materials relevant to an understanding of industry/education/labor collaboration generally and collaborative councils specifically.

Glass, L. W. *School Science and Mathematics.* (EJ 276 925).

> This article provides five reasons why business and industry participate in education: civic duty, career education and employment, equipment and materials, facilities, financial and personnel.

Gold, G. (1982). Public Education and the Private Sector. *Education Leadership,* 40(2), 4.

> A consensus among government, the private sector, and education recognizes that youth socialization and skill development are critical to the future direction of all social institutions and must be shared through a new set of multi-institutional relationships. The author worries about the promotion of more Adopt-A-Schools without a clear evaluation of their value.

Gold, G. *Industry-Education-Labor Collaboration: Designing Mechanisms for Sustained Impact.* (ERIC Document Reproduction Service No. ED 201 743).

> The author describes the opportunities for collaboration among and within education, business, labor, and government, as well as the barriers to such interaction. He describes the mechanisms known as collaborative councils, and the ways they differ from other organizations designed to promote interinstitutional participation.

Gonder, P. O. (1982). Corporations Can Be Real Angels When It Comes to Financing School Construction. *American School Board Journal,* 169(3), 36–38, 45.

> This article details cooperative agreements to finance new schools drawn up by growing school districts in Colorado, and the corporations whose activities are responsible for that growth.

Gonder, P. O. (1981). "Exchanging School and Community Resources," Chapter 10. In Davies, D. (Ed.). *Communities and Their Schools.* New York: McGraw-Hill.

> The author offers a description of several collaborative efforts throughout the country. She believes that the health of a community is tied to the kind of relationships that exist among individuals and institutions.

Gray, S. T. (1984). How to Create a Successful School/Community Partnership. *Phi Delta Kappan,* 65(6), 405–409.

> The Executive Director of the National School Volunteer Program, Inc., Sandra Gray, offers a list of "how to's" for partnering, as well as several mini case studies of effective programs.

Gray, S. T. *Managing School Volunteers—Eight Keys to Success.* (ERIC Document Reproduction Service No. ED 226 463).

> The National School Volunteer Program, Inc. provides technical assistance and trains teams of people to begin or expand school volunteer programs. This article offers eight principles that characterize effective volunteer programs.

Grimshaw, W. F. *Ensuring Educational Excellence through Business and Community Cooperation*. (ERIC Document Reproduction Service No. ED 216 840).

In this paper, the author presents several ways in which rural schools have renewed and strengthened their ties with business and the community. "How to's" for successful partnerships in rural communities are offered, as well as specific examples of school/business/community cooperation in Michigan.

Hart, E. *Blueprint for Partnership: A Process Guide for Organizing Adopt-A-School Programs*. (ERIC Document Reproduction Service No. ED 204 428).

This is a guide for organizing Adopt-A-School programs. The need for active support from both business and school administrators is emphasized, and a program in Washington, D.C., is described.

Hechinger, F. (1985). Turnaround for the Public Schools? *Harvard Business Review, 64*(1), 136–144.

The author provides a brief look at the state of American schools and describes some reasons why the business community cannot ignore the role it has to play in education.

Hemmings, M. (1982). *American Education: An Economic Issue*. Washington, DC: U.S. Chamber of Commerce.

An analysis of business concerns with the American education system and recommendations for business involvement in education programs.

High Schools and the Changing Workplace: The Employers' View. (1984). Washington, DC: National Academy Press.

This monograph describes the skills and competencies that are needed for success at work. According to the authors, employers are much more concerned about how well a prospective worker can think, read, and write, rather than his/her specific job skills.

Hunt, J. (1984). Education for Economic Growth: A Critical Investment. *Phi Delta Kappan, 65*(8), 538–541.

Former Governor Hunt discusses the link between an adequate work force and economic superiority. He describes the ways in which North Carolina business and industry have joined with the public schools.

Kantor, H., & Tyack, D. B. (Eds.). (1982). *Work, Youth, and Schooling*. Stanford, CA: Stanford University Press.

The contributors and editors review the history of vocational education and the vocationalization of schooling in the United States.

Kirst, M. W. (1984). The California Business Roundtable: Their Strategy and Impact on State Education Policy, cited in Timpane, P. M. *Phi Delta Kappan. 65*(6), 391.

The author describes the successful efforts of the California Business Roundtable to secure greater funding for California schools in return for a new set of graduation and attendance requirements for students.

Koch, F. (1979). *The New Corporate Philanthropy: How Society and Business Can Profit*. New York: Plenum Press.

The author describes the mechanisms for corporate philanthropy in general and gives some attention to the role of the corporation in the public schools.

Lacey, R. A. (1983). *Becoming Partners: How Schools and Companies Meet Mutual Needs.* Washington, DC: National Commission for Employment Policy Research Report Series, RR–83–33.

> The author contrasts public/private activities in five cities—Boston, Chicago, Memphis, New York, and Salt Lake City. He concludes with recommendations for policy makers, highlighting the need for networking, personal commitment, and systematic management.

Langpap, W., et al. *Practical Handles #2. Public Involvement. The Home-School-Community Partnership.* (ERIC Document Reproduction Service No. ED 198 115).

> This booklet provides summaries of 36 practitioners' workshop presentations on promoting interrelationships among the home, the school, and the community.

Levine, M. (Ed.). (1985). *The Private Sector in the Public School: Can It Improve Education?* Washington, DC: American Enterprise Institute for Public Policy Research.

> The competing views of business, labor, policy makers, academics, and practitioners are presented in this work, which discusses the fundamental philosophical, institutional, and policy implications of public/private sector interaction.

Levine, M. (1984). *Excellence in Education: Some Lessons from America's Best-Run Companies and Schools.* Washington, DC: Committee for Economic Development. Unpublished manuscript.

> Using the work of Peters and Waterman as a model, the author describes how the schools may profit from the practices learned by the "excellent companies."

Levine, M. (1983). *School Reform: A Role for the American Business Community.* Washington, DC: Committee for Economic Development. Unpublished manuscript.

> The author describes some of the ways that the business community can participate in the improvement of American schools.

Levine, M., & Trachtman, R. (1985). *Business and the Public Schools: Sharing New York's Future.* New York: New York City Partnership, Inc. Unpublished manuscript.

> The authors describe a role for the business community in New York for the improvement of the public schools.

Loozen, L. V. *Looking for Resources? Try Business.* (ERIC Document Reproduction Service No. ED 224 088).

> This article identifies many programs in which businesses are helping schools, lists tips for schools beginning a school/business partnership, and advises school boards to have up-to-date written policies that outline the type of partnerships they will encourage.

Lund, L., & McGuire, E. P. (1984). *The Role of Business in Precollege Education.* New York: Conference Board.

> This is a report based on a survey completed by 514 corporate public affairs

and personnel officers. The survey asked them to evaluate the abilities of newly hired high school graduates and the effects on company hiring policies.

Lusterman, S. (1975). *Education in Industry*. New York: The Conference Board.
A study of business executives revealed their discontent with the performance of schools and colleges in preparing people for work. The author
includes specific criticisms leveled at educational institutions as well as
suggestions made by executives that some of the training methodologies
that they have used successfully could be adapted for use in schools.

Lusterman, S., & Gorlin, H. (1980). *Educating Students for Work: Some Business
Roles*. New York: The Conference Board.
These authors suggest that there is a real and necessary role for the private
sector in public school education. "Insofar as the schools are not adequately
performing their work-preparation role . . . business has an obligation to
encourage and support appropriate change."

Mann, D. (1984). *All That Glitters: Public School/Private Sector Interaction in
Twenty-three U.S. Cities*. New York: Teachers College, Columbia University.
In order to understand the perspective and perceptions of school leaders
regarding business involvement in public school education, Mann interviewed several school personnel in each of 23 large American cities. His
sobering conclusion was that the potential for these involvements has still
not been realized.

McKenzie, F. D. (1983). Forging Partnerships between Schools and Businesses.
The Executive Educator, V, 32–34.
The superintendent of the Washington, D.C., public schools believes that
corporate involvement in education will result in decreased future training
costs for the private sector as well as more productive employees. The
author offers six ways in which the public and private sectors can collaborate.

McNett, I. (Ed.). (1982). *Let's Not Reinvent the Wheel: Profiles of School/Business
Collaboration*. Washington, DC: Institute for Educational Leadership.
Ten model programs of school/business collaborations are presented.

Meyer, J. (Ed.). (1982). *Meeting Human Needs: Toward a New Public Philosophy*.
Washington, DC: American Enterprise Institute.
This work contains a series of essays that describe the role of the private
sector in activities outside the realm of "business as usual."

Miller, L. (1984). *Organizational and political dimensions of private sector/public
school interaction: Focus on urban schools*. New York: Teachers College, Columbia University. Unpublished manuscript.
Based on a series of in-depth telephone interviews, the author discusses
how school-based personnel perceive public/private sector interactions.

Moore, R., et al. (1982). Schools and Community—Partners in Education; Using
Community Assets for Better Learning. *Instructor, 82*(1), 59–62.
A series of short articles describing techniques in involving others in the
community in elementary education—college students, youth groups, industry, service clubs, and church groups.

Moran, M. E. (1983). Improving Schools through Private Sector Partnerships. *American Education, 19*(1), 5–8.

  This article briefly describes President Reagan's Task Force on Private Sector Initiatives. It offers a list of some ongoing public/private partnerships, as well as some suggestions for successful collaborations.

National Commission on Excellence in Education. (1983). *A Nation at Risk: The Imperative for Educational Reform.* Washington, DC: U.S. Government Printing Office.

  Within this document are specific recommendations for the private sector to participate in the improvement of American education.

National School Volunteer Program, Inc. (1983). *Creating and Managing a Corporate School Volunteer Program.*

  This is a 13 stage, step-by-step guide to corporate/school volunteer programs. It describes and analyzes approaches that have proven successful, as well as how excellent programs differ from the others. Copies may be ordered directly from NSVP for $50 each.

National Science Foundation. (1983). *Educating Americans for the 21st Century.* Washington, DC: National Science Foundation.

  One of the reform reports that calls for the involvement of the private sector in the improvement of education.

Nault, W. H. (1984). A Corporate Leader Looks at America's Educational Dilemma. *Journal of Career Development, 11*(1), 42–47.

  A corporate perspective on current education issues. The article cites several examples of innovative programs involving business and industry in the schools.

Neubeck, K. J. (1974). *Corporate Response to Urban Crisis.* Lexington, MA: Lexington Books.

  This work provides several detailed case studies of how corporations responded to the racial unrest of the late 1960s. Chapter 2 offers a lengthy description of Southern Bell's partnership with the St. Louis school system. Neubeck suggests that acts of corporate social responsibility are structured in terms of the perceived needs and capabilities of the individual corporation.

Odom, B. D. (1985). *A Community of Believers. Fourth Anniversary Report.* Atlanta, GA: Atlanta Partnership of Business and Education, Inc.

  The report describes the Atlanta Partnership of Business and Education. It describes the history, purposes, and philosophy of the partnership, as well as specific projects and activities.

O'Connell, C. (1985). *How to Start a School/Business Partnership.* Fastback #226. Indiana: Phi Delta Kappa Foundation.

  A school person's guide to starting a school/business partnership.

Otterbourg, S. D. (1986). *School Partnerships Handbook: How to Set Up and Administer Programs with Business, Government, and Your Community.* Englewood Cliffs, NJ: Prentice Hall.

  A practical guide for school people—with 400 resources identified for working with business and other external groups. Businesspeople will find the information useful as well.

Ozmon, W. (1980). Adopt-A-School: Definitely Not Business as Usual. *Phi Delta Kappan, 63*(5), 350–351.

Ozmon discusses the Adopt-A-School program and lists some of the companies involved and the programs in eight cities. He warns that there is too much business influence on school philosophies and curricula.

Partnerships: Private Initiatives for Public Responses. (March 1982). Conference proceedings. Philadelphia: Atlantic Richfield Company and United States Conference of Mayors.

Partnerships in Education: Education Trends of the Future. (1984). U.S. Department of Education.

A nationwide survey was sent to all public schools to discover the kinds of public/private partnerships in place. The survey reports that there seems to be a national trend toward increased interactions between the two sectors.

Patrick, K. G., & Eells, R. (1969). *Education and the Business Dollar.* New York: Macmillan.

This book describes the historical relationship between education and the business community vis-à-vis corporate philanthropy.

Peters, T. J., & Waterman, Jr., R. H. (1982). *In Search of Excellence.* New York: Harper & Row.

The practices used by the "excellent companies" may prove valuable for educators as well.

President's Task Force on Private Sector Initiatives. (1982). *Summary of Mission, Members and Goals. Report to the President.* Washington, DC.

The President's Task Force on Private Sector Initiatives was organized to promote private-sector leadership and responsibility in meeting public needs and to foster an increased level of public/private partnerships in order to decrease dependence on government.

Pro-Education

This is a magazine devoted to partnerships with education. Articles include discussions of partnerships between education and business, industry, universities, and the community-at-large. According to the publisher, "Our greatest task is to make sure that those in the partnership movement are kept abreast of its progress."

Purcell, E. A. (Ed.). *Partners for the 80's: Business and Education.* (ERIC Document Reproduction Service No. ED 208 222).

Twenty-four profiles of effective cooperative partnerships between business and education are presented.

Putnam, B. *Art Education, 34*(1), 16–17. (EJ 239661).

A secondary school art teacher describes how, when faced with district budget cuts, she developed links with local businesses willing to donate supplies, grants, and display spaces for her art program.

Rath, S. W., & Hagans, R. *Collaboration among Schools and Business and Industry: An Analysis of the Problems and Some Suggestions for Improving the Process.* (ERIC Document Reproduction Service No. ED 178 750).

This paper explores the meaning of collaboration and the issues associated with it. It discusses the need for collaboration, some problems that have been identified, and advice on how to deal with the problems. The collective bargaining model is presented as a way to strengthen and improve the collaborative process.

Rosenau, F. (1982). Beyond Philanthropy. *Educational Leadership, 40*(2), 5–7.
The author presents some reasons for why businesses are joining with schools in new forms of collaboration.

Ruffin, Jr., S. C. (1983). *School-Business Partnerships: Why Not?* Reston, VA: National Association of Secondary School Principals.
This monograph reviews the basic concepts of school/business partnerships. It describes the steps that are needed for building successful partnerships, as well as brief capsules of some successful programs. The author directs his comments specifically to secondary school principals.

Sarason, S. (1983). *Schooling in America.* New York: The Free Press, Macmillan.
This author suggests that education should take place in a variety of community sites, not just within the school building. Unless community members are involved directly in the educational process and are given a role to play, Sarason believes that their understanding and subsequent support of schools will remain limited.

Schilit, H., & Lacey, R. A. *The Private Sector Youth Connection. Volume 1: School to Work. A Planning Manual for Educators and Business People.* (ERIC Document Reproduction Service No. ED 226 074).
The authors provide examples of several types of school/business partnerships, as well as lessons learned during the process. This volume reviews fifty-five tested programs involving seven thousand companies and provides eight generic models of diverse local programs.

School-Community Cooperation: Oakland's Adopt-A-School Program. (ERIC Document Reproduction Service No. ED 199 872).
This bulletin describes the Adopt-A-School program in Oakland, California, and suggests programs, projects, and services that businesses and community organizations might offer to schools.

Schultz, L. (1984). Art Education and Industry: A Case Study of Success. *School of Arts, 84*(3), 14–16.
This article describes an industry-funded, school-based project in elementary art education.

Seeley, D. S. (1983). Education through Partnership. *Educational Leadership, 40*(2), 42–43.
The author points out that in recent reform reports, education partnerships are "either taken for granted or given scant attention." He believes that the partnership model is a way for the public and private sectors to re-open their lines of communication for the improvement of schools.

Seeley, D. S. (1981). *Education through Partnership: Mediating Structures and Education.* Cambridge, MA: Ballinger Publishing Co.
The author tells how families, neighborhoods, churches, and voluntary associations are critical for public school reform.

Shakeshaft, C., & Trachtman, R. (1986). "Corporate-School Partnerships: The

Perspective of Business." Presented at the annual meeting of the American Educational Research Association, San Francisco.

The authors surveyed major American corporations to identify the extent, variability, and motivations for corporate involvement with public schools.

Shanker, A. (1984). Business Is Welcome in School. *Across the Board* (Conference Board magazine), xx(4), 59–61.

The author explores some of the reasons to promote school/business collaborations.

Stein, W. M., et al. *Increasing Guidance Effectiveness through School-Community Cooperation. A Guide to Developing Cooperative Relationships between Schools and Business, Industry and Labor in Rural Communities.* Columbus, OH: National Center for Research in Vocational Education, Ohio State University, 1978.

This book is one of a series designed for rural guidance counselors. It provides guidelines for creating partnerships in rural/small school environments.

Sterling, A. (1982). *Executive Summary of District's Adopt-A-School Program.* Chicago: Chicago Public Schools. Unpublished manuscript.

The coordinator of this Adopt-A-School program describes the relationship between business and the public schools in Chicago, and offers advice regarding positive practices and possible pitfalls.

Synthesizing Work and Schooling: The Roles of Community and Society. Report No. 91. (ERIC Document Reproduction Service No. 143 574).

According to the authors, the separation of schooling and work needs to be challenged and overcome. The changes that need to be effected by the separate institutions in order to accomplish this goal are outlined.

Task Force on Education for Economic Growth: Education Commission of the States. (1983). *Action for Excellence.* Washington, DC: Education Commission of the States.

Several recommendations by the authors of this study point to the need for school/business partnerships to improve the state of school education.

Timpane, P. M. (1984). Business Has Rediscovered the Public Schools. *Phi Delta Kappan, 65*(6), 389–392.

The author describes the renewed corporate interest in public school education. He presents the state of the current activities and points to notable changes from past involvements.

Timpane, P. M. (1982). *Corporations and Public Education in the Cities.* New York: Teachers College, Columbia University.

One of the first major pieces of research to directly address the role of the corporation in public school education. It provides an overview of the historical relationship between these two sectors, as well as a rationale for why present involvements may differ from those of the past. Although Mr. Timpane clearly elucidates the barriers to partnership, he concludes by stating that the potential offered in these relationships may be worth the effort.

Trachtman, R. (1985). *School/Business Collaborations: A Study of the Process and Product.* University Microfilms, Inc.

The author examines the impact of school/business partnerships on school personnel, with particular attention given to the perceptions of participating classroom teachers.

Twentieth Century Fund Task Force on Federal Elementary and Secondary Policy. (1983). *Making the Grade*. New York: Twentieth Century Fund.

This report points to the need for private-sector involvement in the public schools.

Usdan, M. (April 1983). "Private Sector Initiatives in Education: Viewpoints of the Educator." Reston, VA: *National Association of Secondary School Principals Bulletin*, 43–48.

The author indicates that as a result of demographic and political shifts, educators must work vigorously toward involving the private sector in education.

Useem, E. L. (1986). *Low Tech Education in a High Tech World: Corporations and Classrooms in the New Information Society*. Free Press.

Ms. Useem uses the comparison/contrast mode to relate the present inability of schools to respond to the needs of their students and the demands of the economy. She concludes that as an industry group those in high tech have been generally unresponsive to the needs of public education, with most businesspeople unable to spare the time and resources required for collaboration.

Walsh, J. *Crucial Issues Pertaining to the Establishment of Community-Education Work Councils*. (ERIC Document Reproduction Service No. ED 141 591).

This book describes the historical relationships that have existed between industry and education and between labor and education. Section I discusses issues of importance relating to the establishment of community work/education councils. Section II reviews mechanisms similar to the proposed councils.

Wilms, W. W. (1984). Vocational Education and Job Success: The Employer's View. *Phi Delta Kappan, 65*(5), 347–350.

This article points to the need for schools and businesses to join together to improve the skills of future workers. It describes some of the activities in place in California that were initiated to meet this goal.

Wirtz, W. W. (1975). *The Boundless Resource: A Perspective for an Education/Work Policy*. Washington, DC: New Republic Book Co.

In this work the author calls for the establishment of community education/work councils to enlist the participation of the private sector in public education.

Wise, R. T. (1981). Schools, Businesses and Educational Needs: From Cooperation to Collaboration. *Education and Urban Society, 14*(1), 67–82. (EF 257336).

This article discusses some implications of the involvement of business in public education. It also examines requirements for effective school/business partnerships.

Youthwork, Inc. *The Transition from School to Work: The Problem That Won't Take Care of Itself*. (ERIC Document Reproduction Service No. ED 219 521).

This document includes summaries of the four presentations and the two panel discussions at a conference that focused on the need for schools, employment and training systems, business, foundations, and other resources to coordinate efforts to address educational and employment problems of disadvantaged youth.

About the Editors
and the Contributors

David Bergholz is Executive Director of the George Gund Foundation in Cleveland. He was formerly President of the Public Education Fund and Assistant Executive Director of the Allegheny Conference on Community Development. His career has included employment in the areas of housing, community organization, health planning, and music.

Paul Berman received his Ph.D. in political science from the Massachusetts Institute of Technology and is a policy analyst specializing in the study of implementation. He is the author of numerous publications on education and organizational and social change; has been the director of large-scale research projects concerning school improvement; and has been a consultant for federal, state, and local public agencies and private organizations.

Owen B. Butler served as Chairman of the Board of Procter & Gamble Company until his retirement in 1986. Mr. Butler is a member of several boards of directors, including Northern Telecom Limited, The Hospital Corporation of America, Deere & Company, and the Cincinnati branch of the Federal Reserve Board. As a trustee of the Committee for Economic Development, Mr. Butler served as chairman of the CED subcommittees, which produced the studies, *Investing in Our Children: Business and the Public Schools* and *Children in Need: Investment Strategies for the Educationally Disadvantaged.*

Barbara L. Christen has been Principal of the Murry Bergtraum High School for Business Careers since it opened in September 1975. She organized and developed this unique school, which has set a standard for business development of partnerships with corporations in the Wall Street area. Dr. Christen is a member of the National Advisory Panel for the National Center on Employment, as well as the Advisory Boards of the Graduate School of Education of City University of New York, and the Job and Career Center of the New York City Partnership.

Anthony Cipollone is an associate with the Annie E. Casey Foundation in Greenwich, Connecticut, where he coordinates educational activities and educational technical assistance for the foundation's New Futures initiative for at-risk youth in five cities. He was formerly a senior research associate at Education Matters, Inc. in Cambridge, and has been a teacher and administrator at a school for high-risk urban youth in New York City.

Rick Clugston was a Research Associate with Berman, Weiler Associates during the development of *The Minnesota Plan*, and served as a consultant to the Minnesota Business Partnership and the Brainpower Compact regarding its implementation. He was Program Manager for Improving Education in Minnesota, a three-year policy development program of Spring Hill Center, Wayzata, Minnesota. He is a doctoral candidate in higher education at the University of Minnesota.

Eleanor Farrar is an associate professor of education policy at the State University of New York at Buffalo. Dr. Farrar's research interests include the development and execution of federal education policy at the state and local levels, and current efforts to reform education, particularly in urban high schools. She is the author of numerous articles on education policy and school improvement, and the co-author of *The Shopping Mall High School: Winners and Losers in the American Educational Marketplace*.

Barbara Gothard is Director of Public Affairs for the Burger King Corporation. She is responsible for both the Corporate Contributions and Education Programs, and has developed Scholarship Incentive Programs for employees and the first National Recognition Program for teachers and principals. She was instrumental in expanding the focus of Burger King's education programs into a broader, consumer focus to increase public awareness of the importance of teaching and education. Dr. Gothard has had extensive experience as both a teacher and an administrator in several public school systems.

Rita G. Kaplan is a senior consultant at the Minneapolis Foundation, where she works with diverse community leaders to anticipate and define emerging community needs. She was formerly corporate manager of education programs at Honeywell, Inc., where she guided the company's strategies for elementary and secondary education, and served as the CEO's deputy on the Minnesota Business Partnership's education study. She has worked with the Minneapolis schools on Honeywell's strategic plan and on the design of the Summatech magnet program. She is currently Assistant to the President for Community Relations at Augsberg College in Minneapolis.

Marsha Levine, (editor), is an Associate Director of Education Issues at the American Federation of Teachers and Co-Director of the AFT's Center for Restructuring Schools. She was Co-Director of the Committee for Economic Development study *Investing in Our Children* (1985). As a consultant and Visiting Fellow in Education Policy Studies at the American Enterprise Institute, she concentrated on the relationship between corporations and schools. She has been a teacher in public and private schools at the elementary and secondary levels. Dr. Levine's publications include *The Private Sector in the Public Schools: Can It Improve Education?*

Chava Willig Levy, a consultant in Metropolitan Life Insurance Company's Corporate Social Responsibility Division, researches and writes about educational and women's concerns. She also coordinates public service activities at company headquarters for these constituencies.

Valerie S. Lies, former Vice President of the Public Education Fund, Pittsburgh, Pennsylvania, is now President of the Donors Forum of Chicago. She has been the Executive Director of the Otto Bremer Foundation, St. Paul, Minnesota. A graduate of Vassar College, Ms. Lies holds an M.S.W. in planning and administration from the University of Minnesota.

P. Michael Timpane is President of Teachers College, Columbia University. As a college administrator and federal education policy maker and researcher, for the past two decades he has worked extensively with leadership at all levels of education. For the past several years, he has concentrated his research on emerging practices at the state and local levels. His publications include "Business Has Rediscovered the Public Schools," *Phi Delta Kappan*, 1984, and *Corporations and Public Education in the Cities*, a report prepared for the Carnegie Corporation of New York, June 1982.

Roberta Trachtman, (editor), is presently Special Assistant to the Dean for Urban Affairs, City University of New York. As an independent education consultant, her research has focused on interactions between the public and private sectors and the reform of the public schools. She has taught at the secondary school and college levels. Dr. Trachtman is currently investigating the role of teachers as school leaders.

William S. Woodside is Chairman of Sky Chefs, Inc. Previously, he was Chairman and Chief Executive Officer of Primerica Corporation (formerly American Can Company); Chairman of the Executive Committee of Primerica Corporation's Board of Directors, and President of the Primerica Foundation. Mr. Woodside is also a director of James River Corporation, and Chairman of the Institute for Educational Leadership, Inc. of Washington, D.C.

Index